THE ART OF CONTEXTUAL THEOLOGY

The Art of Contextual Theology

Doing Theology in the Era of World Christianity

VICTOR I. EZIGBO

CASCADE *Books* · Eugene, Oregon

THE ART OF CONTEXTUAL THEOLOGY
Doing Theology in the Era of World Christianity

Cascade Books
An Imprint of Wipf and Stock Publishers
199 W. 8th Ave., Suite 3
Eugene, OR 97401

www.wipfandstock.com

PAPERBACK ISBN: 978-1-7252-5928-7
HARDCOVER ISBN: 978-1-7252-5929-4
EBOOK ISBN: 978-1-7252-5930-0

Cataloguing-in-Publication data:

Names: Ezigbo, Victor I., author.

Title: The art of contextual theology : doing theology in the era of world Christianity / by Victor I. Ezigbo.

Description: Eugene, OR : Cascade Books, 2021 | Includes bibliographical references and index.

Identifiers: ISBN 978-1-7252-5928-7 (paperback) | ISBN 978-1-7252-5929-4 (hardcover) | ISBN 978-1-7252-5930-0 (ebook)

Subjects: LCSH: Theology—Methodology. | Christianity and culture.

Classification: BR118 .E95 2021 (print) | BR118 .E95 (ebook)

05/26/21

To Chizaraekpere (Zara) Ezigbo, my beloved daughter

Contents

Acknowledgments

I am indebted to a host of people who have helped me in diverse ways to write this book. I have learned a great deal from students, mentors, and colleagues who are impressive partners and interlocuters in my journey as a Christian theologian. Students at Bethel University, where I teach, have sharpened my thinking and views on many of the issues that are discussed in this book. I thank Dr. Gary Long and Dr. Samuel Zalanga, my colleagues at Bethel University, for reading the drafts of the chapters and for providing insightful feedback, which undoubtedly improved the quality of the final product. Many of my colleagues in the Biblical and Theological Studies department at Bethel University willingly engaged me in discussion when I presented them with several issues that are explored in the book. Dr. Chloe Starr of Yale Divinity School read most of the chapters and provided insightful comments and suggestions. I have benefited from Charlie Collier and his team at Wipf and Stock for their helpful editorial queries and suggestions.

I received an Alumni grant from Bethel University that covered some of the research expenses, for which I am truly grateful. Dr. Miroslav Volf, under the auspices of Yale Center for Faith and Culture at Yale Divinity School, invited me to participate in a two-day consultation on "Jesus as a Moral Stranger" at Yale Divinity School. I presented a large part of chapter 6 at the consultation. I am deeply grateful for the comments and questions of other participants. Many pastors and Christian leaders who participated in the conferences organized by the Center for Research in Global Christianity (CRGC) in Nigeria prompted me to explore further some of the issues covered in this book, chapter 6 in particular.

Finally, I thank my family for the unquantifiable love, support, and encouragement I received over several years as I worked on the book. On many occasions when I lacked the drive to complete it, my family provided the inspirations that I needed.

Introduction

Contextual theologies today consider the *context* as a very important source of doing theology, in addition to scripture and tradition.[1]

S everal years ago, a friend asked me this question: "If all theologies are contextual, isn't contextual theology as a name of a field of study at best redundant?" Another person asked me after I shared with him my interest in contextual theology: "Isn't contextual theology syncretism?" These questions, though misguided, ought to remind contextual theologians to distinguish between the assumed inherent contextuality of theology and the peculiar tasks of the field of contextual theology. In order to get a firm grasp of this distinction, I attempt in this book an extensive discussion on the nature, guiding principles, and tasks that frame *contextual theologizing*— how to intentionally do theology contextually. Since this book is not merely about methodological and procedural issues but also practice in contextual theology, I explore concrete examples that bring into focus the necessity of recognizing and also utilizing the context of a Christian community as an indispensable source of Christian theology.

A central question this book explores is: How might identifying and appraising theological data drawn out from a community's context contribute to Christian theology's content (modes of being) and form (modes of expression)? To answer this question, I have divided the book into two major sections: methodological and procedural issues in contextual theology (ch. 1) and theological case studies that illustrate the practice of contextual theology (chs. 2–6). Brief words about each of these sections and how they fit into the overall goals of this book are in order. Chapter 1 provides a

1. Mulackal, "Women," 152–53.

broader theological background that focuses on the main characteristics and goals of contextual theology. I propose a constitutive genre of contextual theology, distinguishing it from an explanatory genre. The five *theological cases*—issues that raise penetrating theological questions that originate in real-life experiences—I examine in chapters 2–6. These cases provide great insights into the art of contextual theology. Each case study is examined in the following order: a summary of the theological issues, a survey of the historical background of the issues, and discussions on theological responses to the issues. Chapter 2 examines a well-known conversation that Jesus Christ had with an unnamed Samaritan woman about the nature and locale of true worship (John 4). It investigates some echoes of contextual theologizing that might be discerned in Jesus' responses to the theological subject matter of the conversation. Chapter 3 explores caste-based relations in India and the role it plays in Dalit theology. Chapter 4 focuses on the relationship of African indigenous (or traditional) cultures and the project of African theology. In chapter 5, the focal theological issue is the plight of the poor in Latin America and how it provides the impetus for liberation theological discourse. Chapter 6 examines the phenomenon of intermittent abandonment of Jesus in pursuit of spiritual solutions to existential needs that can be discerned in Nigerian Christianity. I explore the causes of this phenomenon and the theological problems it raises for Christian discipleship in the Nigerian context.

1

Theology as a Contextual Exercise

A salient feature of the field of contextual theology is the quest for rediscovering an essential nature of Christian theology: *contextuality*—modes of being and expression that are conditioned by a community's context. Here, the word "context" is used broadly as an umbrella term that encompasses the history, culture (e.g., way of life, language, thought, and intellectual capital), and contemporary state affairs (e.g., life situation and social location). Christian theology's contextuality reminds us that a context orients Christian communities towards a particular way of seeing, interpreting, constructing, and appropriating their knowledge of God-world relations. This chapter discusses Christian theology's contextuality, the features and forms of contextual theology, and the tasks of contextual theologians.

A gathering of twenty-two theologians in 1976, mainly from Africa, Asia, and Latin America meeting in Dar es Salaam (Tanzania), would later become a watershed conference that nudged some theologians to explore the common theological and social concerns of African, Asian, and Latin American Christians.[1] In their communiqué, the attendees of the conference hammered out four objectives that were embedded in their theological questions and quests. These would serve as the guidelines for their future ecumenical theological explorations:

1. Sharing with one another the present trends of interpretation of the gospel in different Third World countries, particularly bearing in mind

1. This was the first of the several theological conferences organized mainly by theologians from Africa, Asia, and Latin America. The conference was held at the University of Dar es Salaam (Tanzania). Of the twenty-two attendees, seven were Africans, seven were Asians, and six were Latin Americans. There was one African American and also one Caribbean in attendance. In terms of ecclesiastical affiliations "there were eleven Roman Catholics, ten Protestants, and one Coptic Orthodox." See "Communiqué," 272.

the roles of theology in relation to other faiths and ideologies as well as the struggle for a just society.

2. Promoting the exchange of theological views through writings in the books and periodicals of Third World countries.

3. Promoting the mutual interaction between theological formulation and social analysis.

4. Keeping close contacts as well as being involved with action-oriented movements for social change.[2]

In these objectives, one can discern a team spirit and camaraderie among the theologians, highlighted by the controversial term "Third World."[3] They shared the desire to challenge colonialism, economic exploitation, domination of foreign powers, and racism in their continents from a Christian theological vantage point. Given that the theologians shared a similar interest in contextual theologizing, albeit for different reasons and at varying degrees, one should not be surprised that the concerns for a "just society," "social analysis," and "action-oriented movements for social change" formed the building blocks of the four objectives. In the "Final Statement," they reiterated the concerns: "We . . . are convinced that those who bear the name of Christ have a special service to render to the people of the whole world who are now in an agonizing search for a new world order based on justice, fraternity, and freedom." The document also states: "We have reflected from our experience as belonging to the oppressed men and women of the human race. We seriously take cognizance of the cultural and religious heritage of the peoples of the continents of Asia, Africa, and Latin America."[4] Though only one of the theologians examined in this book (Gustavo Gutiérrez) was present at the conference in Dar es Salaam, the theological vision of the conference has partly given the impetus for the genre and also the scope of theological exploration I undertake in this book.

Several theological presuppositions derived from Christian Scripture underlie this book, of which three are noteworthy. Firstly, the Christian view of *divine revelation*—God's decision to reveal God's mode of being and operating in the world in ways that are recognizable to human beings— ought to deter Christians from engaging in unfruitful speculations about God's identity. Therefore, the God invoked in the Christian faith should not

2. "Communiqué," 273.

3. For a helpful discussion on the history of the terms "third world" and "third worldism," see Berger, "After the Third World?," 9–39; Hellwig, "Liberation Theology," 137–51.

4. "Final Statement," 259.

be construed as merely a hypothetical concept proposed by Christians as a point of departure in their explorations of the mystery of human existence. On the contrary, the Christian God, as expressed in Christian Scripture, assumes God's self-disclosure through mediated and contextualized avenues. The writer of Hebrews puts it this way:

> In the past God spoke to our forefathers through the prophets at many times and in various ways, but in these last days he has spoken to us by his Son, whom he appointed heir of all things, and through whom he made the universe. (Heb 1:1–2 NIV)

The guiding theological question about the Christian God in the field of contextual theology ought not be: What is the individual essence of the Christian God?[5] A more appropriate question should be: Why the Christian God? To put it differently, why this God that Christians pray to, believe in, sing to, and worship? The "why" question is not really about *epistemic rights*—the rights of Christians as members of a particular religious community to propose a particular God as a theory for explaining the origins of the cosmos. On the contrary, it is about *epistemic praxis*—knowledge of doing—that is grounded in a mediated divine presence embodied by Jesus Christ who summons his followers to participate, as a form of worship, in the work of healing the ills of this world (see Matt 5:13–16; cf. John 17; Eph 2:8–10; Jas 2:14–19).

Secondly, Christian theology is in some ways a commentary on Christians' beliefs about God's proclamation of good news to this world (John 3:16), which is embodied by Jesus of Nazareth (Luke 4:16–21). He should be Christians' window on God's mediated presence in the world (Heb 1:1–4).[6] Philip's request: "Lord, show us the Father and that will be enough for us" and Jesus's response: "Anyone who has seen me has seen the Father. How can you say, 'Show us the Father'?" (John 14:8–9 NIV) suggests that Christian theology will be overreaching itself if its aim is to penetrate the unmediated mystery of God's presence and identity. The apostle Paul warned Christians in Corinth against the illusion of those who think they can penetrate the unmediated and unrevealed mystery of God thorough theological reflections and through their spiritual gifts (1 Cor 13:8–12).

5. This is an important theological question that philosophical theology and systematic theology are better equipped to answer. For helpful discussions on the *what* and *who* questions about God's essence and existence, see Kung, *Does God Exist?*; Plantinga, *Warranted Christian Belief.*

6. In *Re-imagining African Christologies* and in some of my other writings, I argue that Jesus functions as a "revealer" (one who communicates, interprets, and redirects knowledge about) divinity and humanity for Christian communities. I will return to this christological proposal in ch. 6.

Thirdly, as an essential component of the Christian life, theologizing should be grounded in a commitment to explore and experience a relationship with God (the Triune God, in Christian parlance) and a commitment to neighbors—that is, all humans, since all human beings, as Christian Scripture teaches, are creatures and imagers of God (see Gen 1:26–27; 5:1; Mark 12:29–31). Theologizing becomes a commitment to God when it is done for the purpose of glorifying God and promoting the worship of God. Theologizing becomes a commitment to human neighbors when it is done to promote the well-being—spiritual, mental, physical, economic, and social health—of people. Given this commitment to human neighbors, *grassroots* Christian theologies—the theologies that are being worked out daily largely by Christians with no formal theological education—should be of prime concern to theologians. This means that training in fieldwork tailored toward collecting, collating, and analyzing theological data from grassroots theologies is essential to the field of contextual theology. A contextual theologian should bridge the gap between armchair theologians (individuals whose writings are based primarily on bare abstraction rather than on the practical experience of Christian communities) and fieldwork theologians (individuals who see the living and changing situations of Christian communities as the primary workshop of theology). To explore this claim further, I will examine some essential features of contextual theology.

What Is Contextual about Theology?

Theology emerges and indeed finds its voice within the matrix of different, albeit mutually complementary sources. Theologians who attend to the contextual affairs of their community are confronted by theology's contextual face: its invitation to theologians to explore how the context of a Christian community is an essential *locus theologicus* (source of theology). Theologies profoundly reveal (or betray) theologians' particularities in terms of their choice of hermeneutical approaches, choice of theological data, and selective appropriation of theological data. All theologies have what may be described as a contextual accent: an identity marker that points to the historical, social, political, and religious currents of the context *from* and *for* which they are produced. For example, Ghanaian Christians who attempt to negotiate their christological beliefs in light of the Ancestral Stool tradition will face a different theological issue from American Christians who negotiate their christological beliefs in light of the impact of capitalism on the values of the United States of America. While, for instance, such Ghanaian Christians may explore how Jesus of Nazareth qualifies as an ancestor, American Christians may be preoccupied with an exploration of the relevance of Jesus's sayings about poverty to contemporary discourse on American capitalism. These different theological concerns ought to remind theologians that one of the goals of doing theology is to guide Christian communities in the enormous task of working out their identity within their own historical milieu as the "church," to use the words of the Indian theologian M. M. Thomas, called to live the life of "fellowship (*koinonia*) . . . preaching (kerygma), teaching (*didache*), and service (*diakonia*)."[7]

If theologians are conditioned by their contexts, no theology is context-free. Yet some theologians tend to reject context as an essential source of Christian theology. Some disregard the context of a Christian community in favor of other sources such as Scripture, church tradition, and reason. Others relegate context to the margins as if it were only epiphenomenal. Since the mid-twentieth century, however, many theologians from Africa, Asia, and Latin America have pursued with rigor theological activities that aimed to properly account for the contributions of the context to Christian theology. The emergence of African theology in the late 1950s, Latin American liberation theology in the late 1960s, and Dalit theology in the early 1970s has exposed the imperial agenda that lurked in the quest for a universal theology. As Robert Schreiter has noted, the so-called universal theologies were

> in fact *universalizing* theologies; that is to say, they extended the results of their own reflections beyond their own contexts to other settings, usually without an awareness of the rootedness of their theologies within their own contexts.[8]

Though all theologies are inherently contextual, they can also speak meaningfully to issues that are outside of their contexts of origin. However, expecting a theology to be supra-contextual and also to rule over other theologies is deeply misguided. In the end, the so-called "universal theology," which the discourse on world Christianity has amplified, is really a contextualized theological expression that is intended to rule out its limitedness and also to sanitize or erase the peculiarities of the theologies of other Christian communities.

The phenomenon of "world Christianity" has prompted many theologians to explore the role that theological beliefs play in the different forms of expression Christianity takes when it encounters new cultures.[9] Some

7. Thomas, *Acknowledged Christ of the Indian Renaissance*, 297.

8. Schreiter, *New Catholicity*, 2.

9. The term "world Christianity" is used here to describe the phenomenon of the expansion of Christianity in different parts of the world through a process of

missiologists and historians of Christianity with enough interest in Christian theology have predicted and sometimes expressed optimism about a future realization of the theological implications of world Christianity: the realization of the necessity of multiple and interdependent theological centers of Christianity in different regions of the world.[10] Another possible theological implication, as Kevin Vanhoozer has noted, is to abandon the assumption of a universal (Western) theological "rule" that is intended to "rule over" all theologians, especially theologians from the regions of Africa, Asia, and Latin America. Vanhoozer has argued that the "struggle to assert one set of categories over another is often not merely theoretical but is linked to issues of power and control."[11] A real temptation, which should be avoided, is to use Western theologies as the standard for measuring the adequacy of other theologies.[12] What is needed, however, is the openness of Christian theological communities to explore the benefits of mutual exchanges and criticisms. A potential benefit of such exchanges and criticisms is the possibility of deepening one's knowledge of the globality and common features that characterize the diverse forms of existence that the Christian faith has assumed in different cultures.

Theological beliefs have played and continue to play an essential role in the global expansion of Christianity. Why is theology capable of impelling such expansion? Also, what form of theology makes Christianity feel at home in different cultures? In the past few decades, church historians have discussed the historical process and consequences of the early church's understanding of the Christian faith as "a religion destined for all time and for the whole world, and not just for one time, place, or people."[13] What might such historical process and consequences of the universal outlook of Christianity say about the very nature of Christian theology? This book attempts to demonstrate that theology should be an art of formulating responses to the theological needs of a community with theological materials harvested and harnessed in Scripture, church traditions, and changing

---

contextualization—the different forms of expression the Christian faith has taken, which are informed by the context of a local community. For discussions on the different ways missiologists and historians of Christianity use the terms "world Christianity" and "global Christianity," see Ott and Netland, *Globalizing Theology*; Irvin, "World Christianity," 1–26.

10. See Tienou, "Christian Theology in an Era of World Christianity," 37–51.

11. Vanhoozer, "One Rule to Rule Them All?," 95.

12. The term "Western theologies" is used broadly to describe the diverse (and sometimes competing) theological works that are written from within and primarily for North American and European contexts.

13. Sanneh, *Disciples of All Nations*, 3.

human contexts. This way of understanding theology requires moving beyond the form of contextual theology that focuses on "making sense of the Christian message in local circumstances" to a new form of contextual theology that uses data from theological sources to construct a Christian message.[14] In other words, theologians are to ask penetrating theological questions of their context, Scripture, and ecclesial tradition as they develop fresh theological answers for their communities. I explore this line of thinking in the remainder of this chapter.

Rethinking Contextual Theology: From Explanatory Genre to Constitutive Genre

The life situations of Christian communities, as Andrew Walls argues, should function as the workshop of theology:

> The laboratory space for theology is not in the study or the library. The major theological laboratory—workshop might be a more appropriate term—lies in the life situations of believers or the church. Theological activity arises out of the Christian mission and Christian living, from the need for Christians to make Christian choices and to think in a Christian way. This compulsion to think in a Christian way becomes more powerful and more urgent whenever the gospel crosses a cultural frontier, since the process of crossing cultural frontiers almost inevitably creates situations not previously encountered by Christians, and a different climate of thought poses intellectual questions not considered before. Cross-cultural encounter is therefore a spur to theological creativity.[15]

Walls' words above highlight two different paths that theologians can follow to construct Christian theology. On the one hand, Christian theology may be understood as the contextualization of established doctrines, beliefs, and practices. On the other hand, Christian theology may be imagined as an ongoing reflection on God-world relations from the context of a Christian community, along with its Scripture, and ecclesial tradition. Theologians who follow the first path aim to contextualize (to make relevant) the existing theological beliefs in ways that answer new questions of a Christian community. Theologians who follow the second path seek to construct new theological

14. Robert Schreiter is an example of some theologians who see contextual theology or "local theology" as the act of making sense of the Christian message in a local context. See Schreiter, *Constructing Local Theologies*, 2.

15. Walls, "Rise of Global Theologies," 19–20.

beliefs and practices that are thoroughly grounded in the context of a Christian community in response to new theological issues.

Historically, many theologians, especially theologians from Western Europe and North America, have conceived theology in a manner that is commensurate with the *first path*—making the existing theologies relevant to a new theological issue. Paul Tillich's idea of theology in some ways falls within this tradition. For Tillich, theology "is the methodical interpretation of the contents of the Christian faith."[16] Tillich's method of correlation does not quite carry him over to the *second path*—formulating a new theology in order to address a new theological issue—insofar as he understands the task of theologians as pressing an established "Christian message" for answers to "existential questions" implied in "the human situation"—in the ultimate concerns and questions of human beings.[17] The content of the "Christian message" of which Tillich speaks may be summarized as the "*Logos* became flesh, that the principle of the divine self-revelation has become manifest in the event 'Jesus as the Christ.'"[18] Clearly, what Tillich calls the "message" is partly the product of the theological activities of some earliest Christian communities. Since Tillich has highlighted the christological confessions that were informed by the history, experience, vernacular, and culture of the Jewish, Hellenistic, and Greek-speaking Christian communities, should such christological confessions be *the* Christian message? No Christian message is *a*contextual: a message that is not conditioned by the context of the community that constructs and also appropriates it. The content of whatever is called "Christian message" bears the marks of the community that produces it, even if the community is not consciously aware of the influence of its context on the content of such message.

Byang Kato's view of the relationship between Christian theology and the indigenous cultures of Africa is another example of a form of theology that focuses primarily on the task of expressing the so-called Christian message in ways that are relevant to Christian communities. In his critique of African theology, Kato acknowledged "the need for Christian theology to address itself specifically to the African situation."[19] Kato highlighted the "principles

16. Tillich, *Systematic Theology*, 1:15.

17. Tillich, *Systematic Theology*, 1:62.

18. Tillich, *Systematic Theology*, 1:16.

19. Kato, "Theological Issues in Africa," 146. In 1969, E. Bolaji Idowu described the central objectives of the project of African theology as follows: "We seek, in effect, to discover in what way the Christian faith could best be presented, interpreted, and inculcated in Africa so that Africans will hear God in Jesus Christ addressing Himself immediately to them in their own native situation and particular circumstances." Idowu, "Introduction," 16.

of interpretation, polygamy, family life, the spirit world, and communal life" as examples of the areas that "should be given serious consideration."[20] He, however, expressed dissatisfaction with the project of African theology because he believed that "many theologians spend their time defending traditional African religions and practices that are incompatible with biblical teaching."[21] For Kato, in order for African theology to become Christian theology, the "Bible must be its absolute source."[22] Sounding a theological alarm warning about the danger of syncretism, Kato asked African theologians, especially Evangelicals, "to express Christianity in the context of the African" while upholding at the same time that "the Bible" is "the absolute source" because the "Bible is God's written Word addressed to Africans—and to all peoples—within their cultural background."[23] Kato concluded:

> It is more appropriate to talk of Christian theology and then to define whatever context it is related to, e.g., reflections from Africa; the context of marriage in Africa; and the spirit world in Africa. But a continuing effort should be made to relate Christian theology to the changing situations in Africa. Only as the Bible is taken as the absolute Word of God can it have an authoritative and relevant message for Africa.[24]

In his criticism of North American and South African versions of Black theology, Kato faults them for not accepting the Bible as the absolute source of authority in matters relating to Christian beliefs and practices. He writes, "For the Christian, the Bible is the absolute authority on which to base all theological and ethical formulations. Black theology, however, sets up human experience as the basic term of reference."[25]

Kato fails to take seriously the complex relationship of the Bible to Christian theology, particularly how exactly the Bible functions as the source of Christian theology. Also, he seemed to have understood Christian theology as a closed reality for which the task of a theologian is to express it in ways that address the changing needs of Christian communities of each era. Kato also fails to see that Christian theology is the product of a complex process, which is deeply informed and shaped by what is written in the Bible and also the currents that shaped theologians' hermeneutics, ecclesiastical traditions, and agendas. Kato speaks of "Christian theology"

20. Kato, "Theological Issues in Africa," 146.
21. Kato, "Theological Issues in Africa," 146.
22. Kato, "Theological Issues in Africa," 147.
23. Kato, "Theological Issues in Africa," 148.
24. Kato, "Theological Issues in Africa," 148.
25. Kato, "Evaluation of Black Theology," 246.

as if it is a single reality. Historically, communities, sometimes those belonging to the same ecclesial tradition, hold competing theological beliefs. For example, while some Pentecostal churches understand the doctrine of baptism in the Holy Spirit as a second experience that is subsequent to a conversion experience, which is marked by an initial sign of tongues, many Evangelical churches argue that baptism in the Holy Spirit is a part of the process of conversion experience in which God the Father baptizes, metaphorically speaking, believers in the Holy Spirit so that they can become members of the body of Christ.[26]

Contextual theology, as I imagine it, requires an inter-contextual activity: bringing the contexts (as well as the theological contents) of *loci theologici* (Scripture, church tradition, reason, and the context a Christian community) into dialogical communication through a process of *theological appropriation*. By "theological appropriation," I mean a reworking of theological data (ideas, thoughts, beliefs, and sayings) derived from *loci theologici* for the purposes of constructing a theology that addresses particular theological needs of a community. It is a theological activity that entails moving back and forth between the context of Scripture, the context of church tradition, and the context of Christian community as a theologian employs reason in collating and analyzing theological data drawn from these sources. Ideally, theological appropriation will require attending to the range of meanings of theological data drawn from theological sources while avoiding the temptation to distort, misread, and misrepresent the data. Theological appropriation requires both *rethinking* (assessing carefully with the intent to show a fresh understanding) and *reconstructing* (remaking something with the intent to improve or make better).

The type of contextual theology I propose here differs from the works of theologians who concede that all theology is contextual but proceed to treat the context of an intended audience of their theology as merely a recipient that ought not contribute to the content of Christian theology. It also differs from an *explanatory genre* of contextual theology: a form of contextual theology in which theologians merely use local metaphors and thoughts to explain the Christian faith to a present-day community. With the exception of the "anthropological model," other models that Stephen Bevans discussed in *Models of Contextual Theology* can be subsumed under the category of the explanatory genre of contextual theology.[27] The term

26. For more discussions on the doctrine of the Baptism in the Holy Spirit, see Macchia, *Baptized in the Spirit*.

27. Bevans, *Models of Contextual Theology*. The "translation model" focuses on transmitting the "essential message of Christianity," which stands above all cultures, to present-day communities.

"explanatory," as used here, implies that a contextual theologian is to be likened to a messenger who has been given the freedom to deliver a message from a foreign source (Scripture and church tradition) to a Christian community in a manner that is understandable to the audience but retains the contents of the message. In the words of Bevans, "There is always a content to be adapted or accommodated to a particular culture."[28]

The Latin American liberation theologian Gustavo Gutiérrez recognizes the usefulness of the explanatory genre of contextual theology, albeit with some caveats:

> Every theology is, and must be, a dialogue with the culture of its age. The dialogue brings into play the theology's capacity for making the gospel relevant in human history. This supposes, on the one hand, a lucid fidelity to the "deposit of faith" [that is, "the revealed source—the scriptures as they live on in tradition"] and, on the other, a great loyalty to the historical moment in which theology is being developed.[29]

The African theologian John Mbiti shares the same assumption about making the teaching or message of the Christian faith relevant to the changing human contexts.[30] Writing specifically about African theology, Mbiti argues that it "must be sufficiently wide to comprehend the depths of the Christian faith and to interpret it to the people in terms of their understanding and needs."[31] The explanatory genre of contextual theology also implies that the task of a theologian is to demonstrate how a message is relevant to the questions of an audience, even though the message was formulated without their concerns in mind.[32] I argue that contextual theologizing that is grounded primarily in the explanatory genre model may lack the necessary impetus for critiquing and reimagining inherited (both local and foreign) theologies insofar as its main goal is to convey a Christian message or doctrine through the means of local languages and thoughts.

In contrast to the explanatory genre of contextual theology, I propose a model that may be described as a *constitutive genre*. This genre of contextual theology sees the context of a present-day Christian community as an essential theological source that should contribute both to the form and content of Christian theology in ways that are different from other sources such as Scripture, tradition, and reason. The constitutive genre is different from the

28. Bevans, *Models of Contextual Theology*, 37.
29. Gutiérrez, *Truth Shall Make You Free*, 89.
30. Mbiti, "Ways and Means of Communicating the Gospel," 331.
31. Mbiti, "Ways and Means of Communicating the Gospel," 332.
32. Kato, *Theological Pitfalls in Africa*, 182.

"anthropological model" described by Bevans insofar as this model's primary concern is the authentic cultural identity of a community.[33] For Bevans,
"the anthropological model" is grounded in the assumption that "human
nature, and therefore the human context, is good, holy, and valuable."[34] Also,
the "anthropological model would emphasize that it is within human culture
that we find God's revelation—not as a separate supra-cultural message, but
in the very complexity of culture itself, in the warp and woof of human relationships, which are constitutive of cultural existence."[35] It is not entirely
clear in the anthropological model how the context of a community functions differently from Scripture and church tradition in Christian theology
if, as Bevans says, this model sees the Bible as "the product of socially and
culturally conditioned religious experience" of the people of ancient Israel
and early Christians, and sees church tradition as the answer to the questions and concerns of Western Europe.[36]

The constitutive genre of contextual theology I am proposing is
grounded in two assumptions; namely, (a) the context of a Christian community is an indispensable theological source, and (b) theological sources
perform different essential functions in the construction of Christian theology. For example, while Christian Scripture performs the task of guiding Christian theologians to construct theologies that are grounded in the
teaching and life of Jesus as expressed in the New Testament, the context
of a Christian community can guide them to construct theologies that are
grounded in their peculiar theological questions their communities address
to Jesus. Christians typically work out such questions as they negotiate the
task of embodying their commitment to Jesus within the matrix of their life
situations, social locations, history, and cultures.

Adopting the constitutive genre of contextual theology requires doing
theology in several theological theaters. I will highlight four such theaters.
First, contextual theology is to be done in the theater of the changing context of life of a community, which either conceals or amplifies the tension
between *what ought to be* and *what really is*. The expression "what ought
to be" refers to the teaching of Jesus (for example, loving one's enemy as
expressed in Matt 5:43–48). The expression "what really is" refers to how
Christians, disciples of Jesus, are in reality working out, appropriating, and
reappropriating his teaching as they negotiate their Christian identity. For
instance, a contextual theologian might ask: How are American Christians

33. Bevans, *Models of Contextual Theology*, 55.
34. Bevans, *Models of Contextual Theology*, 56.
35. Bevans, *Models of Contextual Theology*, 56.
36. Bevans, *Models of Contextual Theology*, 56.

appropriating Jesus's teaching on loving one's enemies in post-9/11 America, which is incredibly shaped by anxieties about terrorism and also belief in America's military prowess?

Second, contextual theology is to be formulated in the theater of *eternal values* and *temporal issues*. To illustrate this claim, a common criticism proffered against Latin American liberation theology is that it focuses primarily on the issues of material wealth and poverty (earthly issues) at the expense of spiritual wealth and poverty (eternal value). Of course, what those who offer such criticism sometimes fail to grasp is that the biblical ideas of salvation are grounded in holistic well-being, which rejects any unhealthy dichotomy between spiritual and physical, between spiritual and emotional, and between spiritual and political (see Luke 4:16–21).[37]

Third, contextual theology is to be developed in the theater of the *past* and the *present*. Theology is always under the threat of dissolution in the face of constantly changing human contexts, for better or worse. To survive, theology must be designed to adapt to the changing terrains of the contexts of Christian communities. Contextual theologians should navigate the complex terrain of the "past" (for example, the Apartheid-era South Africa) and the "present" (for example, post-Apartheid South Africa in which some South Africans are still suffering under dehumanizing residues from the Apartheid era). After assessing the strengths and weaknesses of the Truth and Reconciliation Commission (TRC) in post-Apartheid South Africa, William Danaher observed,

> criticisms [against the TRC] do establish a liminal state of reconciliation in post-Apartheid South Africa. This liminality reflects the fact that the TRC operated with both a minimal view of reconciliation, defined in terms of peaceful coexistence, and a maximal view that sought to transform all structural inequalities.[38]

Fourth, contextual theology is to be formulated in the theater of *armchair* theological research and *fieldwork* theological research. Traditionally, theological studies focus on armchair library research. Theology students are typically taught both biblical hermeneutics and theological hermeneutics, which can help them to exegete biblical texts and also theological (primary and secondary) texts. Such students are rarely taught courses that are designed to equip them with the necessary hermeneutical skills for interpreting the life situations of a Christian community. If, as proposed in this book, the context of a Christian community contains relevant theological

37. For more discussions, see ch. 5.
38. See Danaher, "Music That Will Bring Back the Dead?," 122.

data, theologians should ferret them out and also engage them. Accessing such theological data would require theologians to bridge the gap between armchair theological research and fieldwork theological research. Knowledge in data collection in social sciences through ethnographic fieldwork and data analysis—qualitative analysis or quantitative data analysis—are useful for accessing theological materials that are embedded in the grassroots theologies of Christian communities

To sum up this section, what is contextual about contextual theology is not merely the recognition that theology is to be done with a specific community in mind or that theologians should use local concepts to express such theology. Rather, it is the recognition of a Christian community's context as an essential *locus theologicus* of Christian theology. In other words, like other sources of theology, context generates essential theological materials that can be harvested, harnessed, and used for formulating Christian theology. The four theological theaters outlined above will guide my exploration of theological sources and their functions, which are crucial issues in the constitutive genre of contextual theology.

Theological Sources and Their Functions

In *Models of Contextual Theology*, Stephen Bevans argues that what distinguishes contextual theology from other kinds of theology is the recognition of the validity of another *locus theologicus*: present human experience. Contextual theology, Bevans writes, "realizes that culture, history, contemporary thought forms . . . are to be considered, along with scripture and tradition, as valid sources for theological expression."[39] Bevans sees the three *loci theologici*—Scripture, ecclesiastical tradition, and present human experience—essentially as consisting in the experience of Christian communities. Scripture is the record of the "faith experience of the *past*" Jewish and Christian communities. In ecclesiastical tradition, the faith experience of the past is "kept alive, preserved, defended—and perhaps even neglected or suppressed." The contemporary context of the church is its *present* experience.[40] For Bevans, contextual theology is a consequence of the "incarnational nature of Christianity."[41] God's act of becoming flesh in a particular human being, Jesus of Nazareth, models for theologians the process of becoming particular in their expressions of the beliefs and practices of the Christian faith. Bevans insists that theological contextualization "is

39. Bevans, *Models of Contextual Theology*, 4.
40. Bevans, *Models of Contextual Theology*, 5.
41. Bevans, *Models of Contextual Theology*, 12.

not something on the fringes of theological enterprise. It is at the very center of what it means to do theology in today's world. Contextualization, in other words, is a theological imperative."[42]

How should Scripture, tradition, and contemporary context interact in the process of constructing a Christian theology? Though Bevans does not engage this question directly, in cautioning against mixing "Christianity and culture" when doing contextual theology, he hints at a possible answer to the question on the relationship of the sources of theology. He seems to favor what may be described as the precedence-subsequence principle: the arrangement of *loci theologici* in their order of importance.[43] Bevans writes that there is no doubt, "when a theologian takes context seriously, he or she can fall into the danger of taking these realities more seriously than the Judaeo-Christian tradition as expressed in scripture and church tradition."[44] For him, the Judaeo-Christian faith "expressed in scripture and church tradition" has pride of place. As I have argued elsewhere, a precedence-subsequence mindset is not entirely helpful to contextual theology vis-à-vis the relationships of *loci theologici*.[45] Asking the question, "What function does each source of theology perform in the process of constructing Christian theology?" rather than, "Which source of theology is primary or secondary?" opens up new vistas for fresh theological ideas and fresh paths to theological exploration. Framing the relationship of the sources of theology in terms of "which is more important" can conceal the strengths and weaknesses of each source. The Bible, for instance, may not be entirely helpful in deciding if a theology passes the "test of relevance"— if it addresses the *actual needs* of a present-day Christian community.[46] The books of the Bible were written from specific contexts and were addressed to specific communities that do not share the same history and cultures with the twenty-first-century Christians. Therefore, proposing that the Bible is the primary source of theology does not really get us very far unless we are also ready to answer the question: "Primary in what sense?" While Scripture may be construed as the primary source of Christian theology in relation to biblical identity, it may not be the primary source in relation to theology's relevance to the theological needs that are embedded in the life situations of a present-day Christian community.[47]

42. Bevans, *Models, of Contextual Theology*, 15.
43. Ezigbo, "Contextual Theology," 107–8.
44. Bevans, *Models of Contextual Theology*, 24.
45. Ezigbo, "Contextual Theology," 107–8.
46. Ezigbo, *Introducing Christian Theologies* 1:13–14.
47. Ezigbo, *Introducing Christian Theologies* 1:12–13. According to Rowan Williams,

Theology emerges from and within the matrix of different sources. The term "source" may be used in three ways that are relevant to the discourse on theological sources. First, it can mean a fountainhead from which something or an idea originates. In this sense, a source is that which generates information about something or someone. A theological source generates theological materials. I use the term "theological materials" here for the raw or processed theological ideas, thoughts, and concepts from and with which a Christian theology can be formulated. None of the three sources of theology singled out in this book—Scripture, church tradition, and context— presents an unmediated knowledge about God. Though a person can attain knowledge of God by studying Scripture, church tradition, and the context of a Christian community, these sources only play a mediatory role. They do not provide an unequivocal access to God and knowledge of God. In a typical dialectical fashion, Karl Barth describes God as the being who is at once knowable and unknowable to human beings. "When God enters, history for the while ceases to be, and there is nothing more to ask; for something wholly different and new begins—a history with its own distinct grounds, possibilities, and hypotheses."[48] Barth also says, "to speak of the glory of God in creation, for example, [is] to pass immediately to emphasizing God's complete concealment from us in that creation (as in Romans 8)" and that the "Word, the word of God, which we ourselves shall never speak, has put on our weakness and unprofitableness so that *our* world *in* its very weakness and unprofitableness has become capable at least of being the mortal frame, the earthen vessel, of the word of God."[49]

Second, a *source* can designate a body of knowledge about someone or something that is generally accepted as authoritative. A source, in this sense, can perform a hermeneutical task. Scripture, church tradition, and the context of a Christian community not only generate theological materials for constructing Christian theology but perform interpretative tasks. They can supply helpful principles and categories for how to utilize the theological materials they generate. Scripture constantly nudges theologians to keep their focus on the biblical ideas of God-world relations when constructing theology. Church tradition ought to remind theologians to enter into dialogical communication with the established and authoritative teaching of the church. As a source, context ought to press upon theologians to

---

"'becoming contemporary' [with Jesus] involves an openness to those other believers, past as well as present, in whom Jesus is believed to be active. Mature Christian identity is at home with the past—with diverse aspects of it, in diverse ways, but always as posing the question of relation with Jesus." See Williams, *Why Study the Past?*, 91.

48. Barth, *Word of God and the Word of Man*, 37.

49. Barth, *Word of God and the Word of Man*, 207, 216.

construct theologies that attend to the changing questions and needs that are present in the life situations of a Christian community.

Third, a *source* can equally function as a canon—that is, a standard principle for assessing something. Scripture, church tradition, and the context of a Christian community qualify as sources of theology in these three usages, albeit in varying ways. They generate theological materials, guide one's understanding of theology, and serve as the measuring grids for testing the identity and utility of a given theology. When the relationship of these three theological sources is construed in terms of the task each performs rather than in terms of a hierarchical order of importance (i.e., a primary-secondary relation), together they can provide helpful tools for assessing the identity and utility of Christian theology. A contextual theologian does not focus primarily on established church dogmas but rather on new ways to construct a Christian message that is faithful to Christian Scripture, in dialogue with church traditions, and relevant to the changing theological needs of Christians embedded in their contexts. This means that contextual theology ought not to be construed as an afterthought. It is central to the very nature of Christian theology and also to its continued viability in the constantly changing human world.

How are theological sources to be used in contextual theology? To answer this question, I will focus on how Scripture, church tradition, and a Christian community's context qualify and also are to be used as theological sources.

Scripture

Is Scripture's integrity or uniqueness compromised in the constitutive genre of contextual theology? A latent temptation lurking behind theologians is the use of Scripture to sanction preconceived theological beliefs rather than pressing it for theological materials for constructing Christian theological beliefs. In *The Uses of Scripture in Recent Theology*, David Kelsey shows the different, sometimes disparate, ways theologians, particularly Protestant theologians, use Scripture to "authorize" their theological positions or proposals. Some construe Scripture as authoritative because of its doctrinal content and its "intrinsic property" as a divinely inspired (revelatory) text.[50] Some ground Scripture's authority in its narrative force ("construed as confessional recital") that calls a Christian's attention to the acts of God in human history. In this view, God does not reveal Godself

---

50. Kelsey, *Uses of Scripture in Recent Theology*, 29.

doctrinally but narratively, for example, in the event of Jesus Christ.[51] Others imagine the authority of Scripture in ways in which it occasions "a new self-understanding" and transforms the life of its readers.[52] Kelsey clearly shows that theologians are conditioned by their own agendas and goals. How, then, should theologians ensure that the integrity and authority of Scripture will not be compromised in their theological formulations? To answer this question, it will be useful to explore how exactly Scripture (Bible) qualifies as a source of theology.

What qualifies Scripture as a source of theology? For many Christians with no formal theological education, the answer to this question is fairly obvious because the Bible is the "word of God." However, the differences in the genres of the diverse collection of books that make up the Bible require us to qualify the usage and meaning of the phrase "word of God." Should it be understood metaphorically when describing how the words of the Bible, which were written by human beings, could be taken up by God to accomplish specific tasks in the life of a person or Christian community? Or should the phrase be understood in an ontological sense, implying that the words of the Bible have divine origins? Robert Stein has argued that Christian

> scripture does not claim God as its immediate author. Paul's letters do not begin, "God, the Father, Son, and Holy Spirit, to the church at Rome." No book of the Bible claims God as its immediate author! Christians, of course, believe that behind the books of the Bible stands the living God, who has inspired his servants [authors of the Bible] in the writing of these books.[53]

Taking into account the common belief among many Christian communities that the Holy Spirit inspired human beings who authored the Bible, the phrase "Word of God" should not be taken literally or at least without significant qualifications.

Any view of the Bible as the sacred book that has authority over Christians ought to simultaneously uphold it as the "Word of God" and the "word of humans" because it was authored by real human beings whose thoughts and ideas were inspired by the Holy Spirit (see 2 Tim 3:16; 2 Pet 1:20–21). Many Christians read the canonical texts of their traditions with the expectation of hearing God's voice and words. But how exactly are the words of the Bible, which were written by human beings, God's words? Traditionally, theologians appeal to the idea of divine inspiration as a theological warrant

51. Kelsey, *Uses of Scripture in Recent Theology*, 33.

52. Kelsey, *Uses of Scripture in Recent Theology*, 84.

53. Stein, *Basic Guide to Interpreting the Bible*, 28.

for the claim that the Bible is God's word. Theologians, of course, do not agree on the nature of the inspiration of the Bible. For some, inspiration consists in God's miraculous act of stirring in the hearts of the authors of the Bible some ideas but granting them the freedom to express such ideas in writing from their own expertise, culture, and limited experience.[54] Others claim that the inspiration of the Bible consists in God's miraculous act of suspending the natural abilities and freedom of the writers of the Bible and empowering them to receive words from God and to write down the words without the possibility of addition or subtraction.[55] Theologians who hold this view of the inspiration of the Bible construe God's revelation in propositional terms: God reveals Godself through the Bible, which makes true assertions about God-world relations. Yet other theologians deny that a special relationship existed between the authors of the Bible and God.[56] However one construes the inspiration of the Bible, what is important, theologically speaking, is that part of "what it means to call a text or a set of texts 'scripture' is that it is 'authority' for the common life of the community" and it is "essential to establishing and persevering the community's identity."[57] James Barr makes a similar point about the authority of the Bible. He writes,

> [T]he Bible has authority because its authority, in some form or other, is built into the structure of Christian faith and the Christian religion. Being a Christian means—among other things—being tied up with the God of the Bible, with biblical ideas of God and tradition about him, with Jesus Christ, about whom almost our only source of guidance lies in the Bible as primary written source.[58]

In addition to the doctrine of inspiration, I would like to suggest another reason the Bible qualifies as an indispensable source of Christian theology. As followers of Jesus Christ, Christians are to return to his teaching in their practice of theology. Jesus's understanding of God-world relations, which is preserved in some of the New Testament books, ought to be the grounds for and the circumference of Christian theology.[59] Notwith-

54. This view of the inspiration of the Bible is called the dynamic theory.

55. Mechanical theories of inspiration such as dictation theory and verbal theory, with some modifications, fit this description of the inspiration of the Bible.

56. For discussions on the different theories of inspiration, see Gaussen, *Divine Inspiration of the Bible*; Trembath, *Evangelical Theories of Biblical Inspiration*; Vanhoozer, *First Theology*; Ezigbo, *Introducing Christian Theologies* 1:65–108.

57. Kelsey, *Uses of Scripture in Recent Theology*, 89.

58. Barr, *Scope and Authority of the Bible*, 52.

59. Following some earliest ecumenical councils' interpretations of some biblical

standing their imperfections, the first-generation disciples of Jesus Christ
preserved reliable accounts of Jesus's practices and teaching in the New Testament. The canonical Gospels preserved for future generations reliable *accounts* (descriptions, theological reflections, and commentaries). However,
it is noteworthy that the publication of the book entitled *The Five Gospels*,
which aimed to separate the authentic sayings of Jesus from the unauthentic
sayings that are attributed to him in the four canonical Gospels, highlighted
some textual issues that have concerned many biblical scholars working in
the field of the New Testament.[60] *The Five Gospels*, however, has not done
any irreparable damage to the credibility of the traditional four canonical
Gospels and the words they ascribe to Jesus. One critic argues that *The Five
Gospels* "finds substantial contradiction in scholarly literature" and also "the
one-sided and sometimes flippant way in which [it] frames its presentation
has more tenuous footing in solid academic learning than it claims."[61] Many
scholars, some of whom see the claims of the authors of *The Five Gospels* as
overly ambitious and untenable, acknowledge that the four Gospels present Jesus Christ (his words and deeds) primarily in theological terms. Luke
Timothy Johnson argues that the

> four canonical Gospels are remarkably consistent on one es-
> sential aspect of the identity and mission of Jesus. Their funda-
> mental focus is [neither] on Jesus' wondrous deeds nor on his
> wise words. Their shared focus is on the character of his life and
> death. They all reveal the same pattern of radical obedience to
> God and selfless love toward other people. All four Gospels also
> agree that discipleship is to follow the same messianic pattern.[62]

The Bible is not an uncomplicated *locus theologicus*. It is not an examination toolkit containing theological questions and answers. Therefore,
claiming that the Bible is the final source of authority in theological matters does not quite settle the issue of its function as a source of Christian

---

passages such as John 1:1–14 and Phil 2:5–11, many Christians believe that Jesus Christ
is ontologically, not merely functionally, divine. However one appropriates these christological claims, they show that many Christian communities believe Jesus taught true
things about God-world relations. If it is true that Jesus is God incarnate, what he says
about God-world relations should be essential to Christian theology. For more discussions on the Christologies of the Council of Nicaea (325 CE), Council of Constantinople (381 CE), Council of Ephesus (431 CE), and Council of Chalcedon (451 CE), see
Kelly, *Early Christian Doctrines*; Grillmeier, *Christ in Christian Tradition*; Hurtado, *How
on Earth Did Jesus Become a God?*

60. Funk et al., *Five Gospels*.

61. Yarbrough, "Gospel according to the Jesus Seminar," 8–20.

62. Johnson, *Real Jesus*, 157–58.

theology. Even the most optimistic views of the inspiration of the Bible that claim its words are God's and not human's do not convincingly show that it is an uncomplicated source of theology.[63] It is not as if there is a straight-forward way to ask God and biblical authors if a particular interpretation of a biblical text is correct. Exegesis, as Karl Barth has reminded us, is a process of "taking and giving, of reading out and reading in." As such, all "exegesis can become predominantly interposition rather than exposition and to that degree it can fall back into the Church's dialogue with itself."[64] One's theological hermeneutics is deeply shaped by one's history, agenda, experience, and culture. For example, some scholars that use a postcolonial theological hermeneutics have pointed out that European territorial and intellectual colonization of African, Asian, and Latin American continents affected how the Bible was presented by European missionaries and how Latin Americans, Asians, and Africans received them. Noting the role the Bible played in the European colonial project, R. S. Sugirtharajah argues that colonialists' dehumanizing binaries between colonizers and the colonized shaped early European missionaries' interpretations of Scripture and the theologies they extrapolated from it:

> Colonialists often discursively constructed paradigms such as Christian/savage, civilized/barbaric, and orderly/disorderly in order to define themselves, and also to explain the dominance and acceleration of colonial rule. Such contrastive pairings helped to condemn the other as inferior and also helped to determine the nature of their hold over the people they subjugated. The early missionary hermeneutics which abetted in this enterprise extrapolated this binary view to inject its own biblical values into the private and public lives of the colonized, and for the good of nations which were still living in a "savage" state.[65]

Sugirtharajah went on to highlight what he believed were the "marks of colonial hermeneutics," which include the use of the Bible as a "vehicle for inculcating European manners," encroachment—the introduction of "alien values under that guise of biblicization"—and the efforts to displace local cultures that were judged to be "undermining the viability of Christian virtues and the colonial project."[66] Sugirtharajah also noted that some European missionaries juxtaposed "biblical and secular

---

63. Verbal theories of the inspiration of the Bible claim that the Holy Spirit chose both thoughts and words for the human writers of the Bible.

64. Barth, *Church Dogmatics*, 106.

65. Sugirtharajah, *Bible and the Third World*, 62–63.

66. Sugirtharajah, *Bible and the Third World*, 63–66.

history as a convenient weapon against those who dared to resist colonial intervention."[67] He observed that "textualization" (privileging written text over oral tradition) was a "characteristic of colonial hermeneutics."[68] Finally, he noted that "historicization of faith"—the presentation of "biblical religion and a historical faith"—led colonial interpreters to "portray non-biblical religions as the pagan 'other' of Christianity, needing deliverance."[69] Sugirtharajah showed convincingly that some early European missionaries superimposed their own interpretations of Scripture and cultures on the way of life of the colonized communities.

Returning to the discussion on the Bible's role in formulating Christian theology, it is worth noting at this point that the belief in a closed biblical canon saves contemporary Christian communities the headache of adding to or removing books from their own Scripture. A closed canon, however, does not entail that God no longer does new things in and through the believing communities or in the world. If God continues to act in the world in ways recognizable to human beings, as many Christian communities claim, it is reasonable to expect that such divine acts would spur fresh theological activities. Consider, for example, a student that turned down her parents' request to spend holidays with them because she believed God wanted her to stay back to serve food to the homeless in the city where her university was located. Clearly, her reason for turning down the request was theological: she was convinced God would want her to stay back and minister to the homeless in a particular city. The student's parents may struggle to understand why God led their daughter to act in a manner that goes against their good desire for her. Also, the student's parents and the student may also wonder why God would care so much about the homeless and homelessness. Her parents may also wonder how they are to theologically verify their daughter's claim; after all it is not as if they can get direct answers to their questions by reading the Bible.

If theological materials and issues can be discerned in the living experience of Christian communities, what tasks exactly should the Bible perform when doing contextual theology? I argue that it should perform two related tasks. Firstly, as a theological source, it supplies essential theological materials (raw and processed) to theologians. The Bible is an essential source of Christian theology because it is the fountainhead of the Christian ideas of God-world relations. Secondly, when interpreted correctly, it should function as a *judge*—providing guidance and corrective measures

67. Sugirtharajah, *Bible and the Third World*, 66–67.

68. Sugirtharajah, *Bible and the Third World*, 68–69.

69. Sugirtharajah, *Bible and the Third World*, 70.

on how Christian communities can live as disciples of Jesus. The Bible, for many Christians, has remained a constant in the elusive quest of the people of faith to know God. Therefore, any reflection that poses a threat to its constancy is hardly welcomed by many Christians. Even Karl Barth who took seriously the human origins of the Bible, argued that it should remain a constant in the church's life:

> With its acknowledgment of the presence of the Canon the Church expresses the fact that it is not left to itself in its proclamation, that the commission on the ground of which it proclaims, the object which it proclaims, the judgment under which its proclamation stands and the event of real proclamation must all come from elsewhere, from without, and very concretely from without, in all the externality of the concrete Canon as a categorical imperative which is also historical, which speaks in time. And with its acknowledgment that this Canon is in fact identical with the Bible of the Old and New Testaments, with the word of the prophets and apostles, it expresses the truth that this reference of its proclamation to something that is concretely external is not a general principle, nor a mere determination of form whose content might be this or might be quite different, but . . . that this part of past history consisting of specific texts constitutes the working instructions or marching orders by which not just the Church's proclamation but the very Church itself stands or falls . . .[70]

For Barth, the Bible protects Christian communities from deviating from the narrative of the life of the church. As the canon—a constant criterion—the Bible should not be "taken prisoner by the Church, that its own life will be absorbed into the life of the Church, that its free power will be transformed into the authority of the Church, in short that it will lose its character as a norm magisterially confronting the Church."[71] Appealing to its "writtenness," Barth argues that the Bible is a concrete criterion with which the Church can judge its proclamation, self-dialogue, and traditions.[72]

The knowledge of God that flows from the Bible is to be expected to supply reliable, although not uncomplicated, knowledge of God for Christian communities. However, theologians should resist the temptation to sanitize the Bible, purging it of its diverse and sometimes disparate portrayals of God-human relations. Beneath the messiness, roughness, and

---

70. Barth, *Church Dogmatics 1.1*, 101.

71. Barth, *Church Dogmatics 1.1*, 106.

72. Barth, *Church Dogmatics 1.1*, 106–7.

complications of Scripture lies theological richness: its constellation of plentiful ideas of God-world relations. Christian theologians should excavate Scripture, harness its theological resources, and utilize its theological materials to formulate theologies for their communities. I will now turn attention to the role that church tradition plays in the process of formulating Christian theology.

Church Tradition

Much of what constitutes the theological tradition of an ecclesial community is derived from Scripture. As David Fergusson has noted, "The reading of sacred texts takes place within communities of faith with their traditions and practices of interpretation. The text is not merely read but is used in prayer, sacraments, creedal statements, liturgy and rituals."[73] One way to differentiate the difference between Scripture and church tradition, when understood as sources of theology, is that the former mainly contains *raw theological materials* (undeveloped theological ideas and concepts) while the latter is largely processed theological products. Another difference is that many communities see Scripture as a closed canon and church tradition as an open canon. Of course, the idea of a closed-church tradition could be theologically dangerous. It would close the door to a fresh look at Scripture, particularly as a Christian community dialogues with its theological ideas in light of its changing life situations. Doing so would also close the door to fresh theological ideas, beliefs, and the possibility of dropping a theological belief, doctrine, or practice that a community may discover is either theologically unwarranted or useless. To cite one example of how the idea of an open tradition can give Christian communities the chance to rethink, revise, and when necessary remove a belief or practice from their theological repertoire, the Roman Catholic Church has held the theory of the Limbo since the medieval period.[74] This belief deals with the question of the salvific fate of infants who died without undergoing the sacrament of baptism. The Limbo is an intermediate state between heaven and hell that supposedly housed infants who died without being baptized. But in 2007, Pope Benedict XVI endorsed the conclusion of the International Theological Commission: the "idea of Limbo, which the Church has used for many centuries to designate the destiny of infants who die without Baptism, has no clear foundation in revelation, even though it has long been used in

73. Fergusson, *Faith and Its Critics*, 153.

74. For a survey of the theory of the Limbo, see Sullivan, "Development of Doctrine about Infants," 3–14.

traditional theological teaching."[75] Pope Benedict XVI effectively abolished the theory of the Limbo that had been in the Roman Catholic Church's theological repertoire for decades.

Christian denominations—for example, the Coptic Church, Roman Catholic Church, Anglican Church, Pentecostal churches, and Greek Orthodox Church—have different bodies of teaching that their members are expected to adopt as reliable theological guides in matters of faith and practice. What the term "tradition" means theologically and also in relation to ecclesial communities varies from denomination to denomination. Aristotle Papanikolaou has observed that many theologians of Orthodox Churches sometimes imagine tradition in ways that differ from its nature and functions in Protestantism and Roman Catholicism:

> Against the Protestants, the Orthodox authors affirm the indispensability of tradition; against the Roman Catholics, they reject the juxtaposition of tradition and scripture as two necessary forms of the truths about the revelation in Christ.[76]

Papanikolaou also highlights the different ways in which tradition is understood in Orthodox Churches, which for him, share a similar root:

> That which unites all these contemporary Orthodox theologians is an understanding of tradition in terms of divine-human communion, or *theosis*, which has also been used as a marker of difference by almost all contemporary Orthodox theologians against Protestant and Roman Catholic theologies.[77]

Though Papanikolaou concedes the importance of *theosis* and "lived-experience," he suggests that Orthodox Churches need to use "contemporary forms of philosophy" to rediscover that they have a "tradition of enquiry."[78] Reason and rationality, according to Papanikolaou, should not be underemphasized in the imagination of Orthodox Churches' understanding of tradition. He writes,

> [The] link between theoretical and practical reason within the Orthodox tradition is remarkably consistent and coherent, because insofar as rational enquiry into the God-world relations resulted in the Christian conceptualization of God as Trinity, this particular understanding of the God-world relations

75. See International Theological Commission, "Hope of Salvation for Infants."
76. Papanikolaou, "Tradition as Reason and Practice," 92.
77. Papanikolaou, "Tradition as Reason and Practice," 93.
78. Papanikolaou, "Tradition as Reason and Practice," 94.

identifies the human good as one of communion with the living
God, and the ascetical tradition can thus be seen as an extended
moral enquiry into how one lives the dogma.[79]

Some scholars, while agreeing with the proposal of Papanikolaou, have noted that his conception of reason and rationalization and the role they play
in the tradition of Orthodox Churches can be misleading. Davor Dzalto, for
example, warns against the assumption that "reason" and "rationality" can
be the basis of the Christian faith or as indispensable tools for explaining
Christian doctrines. He writes,

> [P]arallel to the "tradition of reason," one can also follow another
> tradition in Christian theology, which goes back to the earliest
> days of Christianity. It points to the limits of rational under-
> standing, bringing forth faith and love as those capacities that
> can only bring us to the true "knowledge"—the knowledge and
> the experience of God, which is also the true knowledge of our-
> selves. Such knowledge overcomes this world and our reason.[80]

Reason ought not be construed as the most valuable source of Christian
theology. Also, it should not lead to the silencing of the messy and untidy aspect of the Christian life that is grounded in God's ability to show
wisdom and power through the "foolishness" of the cross of Jesus Christ
(1 Cor 1:18–31).[81] This, of course, does not mean that "reason" is not construed as a source of theology in Dzalto's imagination of the theologies of
Orthodox churches. Rather, he recognizes, and rightly so, the limitations
of reason in the formulation of Christian theology. Reason should not be
viewed as *the* source of Christian theology. It is only one of the sources of
Christian theology.

   In light of the constitutive genre of contextual theology I present in
this book, church *tradition* may be described as a Christian community's
practice of conserving the theological thoughts, doctrines, creeds, litur-
gies, confessional statements, beliefs, and practices of older generations
of Christian communities, sometimes stretching back to the teaching of
Jesus of Nazareth and his earliest disciples. "Conserving" does not imply
passiveness on the part of a present-day Christian community. Church
traditions have emerged in most cases as a result of episcopal, theological,
and political crises. The attempts to conserve the teaching of the earliest
Christian communities have sometimes led to schismatic events. In some

---

79. Papanikolaou, "Tradition as Reason and Practice," 98–99.

80. Dzalto, "Logos as Reason and Love," 116.

81. Premawardhana, "Between Logocentrism and Lococentrism," 399–416.

ways, the Protestant Reformation of the sixteenth century CE arose as a result of the attempts of some Christians from Western Europe to appropriate the spirit of *ad fontes* (returning to original sources) that characterized the Renaissance era that began in the fourteenth century CE. Church tradition functions as a church's living memory that partly conditions its life and identity. It also guides the church's participation in the historical roots of the Christian faith as it negotiates its alliance with some older Christian communities, especially their theological thoughts, doctrines, beliefs, and practices. As a church remembers its Christian roots, which involves interpreting, assessing, and appropriating, it contributes to the subsistence of its tradition. It is worth noting that the desire to iron out the relationship of Scripture to church tradition was a major issue in the Protestant Reformation and also the Church of Rome's Reformation (sometimes called Counter-Reformation).

Tradition is also a constellation of a church's teachings, which are grounded in a continuum from the *past* (what is handed down from a previous generation) to the *present* life situation, that it considers an authoritative source in matters of faith and practice. The *past* here should be understood as the diverse stories of Christians that ought to include the interpretations of Scripture and traditions by earlier Christian communities. The stories of earlier Christians should remind a present-day Christian community of its ancestors and also should encourage the community to contribute to the stories as it works out its identity within the matrix of its own life situations (see Heb 11–12; 1 Cor 15).

Church traditions perform several functions in contextual theology. I will describe briefly three such functions. Firstly, and perhaps most noticeably, church traditions present us with some templates of Christian theology. Most church traditions contain finished theological products insofar as they are comprised of doctrines and practices that are thoroughly grounded in Scripture and theological reflections. The doctrine of the Trinity is a good example. Though the term "trinity" does not appear in the Bible, many Christian theologians, going back to the days of the North African theologian Tertullian, construed it as an appropriate term for describing God's mode of being and the relationship between the three New Testament figures—Father, Son, and Holy Spirit (Matt 28:19; Rom 15:30; Gal 4:4–6).[82] Secondly, church traditions should be mined for theological raw materials—the unprocessed or undeveloped theological ideas, beliefs, and concepts that are expressed in creeds and faith confessions. No church tradition has the final word on the contents of Christian theology. As a community

82. See Tertullian, *Against Praxeas.*

attends to the particular needs of its own context, it will be confronted with the need to develop fresh theologies that satisfy its new needs. Sometimes satisfying a particular theological need requires constructing new doctrines. A doctrine (an official and authoritative teaching of a church) is a finished theological product that is formed with theological materials collected and collated from Scripture, ecumenical councils' theological rulings, writings of the Church Fathers and Mothers, and a community's theological reflections. For example, the doctrine of the "preferential option for the poor," which was adopted by the Latin American Roman Catholic Bishops, was formulated with theological materials that were collected and collated from Scripture and the living experience of Latin American churches as they reflected on what it means theologically to confess that God is a loving Father in the face of poverty on a massive scale.[83] Thirdly, church traditions function as guardrails that can guide Christian theologians in their pursuit of the dual responsibilities of producing theologies that are at once faithful to the Christian faith and relevant to the peculiar needs of their communities. A theology that rejects the distinctive teachings of Christianity (e.g., the doctrine of God incarnate) that have been handed down from generation to generation would need to show why it is worthy of the name "Christian." A theology that is intended for a Christian community but totally disregards the peculiar theological needs of its audience would need to show why it is relevant to the community. As Paul Meier argues, "any argument from Scripture or tradition or nature is filtered through the philosophical presuppositions of the person arguing."[84] The "philosophical presuppositions" and theological agenda of theologians are profoundly affected by their context. How does the context of theologians shape and inform their theological agenda? I explore this below.

Context

Theology is deficient in terms of utility when formulated for a particular community without intentionally and directly engaging theological questions and data embodied by the community. Beyond asking theological questions of the *context* (history, culture, and contemporary state affairs) of their intended audience, contextual theologians formulate theologies with

83. See "Missionary Church Serving Evangelization in Latin America," IV.1.1134, in Third General Conference of Latin American Bishops, *Puebla*, 179; Gutiérrez, *Theology of Liberation*, 171–72.

84. Meier, "On the Veiling of Hermeneutics (1 Cor 11:2–16)," 217.

the materials they gather from the context.[85] For far too long, Christian theology has been imagined, especially in some parts of the Western world, as a field of study that deals with the exegesis and appropriation of "the statement of truth of the Christian message" and also how to present the product of such theological exegesis in a manner befitting to "every generation."[86] This way of imagining Christian theology is grounded in the assumption that theology's task is to present the Christian message, which is supposedly universal and unchanging, in ways that are understandable and coherent to the changing human situations. The Christian message, for many theologians that think in this way, has been expressed in various Christian doctrines on which theological activity should focus. Sometimes theologians speak of the "gospel" as what Christian theology seeks to expound and commend; the gospel that has the capacity "for being at home in more than one cultural environment" but "can be rediscovered at the end of a long and exotic detour through strange idioms and structures of thought."[87]

The context of a Christian community should not be seen as a superfluous source of Christian theology. It should be treated as indispensable source of Christian theology. On the contrary, it is not possible to construct *a*contextual theology—a theology that does not arise from a human context.[88] In his theological reflection on race-constructs and the experience of black people, J. Kameron Carter argues,

> [A]s a twenty-first-century discourse, Christian theology must take its bearings from the Christian theological languages and practices that arise from the lived Christian worlds of dark peoples in modernity and how such peoples reclaimed (and in their own

85. Ada Maria Isasi-Diaz has argued that theologians constructing "*mujerista* theology have developed a method that provides opportunities for and enables grassroot Hispanas/Latinas to speak about themselves and their religious understandings and practices." Also, *mujerista* theologians have created ways to bring the voices of Hispanas/Latinas "to 'official' theological arenas" and have insisted they be "heard and that their lived-experience must be taken in consideration." Isasi-Diaz, *La Lucha Continues*, 93.

86. Tillich, *Systematic Theology*, 1:3.

87. Williams, *On Christian Theology*, xiv. In *Principles of Christian Theology*, John Macquarrie argues that Christian theology "aims not only at showing the internal coherence of the Christian faith, that is to say, how the several doctrines constitute a unity, but also at exhibiting the coherence of this faith with the many other beliefs and attitudes to which we are committed in the modern world." Macquarrie, *Principles of Christian Theology*, v.

88. Oduyoye, "Doing Theology from Beyond the Sahara," 163.

ways salvaged) the language of Christianity, and thus Christian theology, from being a discourse of death—their death.[89]

Carter's point is that Christian theology should attend to the context of its constructors and audience. Human beings are products of their contexts. Given that theologies do not arise in a vacuum, all theologies are inherently contextual. As Paul Matheny rightly points out, "Christian theology has always been contextual . . . for theology has always responded to the questions of the faithful of local congregations and ecclesial communities."[90] Yet it is important to differentiate the claim that theology is inherently contextual from the genre of contextual theology. As stated earlier, contextual theology is the form of theology that recognizes and also uses the context of a community as an essential source of Christian theology. A contextual theologian presses the context of the intended audience of a given theology for theological materials that are useful for constructing fresh theologies. But how does the changing human context generate theological materials? It generates theological materials as Christian communities are working out their commitment to Jesus Christ in the midst of the daily realities of life. In working out their faith commitment, Christians negotiate their Christian identity within the matrix of their history, culture, and contemporary state of affairs. I will describe briefly two main rationales for imagining the context of a Christian community as an essential *locus theologicus* that ought to contribute to the form (mode of expression) and content of Christian theology.

Rationales for Contextual Theology

Ontological rationale: Christian theology is *de facto* contextual. Theology is in its very nature an exercise in contextualization: it is Christians' meditation and reflection on their understandings of God-world relations in light of Scripture, church traditions, reason, and contexts of their communities. Insofar as theologizing does not happen by chance but rather emerges from human beings who are conditioned by their environment, theology is inherently contextual. The "attempt to understand Christian faith in terms of a particular context," Stephen Bevans says, "is a process that is part of the very nature of theology itself."[91] Contextual theology nudges a theologian to rediscover the contextual nature of theology that in many cases has been

---

89. Carter, *Race*, 378.

90. Matheny, *Contextual Theology*, 62.

91. Bevans, *Models of Contextual Theology*, 3.

buried beneath the edifices of some other forms of Christian theology. For example, systematic theology focuses on assembling diverse Christian doctrines into a logical and coherent system.[92] What is usually lost in systematic theology is the particularity of the historical contexts of each doctrine and also the different ways Christian communities adopt, adapt, interpret, and appropriate doctrines to befit their own theological needs.

It is a mistake to present a community's theology as the fixed arbiter of other communities' theologies. For instance, the field of contextual theology has exposed the imperial agenda of some European and North American theologies that were exported to Africa, Asia, and Latin America from Europe and North America during Western missionary expeditions, particularly during Western maritime explorations, conquests, and the slave trade. For instance, several African theologians have pointed out that most European missionaries in the nineteenth century and twentieth century brought to Africa their own theologies, which were wrapped in their cultural and theological garbs, but presented them as *the* Christian theology. In his preface to *African Theology en Route*, Appiah-Kubi described the burden of European theologies on African Christians and the need for African theologians to shake off the burden in order to produce original theological works:

> "How can I sing the Lord's song in a strange land," in a strange language, in a strange thought, in a strange ideology (cf. Ps. 137:4). For more than a decade now the cry of the psalmist has been the cry of many African Christians. We demand to serve the Lord in our own terms and without being turned into European-American or Semitic bastards before we do so. That the Gospel has come to remain in Africa cannot be denied, but now our theological reflections must be addressed to the real contextual African situations. Our question must not be what Karl Barth, Karl Rahner, or any other Karl has to say, but rather what God would have us do in our living concrete condition. For too long African Christian theologians and scholars have been preoccupied with what missionary A or theology B or scholar C has told us about God and the Lord Jesus Christ.[93]

Appiah-Kubi's words highlight what African theologians in the 1970s saw as the need to engage in original theological thinking: theological reflections that attended to the real contextual African situations. It should be pointed out, however, that black liberation theologians and womanist theologians equally raised serious concerns about the form of Christian theologies that

92. Gunton, "Historical and Systematic Theology," 11–20.
93. Appiah-Kubi, "Preface," viii.

overlooked the oppression of African Americans.[94] Appiah-Kubi nevertheless has correctly described the predominant theologies that were brought
to sub-Saharan Africa from Europe and North America. Most of the missionaries repudiated African culture in their attempts to demonstrate the
superiority of the Christian faith over traditional African religions and also
sometimes the superiority of Europeans over Africans.

The rise of African Indigenous Churches (AICs) in the 1800s was,
on the one hand, a protest against Western missionaries' repudiation of
African cultures and, on the other hand, an attempt to make the Christian
faith feel at home in African traditional cultures in ways that attended to
the spiritual needs of Africans.[95] African theology, which I will explore
further in a future chapter, like similar contextual theologies, has shown
that theology ought not be an enterprise that is restricted to an abstract
realm. Theology is embodied: it is expressed concretely in the actual life of
Christians as they continually work out their knowledge of God, language
about God, faith in God, commitment to God's world as stewards, and
commitment to Jesus Christ as the Holy Spirit helps them. Ontologically,
then, Christian theology is *de facto* contextual insofar as it arises from the
life, experience, and belief of Christian communities. Though Christian
theology arises from the communities that follow Jesus Christ in discipleship, it should be designed in a manner that contributes to the process of
promoting healthy societies. I will discuss this task of Christian theology
under the jeremiad rationale.

Jeremiad and prophetic rationale: Christian theology ought to function
as a jeremiad, reminding theologians to heed the theological questions that
are welling up from the life situations of their own communities and empowering Christians, on one hand, to expose societal ills and, on the other
hand, to participate in the larger deliberations on how to overcome the
ills. Christian theologians can contribute to such deliberations being prophetic—calling for repentance, like the Hebrew prophets, from the practices
and beliefs that create and sustain societal ills. Contextual theology requires
a theologian to attend to broader societal issues that inform the life and
struggles of Christian communities. It also nudges theologians to provide
theological guidance on how Christians are to reflect on the contribution
of the Christian faith to the concerted efforts in society at large to create,
promote, and preserve the common good.[96] Of course, Christians may not

94. See Cone, *Black Theology of Liberation*; Grant, *White Women's Christ and Black
Women's Jesus*.

95. Sanneh, *Translating the Message*, 130–56.

96. For further discussions on the common good, see Temple, *Christianity and
Social Order*; Atherton, *Public Theology for Changing Times*; Bishops' Conference of

successfully accomplish this task without being open to what they can learn from (and teach) other non-Christian traditions about the complex process of imagining and promoting the common good. To explore this claim further, it will be helpful to ponder briefly how Christians, as disciples of Jesus Christ, are to understand his instruction to them to be the "salt of the earth" (Matt 5:13) and the "light of the world" (Matt 5:14). Jesus's instruction evokes two disparate cultural spheres or ways of living: a way of living that results in the spiritual, political, and social deterioration of the world and a way of living that will prevent the world from such deterioration (Matt 5:21–48). Jesus's disciples are not immunized against the ways of living that cause great harm to God's creation. In other words, it is possible for a Christian community to live in a manner that does more harm than good to God's creation. Knowing that his disciples are not immunized against the way of living that leads to social, spiritual, and political decay, Jesus instructed them to constantly live in ways that would heal the world of such ruinous degradation. They are not to lose their "saltiness" or cover their light, which ought to reveal and expose social ills. Preserving and healing God's creation of its social, political, and spiritual ills is a humongous task that no group (religious or nonreligious) on its own can successfully accomplish. It is a task that requires interdisciplinary and collaborative efforts. For example, to combat terrorism, poverty and human trafficking, Christian communities should shoulder the responsibility of showing how Christian theo-ethical values and praxis can contribute substantively to the efforts to combat these social problems. To highlight one theo-ethical value, theologians are to explore the role that justice (both retributive and restorative) and forgiveness should play when confronting the perpetrators of terrorism.[97]

Christian ethicists, as well as theologians, have disagreed on how it is exactly the church can concretely be the "salt of the earth" and the "light of the world." I would like to point out two parallel positions that have governed many of the discussions on how Christian communities are to navigate the complicated tasks of being faithful disciples of Jesus Christ (discipleship) and being good citizens of their nations (citizenship).[98] In many parts of the Western world, discussions on the Christian-world relations have followed the trend that pits religion against a secular order or what T. J. Gorringe calls "the sacred-secular divide."[99] For some, the church's task is not to shape

---

England and Wales, *Common Good and the Catholic Church's Social Teaching*; Gorringe, *Common Good and the Global Emergency*.

97. See Ezigbo, "Violent Christians," 236–59.

98. Graham, "Rethinking the Common Good," 133–56.

99. Gorringe, *Common Good and the Global Emergency*, ix.

the secular public square in the image of Christian social ethics but rather to shape individual Christians to attend to their dual responsibilities: to act in the manner that shows they are citizens of their nations and faithful disciples of Jesus Christ. Oliver O'Donovan, in the contexts of the United Kingdom and the Iraq war, argues that Christian Bishops

> may speak as authorized representatives *from* the Christian community *to* the state, or they may speak as pastors *to* the Christian community. But either way, the priority must be to communicate the *moral posture* of those who recognize their responsibilities for Iraq in Christ Jesus, rather than to dictate concrete policy conclusions, which, a month later, are already beginning to look out of date.[100]

Other ethicists and theologians, on the contrary, argue that the church's task includes shaping the social order and nudging the state towards the religious values that promote human dignity. For Rowan Williams, a religious group, firmly rooted in its religious convictions, should participate in public debate and discourse along with other religious and nonreligious groups.[101] He writes,

> [The] significance of the church for civil society is in keeping alive a concern both to honor and to justify the absolute and nonnegotiable character of the human vision of responsibility and justice that is at work in all human association for the common good. It is about concerning the life of civil society with its deepest roots, acknowledged or not. The conviction of being answerable to God for how we serve and respect God's human and non-human creation at the very least serves to ensure that the human search for shared welfare and responsible liberty will not be reduced to a matter of human consensus alone. And if the church—or any other community of faith—asks of society the respect that will allow it to be itself, it does so not because it is anxious about its survival (which is in God's hands), but because it asks the freedom to remind the society or societies in which it lives of their own vulnerability and their need to stay close to some fundamental questions about the nature of the humanity they seek to nourish.[102]

However one construes how the church ought to be the "salt of the earth" and the "light of the world," it is important to recognize that

100. O'Donovan, *Just War Revisited*, 129.

101. Williams, *Faith in the Pubic Square* 302–9.

102. Williams, *Faith in the Pubic Square*, 307.

theologians can best guide Christian communities in this endeavor if they attend to the theological questions embedded in the struggles of the communities to be faithful to Jesus's teaching in bringing about healing to a world being ravaged by social ills. Such questions should not be ignored if theologians want to be relevant to their community. Theologians may well need to construct fresh theologies that are actually relevant and useful to their intended audience. This does not imply that older theologies are irrelevant but rather they may become obsolete and incapable of meeting the current needs of contemporary Christian communities.

To conclude this chapter, I highlight two predominant assumptions governing theological practices of some Christian theologians that this book challenges. The first assumption is that only text-based sources (Scripture and creeds), reason, and ecclesial traditions can supply essential theological data for formulating Christian theology. Theologians operating with this assumption treat the context of a Christian community merely as a testing ground for Christian theology. Essential components of a Christian community's context, such as life situations, are considered in theological construction but only to the extent of how they shape the mode of presentation and not the content of a theology that is worthy of the name "Christian." Contrary to this assumption, I have argued that the context of a Christian community can generate theological data of cardinal importance in formulating Christian theology. The second assumption, which this books challenges, is that the relationship of *loci theologici* (sources of theology) is to be imagined in terms of their order of hierarchical importance. Focusing on the hierarchy of the sources of theology (primary-secondary nexus) rather than on their specific functions hamstrings the interaction of the sources of theology and makes it difficult to do contextual theology. Against the hierarchal ordering of sources of theology, I argue for a function-based relationship. Each source of theology performs some unique tasks in the construction of Christian theology. For example, reason can perform the test of coherence in ways that Scripture and church tradition are unable to do. Also, context can perform the test of relevancy (testing if a particular theology is *actually* addressing contemporary theological needs of a Christian community) in the manner that Scripture, church tradition, and reason are unable to do. In the next chapter, I examine echoes of contextual theologizing in some of Jesus's theological sayings and teaching in the four canonical Gospels with the intent to explore how he might provide guidance to contextual theologians.

2

Echoes of Contextual
Theologizing in Jesus's Teachings

W hat service is theology to render to Christian communities? I argue that it ought to clarify for them how they are to embody Jesus's
theological life as a way of living out their commitment to him (see John
10:7–18) and his vision for the world (see Matt 5:13–16). Jesus's "theological life," in this context, refers to how he lived and also the message he
proclaimed, which is grounded in his understanding of God's relationship
to the world, human beings in particular (see Matt 11:2–6, 25–28; John
5:19–47; 8:12–38; 12:44–50). The cult of the theological guild (the act of
following, venerating, and interpreting works of outstanding theologians)
might have eroded the basic service that Christian theology should render
to Christian communities. This, of course, may be an unintended consequence of theologians' pursuit of theological precision, dialogue, and excel-
lence. Obviously engaging with the established theological traditions and
theological works of great repute is important to Christian theology as an
academic discipline. However, extreme caution is required in order not to
erode the task of showing how Christian theology can help Christian communities to embody Jesus's theological life. One way to avoid such erosion
is to develop theological structures and strategies that equip theologians to
discern the theological needs of Christians, many of whom have no formal
theological education or literacy. Contextual theology, as I have argued
in chapter 1, is equipped to help theologians in this endeavor. Contextual
theologians aim to rediscover the *humanness* of Christian theology—the
reflection of Christians on their various understandings of human existence in light of Jesus's teaching about God and the world as described
and interpreted by some writers of Scripture. Therefore, they are usually
preoccupied with the task of freeing Christian theology from the prison of

the esoteric and bare abstraction. They help lead the investigation into the reasons and conditions of theology's imprisonment, which they hope will unearth the evidence that will liberate it.

Theologians that formulate Christian theology in ways that confine it to the prison of esotericism have failed to learn from Jesus's theological life. As I argued in chapter 1, Christian theology is an essential feature of the Christian life—the way of living, believing, thinking, and relating that are grounded in the person, work, and significance of Jesus Christ. It is appropriate, therefore, to begin an exploration of theology with Jesus of Nazareth because, as I will show in this chapter, he ought to be the defining content and parameter of Christians' reflections on *God-world relations*. The expression "God-world relations" is used broadly in this book to describe the diverse ways of imagining the cosmos as God's project: God's ongoing work of remaking the world in which God has invited humans to enjoy it, learn about it, explore it, protect it, and participate in building it and making it enjoyable for its inhabitants.

If theology is defined broadly as the discourse about God and God's relationship with the world, Jesus merited the title *theologian*. He was a theologian insofar that he invited his followers and disciples to believe in a certain way by accepting his teaching about God-world relations.[1] Clearly, he reflected on God's mode of being and operating in the world. Many Christians who accept the divine-human ontology of Jesus of Nazareth may be tempted to focus only on his final theological product—what he said about God's relationship to the world and also his place in framing and shaping such relationship for his disciples. This is, however, a theological mistake insofar as this way of thinking nudges Christians away from Jesus's theological activity and habit—*how* he actually produced his theological sayings and beliefs. The main question with which I am concerned is: How did Jesus draw upon and also use theological data from Hebrew Scripture, Jewish tradition, and the context of his Jewish community to construct his own theological sayings and beliefs? This is a difficult question to answer for at least two reasons. First, those who desire to write about Jesus's theology are at a considerable disadvantage because he did not write books on theology (or write any books on any subject). Speculations and conjectures about his reasons for not writing any text need not detain us. My primary aim is to highlight the secondary nature of our sources of Jesus's teachings and theological sayings. In other words, what we have as the sources of Jesus's theology are the different portrayals of his life, teaching, and experience by

---

1. In a way, Jesus's sayings about the kingdom of God are his theological commentary on God's relationship to the world.

some of his earliest disciples who wrote primarily to meet the particular needs of their own audiences.[2] At best, what we have are "the sayings of, and reports about, Jesus of Nazareth, which were remembered and developed in oral form until written down" in the canonical and noncanonical texts.[3] Richard Hays in *Echoes of Scripture in the Gospels* shows convincingly that the Evangelists who wrote the four canonical Gospels—Matthew, Mark, Luke, and John—used "figural christological reading" to connect the Christ-event to the Hebrew Bible. By "figural reading," Hays means a hermeneutical act of "reading backwards" or retrospectively (through the means of quotation, allusion, and echo) in order to uncover a "pattern of correspondence" between two or more events that are separated in time.[4] A "figural reading" is also a "process of reading backwards in light of new revelatory events."[5] As the differences in such portrayals of Jesus in the Gospels show, those earliest disciples were selective in the materials they presented, which were profoundly affected by the needs of their own audiences and personal interests.[6] Therefore, theologians who wish to write on Jesus's theology should approach cautiously while attending to the difficulties of discerning his theology through the particular lenses of his disciples who painstakingly preserved for future generations some of his deeds, sayings, and experiences (see John 20:30; 21:25).

The second difficulty that confronts those who wish to write about Jesus's theology is the absence of a developed theological system. Jesus did not leave behind a system of theology. In many cases all we have are terse theological sayings or expressions without expatiation. It would be unwise to treat Jesus's theological sayings as if they are well-developed theological ideas that cohere in a theological system. Theologians should avoid superimposing an arbitrary theological system on Jesus's teaching and sayings.

2. Richard Bauckham's observation is helpful: "[The] full reality of Jesus as he historically was is not, of course, accessible to us . . . Like any other part of history, the Jesus who lived in first-century Palestine is knowable only through the evidence that has survived. We could therefore use the phrase 'the historical Jesus' to mean, not all that Jesus was, but Jesus insofar as his historical reality is accessible to us. But here we reach the crucial methodological problem. For Christian faith this Jesus, the earthy Jesus as we can know him, is the Jesus of the canonical Gospels, Jesus as Matthew, Mark, Luke, and John account and portray him." See Bauckham, *Jesus and the Eyewitnesses*, 2.

3. Horsley and Hanson, *Bandits, Prophets, and Messiahs*, xiii.

4. Hays, *Echoes of Scripture*, 2–3.

5. Hays, *Echoes of Scripture*, 5.

6. As John Crossan has observed, "The New Testament itself contains a spectrum of divergent theological interpretations, each of which focuses on different aspects or clusters of aspects concerning the historical Jesus, or better, different historical Jesuses." Crossan, *Historical Jesus*, 423.

As I noted in the first difficulty stated above, there are diverse portrayals of Jesus in the writings of the four canonical Gospels. Modern scholars who aim to find one overarching portrayal of the so-called "historical Jesus" soon will find out that there is no single picture of him in the writings of the New Testament. Numerous works produced by the scholars of the historical Jesus quests show that there is no common portrait of him.[7] In the words of John Crossan, "Even under the discipline of attempting to envision Jesus against his own most proper Jewish background, it seems we can have as many pictures as there are exegetes."[8]

Taking into account the two difficulties described above, I will focus on a modest task of discerning and delineating Jesus's theological ideas in three pericopes from the canonical Gospels (Mark 7:1–15; Luke 4:16–21; John 4:7–26). I do not attempt to present a comprehensive account of Jesus's theology on all the theological themes highlighted in these passages. Rather, I focus on what they tell us, exegetically and theological speaking, about Jesus's theological life. Though I will from time to time reference relevant ideas from other parts of the New Testament, the scope of this exploration is restricted to what the three passages tell us about how Jesus drew upon theological data of Hebrew Scripture, Jewish religious tradition, and the context of his own Jewish community to formulate and express his theological sayings. I will also discuss Jesus's use of the principle of theological appropriation to analyze and also to reimagine theological data from these sources. In chapter 1, I described *theological appropriation* as a theological activity that requires both rethinking (assessing carefully with the intent to show a fresh understanding) and reconstructing (remaking something with the intent to improve or make better). I will now turn attention to the main theological issues that are present in the three passages.

Theological Case: The Place of Traditions in True Worship and Ethical Living

Summary of the Issues

- The nature of true worship and also the roles of Mt. Gerizim and Jerusalem in the worship of Yahweh.
- The place of traditions and God's commandment in the imagination of ethical living.

7. See Schweitzer, *Quest of the Historical Jesus.*
8. Crossan, *Historical Jesus,* xxviii.

Historical Background

Jesus's attitude toward and usage of Hebrew Scripture, Jewish religious traditions, and theological questions embedded in the life of his Jewish community displayed his proclivity for what we now know as contextual theology and contextual theologizing. I argue that his theological activity and habits qualify him both as a precursor of contextual theology and a model for contextual theologians. He deliberately entered into the theological space of the Jewish experts of his day—namely, rabbis, scribes, and Pharisees—sometimes with the intent to engage them in theological matters.[9] I will show that Jesus engaged in inter-contextuality, which displayed his willingness to use and also dialogue with theological sources both to formulate and express his theological ideas and beliefs. He neither drew upon theological data of Hebrew Scripture, Jewish tradition, and context of his community merely for heuristic purposes, nor to dismiss them as irrelevant to his own teaching. On the contrary, he analyzed and utilized the theological data he collated, separating the data that are relevant to his theology, which directly or indirectly shed light on his own theological insights.

Three pericopes below provide us some insights into Jesus's theological life and activity. I do not attempt to unearth the theological content of Jesus's sayings beneath the representations of the writers of the Gospels because, as the Quests for the Historical Jesus reveal, no such content in its pristine condition is accessible to readers and interpreters. Also, I do not intend to show a common theological theme in all of Jesus's theological sayings or teaching.[10] It is, of course, debated whether a core of Jesus's message even exists.[11] My goal is rather to identify Jesus's contextual theological life (activity and habit) as can be seen in the pericopes, focusing on the Gospel writers' representations of his use of theological data from Hebrew Scripture, Jewish religious traditions, and the context of his own community.

9. For discussions on Jesus's conflict with Jewish scribes of his day, see Keith, *Jesus against the Scribal Elite*; Horsley, *Archeology, History, and Society in Galilee*.

10. For Rudolf Bultmann, the reign of God is the dominant message of Jesus: "The dominant concept of Jesus' message is the Reign of God. Jesus proclaims its immediately impending irruption, now already making itself felt. Reign of God is an eschatological concept. It means the regime of God which will destroy the present course of the world, wipe out all the contra-divine, Satanic power under which the present world groans—and thereby, terminating all pain and sorrow, bring in salvation for the People of God which awaits the fulfillment of the prophets' promises. The coming of God's reign is a miraculous event, which will be brought about by God alone without the help of men." Bultmann, *Theology of the New Testament*, 4.

11. For more discussions on the issue of the core of Jesus's message, see Caird, *New Testament Theology*, 15–17.

Mark 7:1–15

Now when the Pharisees and some of the scribes who had come from Jerusalem gathered around him, they noticed that some of his disciples were eating with defiled hands, that is, without washing them. (For the Pharisees, and all the Jews, do not eat unless they thoroughly wash their hands, thus observing the tradition of the elders; and they do not eat anything from the market unless they wash it; and there are also many other traditions that they observe, the washing of cups, pots, and bronze kettles. So the Pharisees and the scribes asked him, "Why do your disciples not live according to the tradition of the elders, but eat with defiled hands?" He said to them, "Isaiah prophesied rightly about you hypocrites, as it is written, 'This people honors me with their lips, but their hearts are far from me; in vain do they worship me, teaching human precepts as doctrines.' You abandon the commandment of God and hold to human tradition." Then he said to them, "You have a fine way of rejecting the commandment of God in order to keep your tradition! For Moses said, 'Honor your father and your mother'; and, 'Whoever speaks evil of father or mother must surely die.' But you say that if anyone tells father or mother, 'Whatever support you might have had from me is Corban' (that is, an offering to God)—then you no longer permit doing anything for a father or mother, thus making void the word of God through your tradition that you have handed on. And you do many things like this." Then he called the crowd again and said to them, "Listen to me, all of you, and understand: there is nothing outside a person that by going in can defile, but the things that come out are what defile." (NRSV)

Luke 4:16–21

When he came to Nazareth, where he had been brought up, he went to the synagogue on the sabbath day, as was his custom. He stood up to read, and the scroll of the prophet Isaiah was given to him. He unrolled the scroll and found the place where it was written: "The Spirit of the Lord is upon me, because he has anointed me to bring good news to the poor. He has sent me to proclaim release to the captives and recovery of sight to the blind, to let the oppressed go free, to proclaim the year of the Lord's favor." And he rolled up the scroll, gave it back to the attendant, and sat down. The eyes of all in the synagogue were fixed on him. Then he began to say to them, "Today this scripture has been fulfilled in your hearing." (NRSV)

John 4:7–26

A Samaritan woman came to draw water, and Jesus said to her, "Give me a drink." (His disciples had gone to the city to buy food.) The Samaritan woman said to him, "How is it that you, a Jew, ask a drink of me, a woman of Samaria?" (Jews do not share things in common with Samaritans.) Jesus answered her, "If you knew the gift of God, and who it is that is saying to you, 'Give me a drink,' you would have asked him, and he would have given you living water." The woman said to him, "Sir, you have no bucket, and the well is deep. Where do you get that living water? Are you greater than our ancestor Jacob, who gave us the well, and with his sons and his flocks drank from it?" Jesus said to her, "Everyone who drinks of this water will be thirsty again, but those who drink of the water that I will give them will never be thirsty. The water that I will give will become in them a spring of water gushing up to eternal life." The woman said to him, "Sir, give me this water, so that I may never be thirsty or have to keep coming here to draw water."

Jesus said to her, "Go, call your husband, and come back." The woman answered him, "I have no husband." Jesus said to her, "You are right in saying, 'I have no husband'; for you have had five husbands, and the one you have now is not your husband. What you have said is true!" The woman said to him, "Sir, I see that you are a prophet. Our ancestors worshiped on this mountain, but you say that the place where people must worship is in Jerusalem." Jesus said to her, "Woman, believe me, the hour is coming when you will worship the Father neither on this mountain nor in Jerusalem. You worship what you do not know; we worship what we know, for salvation is from the Jews. But the hour is coming, and is now here, when the true worshipers will worship the Father in spirit and truth, for the Father seeks such as these to worship him. God is spirit, and those who worship him must worship in spirit and truth." The woman said to him, "I know that Messiah is coming" (who is called Christ). "When he comes, he will proclaim all things to us." Jesus said to her, "I am he, the one who is speaking to you."

Just then his disciples came. They were astonished that he was speaking with a woman, but no one said, "What do you want?" or, "Why are you speaking with her?" (NRSV)

In what follows I describe Jesus's attitude toward Hebrew Scripture, highlighting how he viewed and also used it to formulate his theological beliefs and sayings.

Jesus and Hebrew Scripture

According to the Gospel of Mark, Jesus proclaimed "the good news of God" that focused on his understanding of the "kingdom of God," which required "repentance" and belief in "the good news" (Mark 1:14–15). Jesus, of course, was not the original progenitor of the concept of the kingdom of God. He borrowed the idea from Hebrew prophetic figures such as John the Baptist. For Matthew, John the Baptist was already preaching about the kingdom of heaven (or kingdom of God) before Jesus arrived on the scene: "In those days John the Baptist came preaching in the Desert of Judea and saying 'Repent, for the kingdom of heaven [*basileia ton ouranon*] is near'" (Matt 3:1–2 NIV). John the Baptist, according to the Matthean account, was carrying out a prophetic task about his role as the forerunner of Jesus Christ (Matt 3:3; cf. Isa 40:3). Yet Jesus did not merely contextualize (make relevant and applicable) *for* his immediate community the theological beliefs of his generation or the generations that preceded him. He did not simply allude to, or quote from, or echo Hebrew Scripture and religious tradition. He also appropriated theological data he collected and collated from these sources and used them to construct his own theological sayings.

Returning to the concept of the kingdom of heaven, Jesus reimagined it in ways that clearly differed from John's understanding of what it entailed. For example, in John the Baptist's view, the nearness of the kingdom of heaven should serve as a serious warning about the impending divine fire and fury that would destroy those who did not bear "fruit in keeping with repentance" (Matt 3:7–10 NIV). Unlike John the Baptist, however, Jesus understood the kingdom of heaven as the reign of God in which God's healing of the broken earth is underway. In response to John the Baptist's inquiry about the identity of Jesus Christ—if he was truly the one "who was to come," he responded:

> Go back and report to John what you hear and see: The blind receive sight, the lame walk, those who have leprosy are cured, the dead are raised, and the good news is preached to the poor.

> Blessed is the man who does not fall away on account of me.
> (Matt 11:4–6 NIV)

These words most likely frustrated John the Baptist since he was probably expecting that Jesus would announce his presence as God's messenger by crushing sinners. Though John and Jesus preached about the same kingdom, they differed in their theological emphases. This is a clear example of Jesus adopting and appropriating a theological concept in the manner that amplified his understanding of God and the world. It also shows Jesus's willingness to learn from and equally engage ideas from Hebrew Scripture. The famous saying "You have heard that it was said [*Ekousate hoti errethe*] . . . but I say to you [*ego de lego humin*]" (Matt 5:21–48) that Matthew attributes to Jesus, when understood in light of Jesus's claim, "Do not think that I have come to abolish the Law or Prophets; I have not come abolish them but to fulfill them," signify theological appropriation. The expression "you have heard that it was said" shows that Jesus was not only referencing Hebrew Scripture, but also how some of its words have to be interpreted and preserved in Jewish traditions, and appropriated in the grassroots theologies of Jewish communities. He used theological data from these sources to formulate his theological sayings in the most befitting manner to his audience.

In one of his notable comments on Hebrew Scripture—the Law and the Prophets—Jesus announced that he did not intend to "abolish" it but rather to "fulfill" it (Matt 5:17–20). He also scolded the Pharisees for focusing more on traditions rather than on the "commandment of God" in Scripture (Mark 7:9–13). His teaching on God is firmly grounded in Scripture. He cited the book of Isaiah to make his theological point against the Pharisees' preoccupation with religious traditions. In Luke 4, he cited Isaiah (61:1–2) in his articulation of his missional vision. Luke does not tell his readers how Jesus came about the Isaiah passage; whether Jesus intentionally looked for it when the scroll was brought to him, or stumbled upon it when he unrolled the scroll's cylinders, or was led to it by the "Spirit of the Lord." How he came upon the passage in Isaiah, however, need not detain us. What is important is that Jesus grounded his vision for ministry in Hebrew Scripture. This is significant for several reasons. By citing and affirming a passage from Hebrew Scripture, Jesus showcased the continuity of his vision for ministry with the sacred text of his Jewish community. He did not seek to repeal and replace the Scripture. When challenged by some Jews who accused him of the crime of blasphemy (John 10:33), he grounded his theological warrant for claiming to be "the Son of God" in Hebrew Scripture. He said to a Jewish audience in Jerusalem: "Scripture cannot be broken" (John 10:35 ESV). Richard Hays rightly notes that here Jesus "articulates a very high view of Israel's Scripture as unbreakable and unimpeachably true."[12]

Jesus was not a literalist. He adopted a nuanced hermeneutics (an art of interpretation) that allowed him to appropriate Scripture by attending to its spirit without limiting himself to its letter in his theological reflections. The word "abolish" that Matthew starkly juxtaposed with "fulfill" merits some attention. To "abolish" (*kataluo*) implies rendering something irrelevant or to relegate something to a non-valuable status. If the Law (the Torah) covers religious codes as wells as "the code of civil and criminal law of the Jewish nations and the national ethos of the Jewish people,"[13] it follows that Jesus was clearly showing his loyalty to the Jewish religious life and also his loyalty to his nation. Yet he did not shy away from critiquing and also refuting some of the theological conclusions of the religious leaders of his era. Christian theologians and biblical scholars have explored what might have occasioned Jesus's announcement that he did not come to abolish "the Law or the Prophets." Was he responding to those who accused him of abolishing the teaching of Hebrew Scripture? Or did Matthew preserve this claim of Jesus (no parallels of Matt 5:17 appear in the other canonical Gospels) in order to show that the Jewish disciples of Jesus, like him, were not abolishing the teaching of Hebrew Scripture? Matthew Thiessen has argued that Matthew was most probably responding to the rumors in the aftermath of the destruction of the Temple in 70 CE that Christians were among the abolishers of the Law who brought God's judgment upon Israel.[14] Thiessen also argues that it was likely that Jesus was responding to the accusation of the scribes and Pharisees (Matt 5:20) that he was abolishing the teaching of Scripture. He writes,

> Considering . . . law abolishment in Jewish history, the dangerous nature of this charge becomes apparent; the consistent emphasis on the Hellenizers of 167 BCE as law abolishers whose actions provoked the Antiochan persecution may stand behind such an accusation. Consequently, such a charge could be deployed in the following way: "Join with us against the law abolishing followers of this law-abolishing Jesus so that we might guard ourselves against God's wrath, which led to the persecution under Antiochus IV."[15]

12. Hays, *Echoes of Scripture*, 299.
13. Caird, *New Testament Theology*, 7.
14. Thiessen, "Abolishers of the Law."
15. Thiessen, "Abolishers of the Law," 551–52.

Whatever the event that occasioned Jesus's public declaration of his acceptance of Hebrew Scripture, he went out of his way to say he has come to "fulfill" (*pleroo*) it. I will return later in this chapter to explore some theological implications of the term "fulfill" in light of Jesus's usage of the principle of theological appropriation.

It is virtually impossible to fully grasp Jesus's understanding of the scope and purpose of his ministry in isolation from Hebrew Scripture. In the pericope from John 4:7–26, Jesus freely alluded to Hebrew Scripture in his theological reflection on the nature of God's salvific work in the world. Hebrew Scripture uses metaphors such as "living water" (flowing water) to describe salvific blessing from God to God's people (see Isa 55:1; Zech 14:8).[16] Although he grounded his ministry in Hebrew Scripture, the freedom with which he interpreted it and also expounded alternative applications perplexed some of his audiences (Luke 4:36–37). To cite an example, he said to the audience in a Nazareth synagogue after reading from the book of Isaiah: "Today this scripture is fulfilled in your hearing" (Luke 4:21; cf. Isa 61:1–2). What exactly was his point in making this claim? If we take Luke 4:16–21 as Jesus's mission *manifesto*—the rough outline of what he planned to accomplish in his ministry—at the very least, by claiming the prophecy of Isaiah has been fulfilled in his audience's hearing, he indirectly announced that his life and ministry will focus on making the ideas of the Jubilee (the year of the LORD) visibly present in his community. The Jubilee, which is grounded in the principles of wellbeing and flourishing, is a socioeconomic arrangement of ancient Israel that was designed to care for the poor and the earth. It was also designed to prevent economic exploitation, servitude, and debt-slavery.[17] The spirit of the Jubilee was the impetus for his miraculous deeds. As Paul Hanson has noted, Jesus's claim implies that his

> life was dedicated to the inauguration of the era of redemption and healing of creation. Given the completeness of that dedication, and the confirmation of Jesus's divine commission associated with his resurrection, it is understandable that the early disciples concluded that God was personally present in Jesus's life "reconciling the world to [Godself]" (II Cor. 5:19).[18]

16. Jer 2:13, for example, states, "For my people have committed two evils: they have forsaken me, the fountain of living waters and hewed out cisterns for themselves, broken cisterns that can hold no water" (ESV).

17. For more dissuasions on the Jubilee, see Bergsma, *Jubilee from Leviticus to Qumran*; Wright, *Mission of God*, 289–323; Olanisebe, "Sabbatical and Jubilee Regulations as a Means of Economic Recovery."

18. Hanson, "Identity and Purpose of the Church," 345.

Some scholars see Jesus's announcement here as a public display of his mission ideas and vision.[19] For Christopher Wright,

> "The Nazareth manifesto" (Luke 14:16–30) is the clearest programmatic statement . . . [it] is the closest Jesus comes to a personal mission statement, and it quotes directly from Isaiah 61, which was strongly influenced by Jubilee concepts.[20]

Jesus firmly kept his eyes on healing the sick that he encountered. He proclaimed liberation to the poor and the oppressed as evidenced in his Sermon on the Mount (Matt 5:1–12; 6–4) and his miraculous deeds. It could also be argued that the spirit of Jubilee functioned as a theological framework for Jesus's conception of the purpose of his life and the nature of his ministry.

Jesus and Jewish Religious Tradition

Jesus had a positive attitude toward many of the Jewish traditions. This should not be surprising because he was born into a devout Jewish family. Like a devout Jew, he prayed, learned, and taught in the synagogue. Given that the Temple was in Jerusalem, the synagogue played important roles in the religious life of the Jews who lived in the region of Galilee, where Jesus grew up and partly conducted his ministry. Apparently, it was Jesus's custom to go to the "synagogue on the Sabbath day" whenever he visited Nazareth, his hometown (Luke 4:16). In some ways, the synagogues bridged the gap between the Jewish communities living far away from Jerusalem (in Israel and the Diaspora) and the Jewish way of life (piety, beliefs, and doctrines) expected of devout Jews.[21]

Archeologists and biblical scholars dispute the existence of synagogues in Israel in the first century CE.[22] Lee Levine summarized the disputes as follows:

> Determining the origin and early development of the synagogue has presented modern scholarship with a seemingly insurmountable challenge. As often happens with institutions, movements, and ideas of revolutionary proportions, the forces which

---

19. Massey, *Dalit Theology*, 188–89.

20. Wright, *Mission of God*, 301.

21. Levine, *Ancient Synagogue*, 124.

22. Olsson and Zetterholm, *Ancient Synagogue from Its Origins until 200 C.E.*; Fine, *Jews, Christians, and Polytheists in the Ancient Synagogue*.

shape new initiatives, especially in their embryonic stages, remain shrouded in mystery.[23]

Some archeologists believe that at the time of Jesus, the synagogues most likely served a dual purpose: they were used for religious meetings and civil events.[24] Focusing on their religious function, the synagogues were the major centers of scriptural and theological instructions. The Pharisees, for example, "exercised their influence through the synagogues, working against the corrupting Hellenizing leaven of the Herods and their circle of wealthy supporters."[25] Jesus's assessment of Pharisees' understanding of piety and scribes' scriptural teaching was based primarily on his firsthand information about them, which he most likely learned by attending their instructions in the synagogues. From an astonishingly early period of his life, he was fascinated by religious and theological activities that were conducted in the synagogues (Luke 2:43–47). Scriptural and theological instruction in the synagogues contributed immensely to Jesus's growth "in favor with God and men" (Luke 2:52).

As an important center of Jewish religious life, the synagogues in Israel provided Jesus with a visible platform to express his theological understandings and insights about God-world relations, especially how his Jewish communities are to understand their relationship with God (Luke 4:14–17; Matt 4:23; John 6:53–59; 18:19–24). According to Mark and Luke, Jesus taught his theological ideas in the Capernaum synagogue (Mark 1:21–28; Luke 4:31–37). Though Mark and Luke did not describe explicitly the content of Jesus's teaching, the mentioning of the "teachers of the law" indicates that his subject matter was religious and theological in nature. The audience's amazement at his religious and theological insights indicates that he was not merely rehearsing the normal teaching of the scribes. Some wondered if Jesus was propounding a "new teaching" (Mark 1:27; Luke 4:36). The audience was astonished not only because of the content of Jesus's scriptural and theological expositions but also his exhibition of his divine authority in the act of healing "a man possessed by a demon, an evil spirit" (Luke 4:33 NIV; see also Mark 1:23–26). In the story of the healing of a crippled woman, the scribes were infuriated by Jesus's departure from the Jewish tradition by working on the Sabbath (Luke 13:10–17).[26] In the peri-

23. Levine, *Ancient Synagogue*, 19.

24. Hachlili, "Synagogues." See also Levine, *Ancient Synagogue*, 124–59.

25. Barnett, *Jesus and the Rise of Christianity*, 137; Levine, *Ancient Synagogue*, 40–41.

26. For discussions on whether the healing actually took place in the synagogues or a Lucan redaction, see Ryan, "Jesus and Synagogue Disputes."

cope from the Gospel of John (4:7–26), Jesus acknowledged that Jerusalem was an important religious site for the Jews, yet he made a theological move that might have baffled the unnamed Samaritan woman and also annoyed many Jews. He relativized Jerusalem and Mt. Gerizim and emphasized the importance of the sincerity of a worshipper over a geographic location of worship. He also reminded the woman that the Samaritans, unlike the Jews, "worship what [they] do not know" and also that God's "salvation comes from the Jews" (John 4:22). Jesus was most likely highlighting a common Jewish belief about the syncretism that characterized the religion of Samaria (2 Kgs 17). I will return later to explore the nature of this syncretism. What is of interest here is that he did not follow traditions legalistically. On the contrary, he constantly returned to the sources of the traditions with the intent to explore their meanings in relation to his immediate context.[27] For example, he broke a cultural tradition by spending time alone with a woman who wasn't his spouse and, more especially, a Samaritan woman. John noted that Jesus's disciples were "astonished" to see that he was alone with the woman (John 4:27).

In the Markan pericope (7:1–15), it is striking that Jesus did not scold his disciples for violating the Jewish religious ritual of ceremonial hand-washing when the Pharisees and scribes brought to his attention that his disciples "were eating with defiled hands, that is, without washing them" (Mark 7:2–5). This pericope is replete with several complexities caused by scribal redactions.[28] Was the encounter between Jesus and *haberim*, a group within the traditions of Pharisees that practiced rigorous purity laws?[29] If this were the case, the claim that the practice of handwashing was commonplace among the Jews would be an exaggeration. Whatever the identity of the Pharisees and teachers of the laws, Jesus problematized the purity law, denouncing simplistic interpretations and application of the laws that were present in the teaching of some scribes, Pharisees, and grassroots theologies of some Jewish communities.[30]

Jesus touched on so many issues in his response to the charges the Pharisees and scribes brought against his disciples. For example, according to Mark's portrait, Jesus contrasted the human tradition of handwashing (which does not infringe on God's commandment) with the *korban*

27. For discussions on Jesus's healing acts on the Sabbath, see Collins, *Jesus, the Sabbath and the Jewish Debate*.

28. For discussions on redactions and textual issues in this pericope, see Booth, *Jesus and the Laws of Purity*.

29. Roger Booth describes "the *haberim* as the Pharisaic group most zealous to avoid defilement." Booth, *Jesus and the Laws of Purity*, 194.

30. Note that Jesus addressed the crowd in verses 14–15.

tradition—a religious maneuvering that allowed people to evade caring for their parents under the guise of setting aside special offering for religious use. As C. E. B. Cranfield notes, "That which is offered to God as a *korban* becomes 'holy' and so is no longer available for ordinary use."[31] Jesus is not criticizing the oral tradition but rather the attitude of some Pharisees and scribes toward such laws, especially its use to circumvent the written law.[32] Also, Jesus makes a theological and an ethical move by comparing two human acts that are indirectly linked to handwashing—*digestion* and *excreta*, albeit in a figural way: "Listen, to me, everyone, and understand this. Nothing outside a man can make him unclean by going into him. Rather, it is what comes out of a man that makes him unclean" (Mark 7:14–15 NIV). The ambiguity of Jesus's theological and ethical move is highlighted by his disciples' confusion about what it is exactly he was intending to convey to the crowd (Mark 7:17). Jesus's explanation clarifies the nature of his theological and ethical reflections on some Jewish religious traditions: "Don't you see that nothing that enters a man from the outside can make him 'unclean'? For it doesn't go into his heart but into his stomach, and then out of his body" (Mark 7:18–19 NIV). He starkly juxtaposes the defilement that is contracted by touching unclean things with the defilement that proceeds from a person's heart.[33] Booth argues that Jesus's aim was to make the case that there "is nothing outside a man which *cultically* defiles him as much as the things coming from a man *ethically* defile."[34] Mark appears to present Jesus as a contextual theologian, to use a contemporary parlance, who attended to the theological issues embedded in the context of his community as he worked out the relationship between Scripture (the Hebrew Bible) and traditions (*halakhah*—"teaching of the elders"—some of which are preserved in the Midrash). The juxtaposition of the "commandment of God" with the "traditions of men" in Mark 7:8 highlights Jesus's criticism of the act of holding on to religious traditions without attending both to the spirit of God's commandment in Hebrew Scripture and to the particularity of a context. I will explore in the next section how Jesus engaged the theological data from his context, especially the data from the grassroots theologies of his community.

31. Cranfield, *Gospel according to St. Mark*, 237.

32. This is an example of how a religious law may not be inherently wrong but could become wrong depending on how it is implemented.

33. For scriptural references on the defilement that is contracted by touching unclean things, see Lev 11–17 and Num 19.

34. Booth, *Jesus and the Laws of Purity*, 214.

Jesus, Context, and Grassroots Theologies

The pericope from John (4:7–26) brings into light the tension between the Jews and the Samaritans. Clearly, Jesus lived at a time when the Jews and the Samaritans saw themselves as enemies (John 4:1–45; 2 Kgs 17; Ezra 4).[35] He also grew up at a time when many Israelites believed that they were the special children of the true God (Yahweh) through whom God would bless other nations (Gen 12; John 4:22). By Jesus's day, many Jews constantly rethought their status before God in light of the Roman occupation and also the strangling influence of the Greco-Roman cultures on the nation of Israel. We can hear a voice full of despair in the words of two followers of Jesus traveling to Emmaus who seemed quite distraught because of his crucifixion: "but we had hoped that he was the one who was going to redeem Israel" (Luke 24:13–21). In the assessment of those two Jewish followers of Jesus, the one whom they hoped would deliver Israel from the Roman occupation and oppression turned out not to be the one—the expected Messiah. Jesus also lived and envisioned a future for the nation of Israel at a time when religious and political groups such as Pharisees, Essenes, Sadducees, and scribes populated the nation of Israel, many of whom had "differing Jewish options about the best vision, program, and leadership for the Jewish future in a very dangerous age."[36] In what ways did the *context* (history, culture, and state of affairs) in which Jesus lived and carried out his ministry shape his theological views and sayings? This is the question that will guide the discussion in this section.

John 4:7–26 contains a powerful story that took place at the famous well of Jacob in the town of Sychar in Samaria. The story begins with a scene of cultural, ethnic, political, and religious tensions: Jesus, a Jew, asked a woman of Samaria, for water to drink. The immediate response of the Samaritan woman to Jesus's request for water brings into focus the religious, political, and social tensions between Jews and Samaritans. The woman said to Jesus: "How is it that you, a Jew, ask a drink of me, a woman of Samaria?" (John 4:9 NRSV). John went out of his way to remind his readers that "Jews do not share things in common with Samaritans" (John 4:9 NRSV). This story brings into light a clash of religions, cultures, and ethnicity: two people, grounded in their own traditions, fought for their own religious and cultural territories. Jesus would eventually make a theological

---

35. Under the leadership of John Hyrcanus, the Jews destroyed a temple on Mt. Gerizim. The destruction of the temple is dated between 128–111 BCE. See Bourgel, "Destruction of the Samaritan Temple"; Sievers, *Hasmoneans and Their Supporters*. See also Josephus, "Antiquities" 13.10.2.

36. Crossan, *Who Killed Jesus?*, xi.

move that transcended the barriers of gender, ethnicity, and religion. However, it is important to explore the clash of cultures, religions, and ethnicity that shaped the conversation between Jesus and the Samaritan woman. It is very likely that Jesus's disciples were "astonished" at Jesus's behavior partly because he violated a social norm by talking with a woman who was alone and especially a Samaritan woman who was, in their estimate, an enemy of the Jewish people (see Ezra 4).

John was not catastrophizing the tension between Jews and Samaritans in this story. The tension can be traced back to the events of 722 BCE that are recorded in 2 Kings 17. King Hoshea who ruled over Israel (the Northern Kingdom) from Samaria incurred the wrath of an Assyrian king (Shalmaneser) by breaking a taxation treaty (17:4). In response, Shalmaneser invaded Samaria, conquered it, relocated some people of Israel to Assyria (17:6), and resettled people from Babylon, Cuthah, Avva, Hamath, and Serpharvaim in the cities of Samaria (17:24). The foreigners brought along with them their religious beliefs and practices to Samaria. The author-complier of 2 Kings explained this horrific event as God's judgment on Hoshea and the people of Israel for their idolatry (17:7–18). The event had disastrous effects on the people of Israel that were left behind in Samaria. They had to endure a form of syncretism that gravely distorted their Jewish faith:

> But every nation still made gods of its own and put them in the shrines of the high places that the people of Samaria had made, every nation in the cities in which they lived; the people of Babylon made Succoth-benoth, the people of Cuth made Nergal, the people of Hamath made Ashima; the Avvites made Nibhaz and Tartak; the Sepharvites burned their children in the fire to Adrammelech and Anammelech, the gods of Sepharvaim. They also worshiped the LORD and appointed from among themselves all sorts of people as priests of the high places, who sacrificed for them in the shrines of the high places. So they worshiped the LORD but also served their own gods, after the manner of the nations from among whom they had been carried away. (17:29–33 NRSV)

This form of syncretism signaled a departure from the Sinai law: "You shall not worship other gods" (17:35; see also Exod 20:2–6). Gradually, the inhabitants of Samaria moved away from many of the Jewish sacred writings and accepted only the Pentateuch as its authoritative Scripture. Also, they rejected Mt. Zion in Jerusalem as the center of religious worship, replacing it with Mt. Gerizim in Samaria. It was this syncretism that made the Judeans who had returned from the Babylon exile to reject the Samaritans' help as they worked on the temple (Ezra 4:1–3).

The version of the origins of the tension between Jews and Samaritans described above fits roughly what John Macdonald calls the "Judaist" tradition.[37] Macdonald notes that Samaritans' version of their own origins presents Shechem, which lay in the valley between Mounts Gerizim and Ebal, as the center of Moses's administration.[38] The tradition of Samaritans traces the sanctuary that was built on Mt. Gerizim to Joshua.[39] The hostility between Jews and Samaritans, according to the Samaritan tradition, was a post-Judges (or kings) era event. Eli was responsible for the religious division among the Israelites for building an alternative (or rival) sanctuary at Shiloh. According to Macdonald, this

> split in Israel, occurring long before the traditional division of Israel after the death of Solomon, is important for the understanding of the Samaritan claim to be the true followers of those who adhered to worship on Mount Gerizim under the High-Priesthood of Uzzi and his successors.[40]

Another turning point in the schism between Jews and Samaritans occurred during the prophetic office of Samuel. While most tribes of Israel demanded for a king to be appointed for them, the "Josephites" (tribes of Ephraim and Manasseh, who largely constituted the Israelite component of Samaria) rejected such an unruly demand from God's prophet.[41] It is noteworthy that in both the Judaist and Samaritan accounts of the origins of Samaria and the schisms between Jews and Samaritans, religious disputes, differences, and conflicts are acknowledged.[42]

John presents Jesus as one who was culturally adventurous. Though Jesus had every opportunity to avoid the Samaritans by taking the Perean route from Judea to Galilee, he chose to go through Samaria. He also could have made preparations to go through Samaria, which was a shorter route, without stopping for food, not to mention starting an unwarranted conversation with a woman (John 4:4–8). Ben Sira cautions men against spending time alone with women who are not their wives:

---

37. Macdonald, *Theology of the Samaritans*, 15, 21–24.
38. Macdonald, *Theology of the Samaritans*, 16.
39. Macdonald, *Theology of the Samaritans*, 16.
40. Macdonald, *Theology of the Samaritans*, 17.
41. Macdonald, *Theology of the Samaritans*, 18.
42. Macdonald, *Theology of the Samaritans*, 24–25.

> Do not be jealous of the wife of your bosom, or you will teach
> her an evil lesson to your own hurt. Do not give yourself to a
> woman and let her trample down your strength. Do not go near
> a loose woman, or you will fall into her snares. Do not dally with
> a singing girl, or you will be caught by her tricks. Do not look
> intently at a virgin, or you may stumble and incur penalties for
> her. Do not give yourself to prostitutes, or you may lose your
> inheritance. (Sir 9:3–6 NRSV)

John does not tell us why exactly it was necessary (*edei*, "had to") for Jesus
to travel through Samaria. It was as if Jesus concluded that the benefits of
going through Samaria outweighed the risks of going through Perea. One
possible benefit is to avoid a circuitous route in order to get to Galilee faster
(geographical reasons). Another possible benefit was the unlikelihood the
Pharisees who had come to investigate him would follow him through Samaria given their proclivity to observe the Jewish purity laws (tactical reasons). It was possible that *edei* was used by John to denote "the situation of
open hostility which existed between" Jews and Samaritans (ethno-cultural
and socioreligious reasons).[43] Teresa Okure argues that it was most likely
that "*edei* refers to the divine will for Jesus" since he "can do nothing except
what he sees the Father doing . . . and there can be no other imperative in
his life than the Father's will" (theological reasons).[44]

That Jesus struck an unwarranted conversation with a woman of Samarian would suggest that it was possible his reason was missional: he
wanted to teach his disciples (and the people of Samaria) to reimagine their
understandings of God-human relations (in the context of true worship)
and human-human relations (in the context of ethnic and religious biases).
Whatever the actual reasons that occasioned the necessity, Jesus was willing
to critique and engage both the Jewish and Samarian religious traditions in
light of his theological reading of Scripture. The tension between Jews and
Samaritans raised some important theological questions that Jesus could not
ignore. The tension raised questions about God's identity, about the nature of
true religious worship (especially the hierarchical relationship between the
right mode of worship and the right location for worship), and about Jesus's
identity in relation to God's gift of salvation. Jesus's conversation with the
woman shows that he drew upon theological data of Hebrew Scripture, Jewish tradition, and the context of his community not merely to express Jewish
theology in the language of his day. On the contrary, he pressed the theological data from these *loci theologici* for useful theological materials, which he

43. Okure, *Johannine Approach to Mission*, 84.
44. Okure, *Johannine Approach to Mission*, 85.

used to formulate his theological beliefs. I will now turn attention to some theological themes in the three pericopes examined in this chapter.

Theological Themes in Jesus's Sayings

I will focus on three themes—true worship and God's freedom, Jesus as fulfiller of Scripture, and Jesus as dispenser of God's salvific blessing.

True Worship and God's Freedom

According to John's account, the Samaritan woman recalled two theological beliefs that were prevalent in the grassroots theologies of the people of Samaria. She deployed the beliefs to stake her claim for the uniqueness of the Samaritans vis-à-vis the Jews. She introduced the first belief in a question format: "Are you greater than our ancestor Jacob, who gave us the well, and with his sons and his flocks drank from it?" (John 4:12 NRSV). She appealed to the authority of her ancestor, Jacob, to counteract what she perceived as Jesus's arrogance or self-conceit. The second theological belief she invoked was that God is to be worshiped at Mt. Gerizim (see Gen 33:18–20; 48:22; Deut 11:29). For the woman, Mt. Gerizim, perhaps like Mt. Zion in Jerusalem, was the rightful center of religious worship. By invoking the two grassroots theological beliefs, the Samaritan woman wanted them to settle the religious and theological issues between Jews and Samaritans within the parameters of traditions marked by the ancestral authority of Jacob, Mt. Gerizim, and Jerusalem. Jesus, however, steered the conversation beyond the parameters of tradition by invoking God's freedom in relation to true worship. The expression "God's freedom" in this context consists in *spatial transcendence*: God can encounter a worshipper at any place and time. Though the traditional places of worship of Samaritans and Jews are important, they are not essential to true worship of God. To put it differently, God, and not a place of worship, should be the focus of true worship.

How are we to understand *true worship*? John 4:22 provides a helpful clue to the nature of true worship. Jesus's claim that Samaritans "worship what [they] do not know" seems to suggest that he imagined true worship as requiring the right knowledge of God. The expression "in truth and spirit" in John 4:23 also suggests that *true worship* is the kind of worship that is firmly grounded in the right knowledge of God and the right attitude toward God. Jesus highlighted God's spatial transcendence by reminding the woman that God is "spirit" and therefore should be worshipped "in truth and spirit." God's mode of being in the world is described with the

word "spirit," implying that God cannot be confined to a space or location of worship. God, as "spirit," can encounter a worshipper in a specific
place of worship (Mt. Gerizim or Mt. Zion) and outside of it. Given that
John does not explain the meanings of "truth" in this context, it would be
helpful to see how he used similar words elsewhere in his Gospel. If we
understand "truth" in the context of worship as reliable and trustworthy
knowledge of God (in both cognitive and relational senses), who is the
object of true worship, it follows that John's description of Jesus as the embodiment of truth provides a helpful clue to truth's role in worship (John
14:6). John appears to position Jesus as one who can guide the worshiper
to and through true worship. According to John 8:31–32, Jesus told his
disciples: "If you continue in my word, you are truly my disciples; and you
will know the truth, and the truth will make you free" (NRSV). The role
that Jesus plays in guiding worshipers (his disciples) to the true knowledge
of God and to true worship of God fits John's theological aim to show that
Jesus was superior to Israel's ancestors such as Jacob (John 4:12), Moses
(John 6:32–59), and Abraham (John 8:53).[45]

The woman's confusion about Jesus's identity—whether he was a
prophet or the Messiah—does not prevent her from witnessing to other
Samaritans about the "man who told [her] everything" she has done (John
4:29). Though Jesus's declaration that he was the Messiah (John 4:26) did
not clear the woman's confusion about his identity and his authority to
challenge the religious tradition of Samaria, she nonetheless shared her
experience with others. Her witness, according to John, resulted in many
Samaritans hearing and believing in Jesus (John 4:39–42). Parodying Jesus's line of theological appropriation that is implied in his expression,
"You have heard that it was said . . . but I say to you" (Matt 5:21–48),
we could assume that he might have said to her: "You have heard that it
was said a location of worship is important, but I say to you, our standing
before God during worship is what is most important." By dismissing both
the religious locations of the Jews (Jerusalem) and the Samaritans (Mt.
Gerizim) as essential to true worship of God, Jesus made it clear that no
religion can encapsulate the mystery of God. True worship is not reducible
to human constructs. God transcends human commentary on his being
and work. God can encounter a true worshiper in places other than official
religious sites. Below I explore the role that Jesus plays in guiding his followers and disciples to true worship, particularly in his understanding of
himself as a fulfiller of Hebrew Scripture.

45. Neyrey, "Jacob Traditions," 420–21.

Jesus as Fulfiller of Scripture

In the Lukan pericope (4:16–21), Jesus said the following words after reading from a scroll containing the book of Isaiah: "Today this scripture has been fulfilled in our hearing" (Luke 4:21 NRSV). What is the theological content of the claim that Jesus "fulfills" Hebrew Scripture? The term "fulfill" here signifies a form of embodiment: Jesus viewed himself as one who embodied the significance of the theological truths in Hebrew Scripture. It is an embodiment of scriptural truths within the theater of expectation and disillusionment occasioned by the Roman occupation of Israel. For some of the contemporaries of Jesus who entertained the idea that he might be the political liberator and national deliverer of Israel, he should show some clear visible signs that would indicate he merited the title "Messiah" such as not dying in the hands of the Romans (Matt 16:21–28; Mark 8:31–38; Luke 24:13–27; cf. Luke 9:22–27). According to such expectations, Jesus failed, for he did not liberate Israel from the hands of the Romans.

To say that Jesus "fulfills" Hebrew Scripture does not mean that he followed the teaching of Scripture legalistically. He moved away from a legalistic reading of Hebrew Scripture to a more robust understanding that addressed the significance of its teaching, especially its significance for forming and sustaining a community of God's people. He was constantly accused of not following the letter of Scripture, for example, when he chose to heal on a Sabbath day (Luke 13:10–17). As the fulfiller of Hebrew Scripture, the totality of his life and experience gives a concrete meaning to and also brings into light some theological truths of Hebrew Scripture. Richard Bauckham observes in his study on the Gospel of John that Jesus fulfills Scripture in the sense that he

> is the true Passover Lamb, slain to effect the new exodus from the empire of sin (1:29; 19:33, 36). He is the true temple of the messianic age from which the water of life flows (7:38; 19:34; 21:11; cf. Ezek 47:1–12). He is the true righteous king of the psalms of David, protected by God even in his abandonment to deathly affliction (13:18; 19:24, 28, 36). He is the truth of Jacob's ladder, raised up on the cross to reach heaven (1:51). By fulfilling scripture, in these and many other ways, Jesus enacts God's faithfulness. In him God proves true to his word.[46]

As the fulfiller of Hebrew Scripture, Jesus embodies God's words to God's people. This embodiment should be understood in the context of Jesus's understanding of the kingdom of God. By invoking the *spirit* (significance)

---

46. Bauckham, *Gospel of Glory*, 74.

of the *letter* (words) of Prophet Isaiah, Jesus clearly announced that God's reign intentionally engages and uplifts those who are being crushed under the weight of poverty, diseases, oppression, and exploitation (Luke 4:18–19; cf. Isa 61:1–2).

It is equally likely that Jesus intended his declaration of the fulfillment of Isaiah's prophecy as a theological invitation: he admonished his hearers to reimagine their theologies of the Jubilee in a new light. Since his hearers did not suddenly experience debt forgiveness and also restoration of health, his declaration would have perplexed them. That they eventually drove him out of town and wanted to murder him (Luke 4:28–30) would indicate that Jesus's theological invitation did not go so well. Some of the hearers questioned his authority to issue such a theological invitation given that neither he nor his family had any scribal pedigree. Such a presumptuous attitude was evident in the question of the crowd: "Isn't this Joseph's son?" (Luke 4:22). Luke obviously did not describe why the crowd was so incensed with Jesus to the point of attempting to kill him. Verses 23–27, however, have helpful clues to the nature of Jesus's invitation to theological reimagination of God's restoration. Two key themes are implied in these verses. First, Jesus's assessment of the crowd's expectation shows he believed that their preoccupation with miracles as a physical evidence that God was working through him was deeply misguided. "Surely," Jesus said, "you will quote this proverb to me: 'Physician, heal yourself! Do here in your hometown what we have heard that you did in Capernaum'" (Luke 4:23 NIV). Challenging Jesus to demonstrate his authority and powers by performing miracles as he did in Capernaum (Mark 1:21–28) signified that the crowd's mindset was grounded in unbelief, which is displeasing to God. Such an unbelieving mindset, for Jesus, constituted the grounds for God's punishment. Second, Jesus invited the crowd to reimagine their understanding of God's restoration and blessings in ways that did not confine God's work only within the nation of Israel. He said to the crowd:

> Truly, I say to you, no prophet is acceptable in his hometown.
> But in truth, I tell you, there were many widows in Israel in the
> days of Elijah, when the heavens were shut up three years and
> six months, and a great famine came over all the land, and Elijah
> was sent to none of them but only to Zarephath, in the land of
> Sidon, to a woman who was a widow. And there were many lepers in Israel in the time of the prophet Elisha, and none of them
> was cleansed, but only Naaman the Syrian. (Luke 4:24–27 ESV)

The words above show that Jesus paid close attention to the grassroots theologies of his audience and engaged them in light of his theological insights and understanding of Hebrew Scripture and God. He also construed God's salvific work in ways that were driven partly by his understanding of his own mission: to proclaim and embody God's news of liberation to the world, especially to the poor, oppressed, and marginalized (Luke 4:16–21).

Jesus as the Dispenser of God's Salvific Blessing

One of the controversial theological insights of Jesus was his claim to dispense God's "living water" or salvific blessing. The Samaritan woman's question highlights the difficulty of understanding Jesus's claim. Obviously, Jesus couldn't possibly be speaking of literal water when he said to the woman he could give her the "living water." It is not surprising that the woman sardonically remarked: "Sir, you have no bucket, and the well is deep. Where do you get that living water? Are you greater than our ancestor Jacob, who gave us the well, and with his sons and his flocks drank from it?" (John 4:11–12 NRSV). Also, she said: "Sir, give me this water, so that I may never be thirsty or have to keep coming here to draw water" (John 4:15 NRSV). The woman clearly misunderstood Jesus's point: the "living water," a metaphor for God's salvific blessing, is more important than the natural water that has temporal value.[47] Jesus responded with these words: "Everyone who drinks of this water will be thirsty again, but those who drink of the water that I will give them will never be thirsty. The water that I will give will become in them a spring of water gushing up to eternal life" (John 4:13–14 NRSV).

Jesus was most probably echoing the figural usages of "living water" in Hebrew Scripture. Though the words "water" and "living water" are sometimes used metaphorically in the Scripture and Judaism to describe a host of things, it is most likely that Jesus and John were referring to God's salvific blessing.[48] This divine blessing should also be understood in light of the already not-yet eschatological nexus that characterizes Jesus's understanding of God's reign in the world. God's salvific blessing is already ongoing, and Jesus construed himself as its dispenser: "If you knew the gift of God, and who it is that is saying to you, 'Give me a drink,' you would have asked him,

47. C. K. Barrett argues that the "living water" in this context is a reference to the "Holy Spirit." See Barrett, *Gospel according to St. John*, 190. As I will show later, a broader understanding of the "living water" as the metaphor for the Triune God's salvific blessing is more fitting in the context of John's Gospel.

48. "Living water" is used metaphorically to describe God (Jer 2:13; 17:13). "Water" is used metaphorically to describe spiritual purification or cleansing (Ezek 36:24–26; Zech 13:1) and the Torah (Sir 24:23–27). In Zech 14:8, "living water" is used to describe God's restorative work. Isaiah 12:3 make an implicit reference to water ("wells") in connection to God eschatological work of salvation.

and he would have given you living water" (John 4:10 NRSV; see also John 7:37–39; cf. Isa 12:3).[49] John 3:16 provides a helpful context for understanding John's understanding of salvific blessing as God's gift to the world. As Teresa Okure observes,

> The purpose of the gift is so that those who believe in him may have "eternal life." A direct link is thus established between [John] 3:16 and 4:10, 14: both passages inseparably link the "gift of God" (understood as "eternal life") with Jesus through whom this gift is given. Put differently, Jesus is God's primary gift without whom the gift of living water/spirit/word is impossible.[50]

John links the "living water," which Jesus was prepared to offer the woman, to Jesus's identity—his person and work (John 3:10, 13–14). Jesus's qualification as the dispenser of God's salvation could be understood in light of the assumption of the woman that he might be the expected Messiah (certainly a prophet) and also Jesus's confirmation that he was indeed the Messiah (John 4:25–26). His qualification as the dispenser of God's salvific blessing could equally be understood in light of John's thesis that *Jesus is superior to Israel's ancestors because he is God incarnate* (John 1:1–18; see also John 4:12; 6:32–59; John 8:53). John's juxtaposition of the sources of the water from the well at Sychar and the living water is noteworthy: Jacob is the giver of the water from the well at Sychar and Jesus is the giver of the living water. John might have included the story of Jesus's encounter with the Samaritan woman in his Gospel narrative to make the theological case for "the Samaritan mission and to establish the full equality in the community between Samaritan Christians and Jewish Christians."[51] In any case, it was part of John's theological strategy to accentuate the centrality of Jesus's identity with the Christian message about God's ongoing work of salvation in the world. God's salvation, in Jesus's theology, is restricted neither to the Jews nor the Samaritans. God's salvific work provided a surplus that transcended ethnic and religious boundaries of both Jews and Samaritans.

What my discussions so far have shown is that Jesus performed his task of theologizing in ways that can serve as a model for how to do contextual theology. But as I noted earlier, the concept of "model" reminds us of similarity-dissimilarity dialectic. As a model for how to do contextual theology, Jesus brought different theological sources into dialogic communication for purposes of both formulating his theological beliefs and

49. For discussions on the possible echo of Isa 12:3 in John 7:38, see Marcus, "Rivers of Living Water," 328–30.

50. Okure, *Johannine Approach to Mission*, 97–98.

51. Schneiders, "Feminist Interpretation of John 4:1–42," 243.

expressing them to his communities and audiences. So far I have explored the similarities between Jesus and contextual theologians. In the next section I pursue the other side of the dialectic—the dissimilarities between Jesus (who is fully divine and human) and contextual theologians who are merely humans. Building on this traditional Christian belief about Jesus's divine-human ontology, I explore the idea that he ought to be the *grammar* of the theologies of Christian communities.

Jesus as Grammar of Christian Theology

The term "grammar" is used here in two senses. First, as the grammar of Christian theology, Jesus (his life, experience, and teaching) sets the boundary for how to properly do a theology that is worthy of the name "Christian." If Christian theology is to be done from the perspectives of the Christian faith and Christian communities, it is reasonable to believe that Jesus ought to govern its contents. Any theology that competes with the life, experience, and teaching of Jesus (as presented in Scripture) should shoulder the burden of demonstrating why it should be called "Christian theology." Second, as the grammar of Christian theology, Jesus constitutes the essential theological data that should put together Christians' theological reflections on God-world relations. A Christian theology should expound on the life, experience, and teaching of Jesus as the principal guide to how Christian communities are to think of God-world relations. Insofar as Christianity emerged as a result of the teaching and experience of Jesus, Christian theology may be defined as Christians' reflections on God-world relations in light of Jesus's understanding of God-world relations. Jesus is the fullness of the language of Christian communities about how God relates to the world. In the words of Karl Barth,

> The question of truth, with which theology is concerned throughout, is the question as to the agreement of the Church's distinctive talk about God with the being of the Church. The criterion of past, future, and therefore present Christian utterance is thus the being of the Church, namely, Jesus Christ, God in His gracious revealing and reconciling address to man.[52]

Those of us who, in accordance with Scripture, confess that Jesus Christ is Lord and also, in accordance with the earliest ecumenical councils, confess that he is truly divine and truly human, face a temptation to

---

52. Barth, *Church Dogmatics 1.1*, 4.

emphasize his divinity at the expense of his humanity or vice versa.[53] Claiming that Jesus is a model for contextual theologians, as I have argued in this chapter, requires holding in tension that he is truly divine and truly human. Jesus was thoroughly grounded in his Jewish roots. We should not be surprised that his earthly parents took him to the Temple for the Feast of Passover (Luke 2:41–51). Luke tells us that "the boy Jesus . . . grew in wisdom and stature, and in favor with God and men" (Luke 2:43, 52 NIV). For Luke, Jesus developed physically, mentally, socially, and spiritually. From at least his teen years, Jesus listened to and most likely learned from the Jewish rabbis: "They [Jesus's parents] found him in the temple courts, sitting among the teachers, listening to them and asking them questions" (Luke 2:46 NIV). Luke tells us that Jesus was an engaging student: "Everyone who heard him was amazed at his understanding and his answers" (Luke 2:47 NIV). Jesus grew in his knowledge of God and developed his theological skills like someone who was truly human. Hebrew Scripture, Jewish religious tradition, and the grassroots theology of his Jewish community aided him in his contextual theological life: his collection, collation, and use of theological data to formulate his theological sayings, which he used to address the theological needs of his audiences.

Unfortunately, many Christians today approach Jesus's teaching mainly from the assumption that he was divine. They pay little attention to the traditional Christian belief that he was equally truly human. Such Christians focus primarily on the content of Jesus's teaching—his final theological product—and the truthfulness of his teaching, but not on the sources of his theology or how he used the sources to construct his own theology. It is worth noting that the issue of how best to reconcile Jesus's divinity and humanity has continued to occupy many Christian theologians. For example, kenotic theologians as well as theologians that hold two-minds Christology uphold Jesus's true humanity.[54] Though Thomas Morris holds the two-minds

53. Since the second century CE, Christian theologians have been fascinated by the metaphysics of Jesus of Nazareth. How was he God incarnate? According to Justin Martyr (died ca. 165), the *Logos* (Word) took shape, became a man, and was Jesus Christ. See Justin, "Apologia I." Two related theo-christological questions have governed Christian theologians' reflections and debates on Jesus's personhood and the two natures that constitute his person. First, how is it possible for two disparate natures (divine and human) to constitute an individual's personhood? Second, was the Incarnation really necessary for God's salvific act of restoring a fallen creation? The Council of Nicaea (325 CE) and the Council of Chalcedon (451 CE) did not quite settle these extremely difficult questions. The debate that preoccupied these councils need not detain us. For discussions on these councils, see Kelly, *Early Christian Doctrines*, 83–343; Grillmeier, *Christ in Christian Tradition*.

54. For example, Gottfried Thomasius argued that God's *Logos* (eternal Son of God) divested himself of his nonessential attributes in order to become fully human. Others

Christology (the belief that Jesus had a divine mind and a human mind), he argues that Jesus lived mainly from his human mind during his earthly life. He writes, "God the Son Incarnate had two minds and chose to live out the life of the body on this earth normally through the resources of the human mind alone. That was the primary font of most of his earthly behavior and speech."[55] Morris, however, argues that Jesus's beliefs and teachings arose from and were approved by his divine mind:

> to say what he, the individual person, believed about this or that, we must appeal to the feature of hierarchical organization endemic to a systems view of mentality and, recognizing the priority of the divine, represent God the Son's ultimate belief state as captured in his divine omniscience.[56]

Morris's claim exemplifies the readiness of some Christian theologians to move rather too quickly to the divine origins of Jesus's theological beliefs without considering the earthly sources of his theology.

One of the implications of the belief in Jesus's full humanity is that he taught and expressed his view of God as a real human being.[57] Jesus was open to being challenged and also to grow in his knowledge about the best way to negotiate his life and vision for the world in light of his inherited Hebrew Scripture, tradition (beliefs, practices, and assumptions), and personal theological insights. For instance, Matthew 15 narrates Jesus's encounter with an unnamed Canaanite woman in the district of Tyre and Sidon (15:21). Surprisingly, in his initial response to the woman's request to "have mercy" on her by healing her daughter who was "oppressed by a demon" (15:22), Jesus echoed or alluded to a derogatory and ethnic slur some Jews used to describe the non-Israelites—the so-called Gentiles (see Jub 22:19–22). According to Matthew, Jesus said to her: "It is not right to take children's bread and throw it to the dogs [Greek *kynáriois*]" (15:26). Dogs, for the Jews, were filthy things: they were "known for their attachment to dung and sniffing other dogs' rear ends" and were commonly "linked

---

argue that God's eternal Son did not relinquish any divine attributes such as omnipotence and omniscience. Rather, he suspended the use of such divine attributes. For other helpful discussions on kenotic Christology, see Evans, *Exploring Kenotic Christology*; Thomasius, "Christ's Person and Work," 31–114; Fee, "New Testament and Kenosis Christology," 25–36.

55. Morris, *Our Idea of God*, 173.

56. Morris, *Our Idea of God*, 173.

57. In Acts, Luke also notes that God anointed Jesus with the Holy Spirit, empowering him to do good works such as "healing all who were oppressed by the devil" (Acts 10:38 ESV).

with birds as scavengers that devoured unburied corpses."[58] Some scholars have attempted to explain away the seriousness of Jesus's unpleasing and disturbing response to the Canaanite woman.[59] Some argue that he simply was intending to send the persistent woman away. Others argue that he was testing the woman's faith (after all the woman could have opted to trade insults). Craig Bloomberg claims: "Jesus apparently wants to demonstrate and stretch this woman's faith."[60] But why would Jesus echo or allude to a slur as a way of either driving the woman away or testing her faith? The seriousness of Jesus's language and treatment of the woman should not be ignored, even if he might have merely alluded to a slur without intending to affirm it as an acceptable way of describing non-Israelites. Also Jesus's choice of *kynáriois* (house dogs or pets) instead of *kyōn* (a street dog) does not diminish the condescending weight of his response. Opting not to trade insults, perhaps for fear that she might end up not getting what she really wanted (the deliverance of her daughter from demonic possession), the woman instead chose to respond with grace, albeit with clear and unmistakable boldness. "Yes Lord," the woman said, "yet even the dogs eat the crumbs that fall from their masters' table" (Matt 15:27 ESV; see also Mark 7:28). As Nancy Klancher has observed, "The Canaanite woman . . . turns the tables, by claiming the rights of a dog to crumbs under the table."[61]

Another possible way of making sense of Jesus's puzzling language, which I believe is more viable than the foregoing explanations, is that Jesus used unfortunate language to reemphasize the narrow focus of his ministry. In both Matthew's and Mark's accounts of the story, Jesus expressed that his mission was first and primarily for Israelites (Matt 15: 24; Mark 7:27). The woman's gracious response to his unfortunate language most likely helped him to realize that the woman might have misunderstood his intentions. Mark ascribed Jesus's change of heart to the woman's gracious response: "And he said to her, 'For this statement you may go your way; the demon has left your daughter'" (Mark 7:29 ESV). That Jesus changed his mind after initially snubbing the woman showed, by opting not to trade insults, she had succeeded in nudging him to show the scope of his mission extended beyond

---

58. Keener, *Commentary on the Gospel of Matthew*, 416–17. First Kings 14:11 describes the scavenging life of dogs: "Anyone belonging to Jeroboam who dies in the city the dogs shall eat, and anyone who dies in the open country the birds of the heaven shall eat, for the LORD has spoken it" (ESV).

59. For the history of the interpretations of this story, see Klancher, *Taming of the Canaanite Woman*.

60. Bloomberg, *Matthew*, 244.

61. Klancher, *Taming of the Canaanite Woman*, 1.

the nation of Israel.[62] God's blessings (signified by the term "bread") extend beyond the people of Israel (signified by the term "children") to include Gentiles (signified by the term "dogs"). Although Jesus, in all likelihood, was aware that his mission extended beyond "the lost sheep of the house of Israel" (Matt 15:24), it was this unnamed Canaanite woman that prompted him to demonstrate publicly a more inclusive and global vision of God's blessings. There is a theological value in juxtaposing Matthew 15:24 with Matthew 28:19: Matthew presents Jesus in a way that clearly shows he extended his vision from the nation of Israel to all nations As Richard Hays notes, the "command to make disciples of all nations" shows that Jesus expected his disciples to carry "the preaching of the gospel beyond the boundaries, both geographic and ethnic, of Israel."[63] The writers of the four canonical Gospels shared a common agenda: to show their audiences, in their own ways, that Jesus of Nazareth was the embodiment of God's good news of salvation to the nation of Israel and also to all nations of the world (Matt 28:19; Mark 16:14–18; Luke 24:46–49; cf. Acts 1:8; John 17).

Jesus is the embodiment of *the* "Christian message" (or Christian gospel)—the totality of what Christians should say about the good news of God's salvific work in the world. This claim implies that the Christian message or gospel is not merely a statement but rather a person: Jesus of Nazareth. The good news (gospel) the angel of the Lord announced, according to Luke, is that a "Savior has been born to you; he is Christ the Lord" (Luke 2:11 NIV). Construing Jesus as the embodiment of the Christian message has several implications for Christian theology. I will highlight some here. (1) Christian theology should be derivative of the teaching, life, and experience of Jesus insofar as Christians are his disciples. As the Christian message, Jesus imposes a boundary on what a Christian community should say about God-world relations. (2) Christian theology is the theological commentary of Christians about God-world relations and as such is essentially duplicative of Jesus's theological life. As duplicative of Jesus's theology, Christian theology is incapable of becoming the Christian message. To put it differently, Christian theology cannot replace Jesus, who is the Christian message. Jesus would always remain a surplus that resists the attempts by

62. William Placher's commentary on Mark's account is helpful in this regard: "If Mark did not show us Jesus' initial harsh remark, we could not see the grace with which Jesus concedes defeat in an argument. That the woman does win the argument is a point any valid interpretation needs to acknowledge. To say that that could not happen is to deny Jesus' full humanity. Here yet again humanity and divinity come together in a single narrative of a single agent—the same Jesus who loses the argument can cure her daughter." Placher, *Mark*, 106.

63. Hays, *Echoes of Scripture*, 183.

a Christian community to colonize him. (3) Contextual theologians ought to see Jesus as the *grammar* of Christian theology. Their theologies should be derivative and duplicative of Jesus Christ's theological life vis-à-vis the matrix of a Christian community.

Seeing Jesus Christ as the grammar of Christian theology, however, raises questions about his universal relevance to the theological conversations of Christians of all times and in all contexts. Why is Jesus, the Jew, universally relevant to the theological discourses of all Christian communities? Why should contemporary Christian communities, especially those with no historical ties to the Jewish context, bring Jesus's life and teaching into their theological activities when addressing theological issues that are peculiar to their own contexts? This is by no means a new theological question. Constructing a theological bridge between Jesus and non-Jewish Christian communities has troubled Christians from the earliest times. Acts chapter 15 reveals the internal struggles of the early church to construct such a theological bridge:

> We have heard that some went out from us without our authorization and disturbed you, troubling your minds by what they said. So we all agreed to choose some men and send them to you with our dear friends Barnabas and Paul—men who have risked their lives for the name of our Lord Jesus Christ. Therefore we are sending Judas and Silas to confirm by word of mouth what we are writing. It seemed good to the Holy Spirit and to us not to burden you with anything beyond the following requirements: You are to abstain from food sacrificed to idols, from blood, from the meat of strangled animals and from sexual immorality. You will do well to avoid these things. (Acts 15:24–29 NIV)

The Jerusalem council was clearly Jewish both in its membership and its theological focus. On the one hand, the council did not want to burden non-Jewish communities with some Jewish laws (Acts 15:19). On the other hand, the council required some laws that are Jewish in nature (Acts 15:20–21; see also Acts 21:25; cf. Lev 3:17; 7:26). However, the council's attempt to clarify the relationship between the law of Moses and the freedom of Christ was a watershed moment in the cross-cultural theological activity of the earliest Christian communities. "Gentile believers," whom God has "purified by faith," should not be burdened with a Jewish legal yoke because, like the Jewish believers, they have been saved "through the grace" of Jesus Christ (Acts15:10–11). Without any precedent, the council made a theological move that would open the door for Christians with no historical ties to the Jewish context to freely express their experience of

God through the Holy Spirit as they commit to Jesus Christ in discipleship (Acts 15:7–9). If the council had ruled in favor of the "party of the Pharisees" that required Gentile Christians to be circumcised according to the law of Moses (Acts 15:5), the non-Jewish early Christians might not have had the courage to express their faith in Jesus in terms of their own history, experience, culture, and social location.

How, then, should Jesus's universal relevance be construed in light of the contextuality of Christian expressions? Traditionally, many Christians have taken what may be described as the *divine-origins* pathway when discussing the universal relevance of Jesus Christ. Citing a christological ode, the Apostle Paul argued that Jesus had the "form of God" (*morphe Theou*) but did not exploit such exalted ontological status for selfish gains (Phil 2:6–9). The Apostle John described Jesus Christ as God incarnate:

> In the beginning was the Word [*Logos*], and the Word was with God, and the Word was God. He was with God in the beginning . . . The Word became flesh and made his dwelling among us. We have seen his glory, the glory of the One and Only, who came from the Father, full of grace and truth. (John 1:1–14 NIV)

In the fourth and fifth centuries, several church councils made the case for Jesus's consubstantiality with God the Father: he was "truly God."[64] James Massey, Kwame Bediako, and Gustavo Gutiérrez, whose theologies I will explore in the next three chapters, ground their understanding of the universality of Jesus Christ in his divinity. According to Bediako, Jesus Christ is unique in relation to the lords of other faiths because he is God incarnate:

> The affirmation that in Christ, God humbled himself and identified with humankind in Christ's birth as a human baby, born of woman, and endured the conditions of "normal" human existence—in other words, the Incarnation is supremely the unique sign and demonstration of divine vulnerability in history.[65]

---

64. See the creeds of the Councils of Nicaea (325 CE) and Constantinople (381 CE), and the christological definition of the Council of Chalcedon (451 CE).

65. Bediako, *Jesus and the Gospel in Africa*, 41–42. Bediako also wrote, "Ancestors are considered worthy of honor for having 'lived among us' and for having brought benefits to us; Jesus Christ has done infinitely more. They [ancestors], originating from among us, had no choice but to live among us. But he [Jesus Christ], reflecting the brightness of God's glory and the exact likeness of God's own being (Hebrews 1:30), took our flesh and blood, shared our human nature, and underwent death for us to set us free from the fear of death (Hebrews 2:14–15)." See Bediako, *Jesus and the Gospel in Africa*, 30.

Massey also invokes the doctrine of the Incarnation to demonstrate the relevance of Jesus Christ to the Dalit experience. He writes, "in the act of incarnation, we do meet God, in full solidarity with us, not just as any human being, but as one who gave up his otherworldly identity completely for our sake and became the poorest of the poor—in a real sense, a Dalit."[66] Gutiérrez sees the Incarnation as God's commitment to human history: "God is manifested visibly in the humanity of Christ, the God-Man, irreversibly committed to human history."[67]

Following the divine-origins path of christological exploration of the universality of Jesus, however, should not circumvent contextual theologizing, especially how his life and teaching are relevant to the context of present-day Christian communities. Christian theologians need not presume Jesus's universal relevance for doing theology by simply invoking his divinity without showing how his life and teaching can be useful to the theological needs of Christian communities of all cultures and times. Theologians should show how Jesus's "works" (*erga*)—his teaching and deeds—testify to his person and significance (John 10:25). To accomplish these tasks, theologians should not treat Jesus Christ—the grammar or language of Christian theology—as a *dead language*: a form of theological language that looks backward but not forward. When we focus only on what Jesus did during his earthly ministry (as recorded in Scripture) and disregard what he is doing in the communities of his present-day followers, we have succumbed to the temptation of treating him as a dead theological language. The concept of discipleship is most helpful in this context. To be a disciple of Jesus Christ is to declare one's allegiance: choosing to enter into a lifelong process of working out one's relationship within the matrix of one's context. Contextual theology reminds us to treat Jesus as a living theological language. Theologians should look both backward and forward as they reflect on the universal relevance of Jesus to theological discourses on religious beliefs and practices. For example, in doing Christology, theologians need to be prepared to exegete both the appropriation of the life and teaching of Jesus by communities of antiquity and also the ongoing appropriation of his life and teaching by his present-day communities.

Though Jesus, as I have argued in this chapter, may be described as a model for contextual theologians, he is unlike them because he is fully divine. To say that Jesus of Nazareth is God incarnate is a confession of faith that is at the heart of theological beliefs of many Christian communities. Since I share this belief about Jesus's divinity, I will highlight its implications

66. Massey, *Downtrodden*, 61.

67. Gutiérrez, *Theology of Liberation*, 109.

for contextual theology. As God incarnate, Jesus's theological insights into Hebrew Scripture, Jewish religious tradition, and the grassroots theologies embedded in the context of his Jewish community should be authoritative for Christian communities. Theologians that hold the two-minds Christologies and kenotic Christologies share the belief that Jesus was *infallible*: his teaching and life were reliable and trustworthy for his disciples. They disagree, of course, on how it was possible for him to be infallible. Those who hold two-minds Christologies would argue that Jesus's divine mind could not have allowed his human mind to teach and live fallibly.[68] The divine mind provided the human mind the protection he needed to live righteously. Kenotic theologians would argue that God the Father and the Holy Spirit provided Jesus the knowledge, power, and ability he needed to live his life and carry out his earthly ministry.[69]

A kenotic Christology that is grounded in the belief (a) that God's *logos* did not relinquish any divine attributes in order to become incarnate as a human being (Jesus Christ) and (b) that in his incarnate state, Jesus depended on the Father and the Holy Spirit for his life and ministry makes the most sense for the portrait of Jesus I present here (Phil 2:5–11). In Luke's Gospel, the Holy Spirit empowered Jesus Christ: he was "full of the Holy Spirit" (Luke 4:1), the Holy Spirit led him (4:1), and he lived in the "power of the Holy Spirit" (4:14). In Acts, Luke also tells us, "God anointed Jesus of Nazareth with the Holy Spirit and power" and he "went around doing good and healing all who were under the power of the devil, because God was with him" (Acts 10:38 NIV). John the Baptist, according to the Gospel of John, claimed to have seen "the Spirit come down from heaven as a dove and remain on" Jesus Christ at his baptism (John 1:32). John also tells us that Jesus will baptize people "with the Holy Spirit" (4:33). Given the kind of kenotic Christology I endorse in this book, it is argued that God (the Father) and the Holy Spirit empowered Jesus Christ to use theological materials from Hebrew Scripture, Jewish religious tradition, and the context of his own community to construct his theological sayings. As God incarnate, Jesus enjoyed a special and exclusive relationship with God (the Father) and the Holy Spirit. This special and exclusive relationship is the grounds for claiming that Jesus, unlike theologians who are merely human beings, produced theologies that should serve as the *grammar* (content and boundary) of Christian theologies.

To conclude this chapter, I have argued that theologians ought not rely solely on the theological questions and assumptions of earlier Christian

68. See Morris, *Our Idea of God*, 158–84.

69. See Fee, "New Testament and Kenosis Christology," 25–36.

generations. They should also discern new theological questions and assumptions that Christians of this era address to the Christian faith. Accessing such contemporary theological questions and assumptions, as I have shown in chapter 1 and in this chapter, requires expanding Christian *loci theologici* to include the changing life situations of present-day Christian communities. Theologians can learn from the echoes of contextual theologizing that are displayed in her or his theological activities.

In the next three chapters, I will explore the ways James Massey, Kwame Bediako, and Gustavo Gutiérrez formulated their theologies by drawing upon the theological data of Christian Scripture, church tradition, and the contexts of their own communities. Massey, Bediako, and Gutiérrez share in common a spirit of theological protest against Western theological dominations that were quenching the embers of theological hope of producing theologies that actually took seriously the contexts of African, Asian, and Latin American Christians. Western theologies and theologians, of course, were not the only targets of their theological protest. They also directed their theological protest against the Asian, African, and Latin American protégés of Western theologians who produced theologies that were helping in perpetuate Western theological domination and hegemony in their countries and continents. Beyond theological protests, Massey, Bediako, and Gutiérrez have shown strong examples of how to construct theologies that are thoroughly grounded in the contexts of their own communities. In the next chapter, I explore Dalit Christians' dehumanizing experience in India and how James Massey engages it in his Dalit theology.

3

Caste and Dalit Theology

I s the belief that Dalits are inherently and irreversibly inferior to people with caste status in the Indian caste system relevant to Christian theology? What form of Christian theological anthropology is befitting to the struggles of Dalits for liberation?[1] How does Dalit (Christian) theology contribute to the field of contextual theology? I explore these questions in this chapter.[2]

Theological Case: Caste Relations in India and Their Impact on Dalits' Full Humanity

Summary of the Issues

- The inherent worth of Dalits as God's image-bearers vis-à-vis the caste-based relations in India.

- Liberation of Dalits from caste-based dehumanization and oppression.

---

1. The 2001 census estimated that these communities constituted about 16.20 percent of Indian population. Clarke et al., "Introduction," 5.

2. I have been wrestling with these questions since 2005. I pondered these questions as I listened to a doctoral student at the University of Edinburgh (Scotland) present some of his research findings over a decade ago. Though I was researching African Christianity and Christology, I became increasingly interested in Dalit Christianity and Dalit theology. Conversing with colleagues at the University of Edinburgh whose research interests were in Indian Christianity and Dalit theology only intensified my hunger to study the Indian caste system and its impact on both Dalits and the Christian faith.

Historical Background

The caste system has devastating outcomes for Dalits who struggle to navigate their place in the social, economic, political, and religious life of India. Some questions about the precise origins of the caste system remain unanswered. Yet questions about the origins of caste-based relations in India should not conceal the ruinous effects of *casteism* on Dalits and also Shudras (the lowest of the traditional four castes), which have taken the form of oppression, dehumanization, marginalization, poverty, and illiteracy. I use the term "casteism" here to describe the kind of life and relationships that are both grounded in and justified by the concept of caste. The English word "caste" has been conventionally used as an umbrella term to describe two Sanskrit terms, namely, *jāti* (birth or lineage) and *varna* (color or estate). The complex history and usage of these terms raise questions about the adequacy of subsuming their meanings and representations under the English word "caste." As David Mosse has noted, "Caste is both a mode of domination and a means to challenge that domination; a discourse of rant but also of rights."[3] Also some scholars have pointed out that the traditional four classifications of castes are not nuanced and flexible enough to account properly for the "variations . . . in the manner in which social relations among different castes have historically evolved."[4] What are these castes? How did they emerge in India? Answering these questions will help clarify how the caste system is interpreted in Dalit theology.

Brahmins, Kshatriyas, Vaishyas, and Shudras delineate different lineages, social ranks or positions, and occupations in India. Sathianathan Clarke, Deenabandhu Manchala, and Philip Vinod Peacok have given a terse, albeit helpful description of the traditional four castes and their hierarchical relations in Hindu cosmology and anthropology:

> Caste communities consist of four castes that are hierarchically ordered. The Brahmins (priests) are the preservers and protectors of the eternal laws of the universe (*dharma*). The Kshatriyas (rulers and warriors) are the defenders and the guarantors of the safety and security of the community. The Vaishyas (merchants) are the conservers and the distributors of wealth. And the Shudras (the laborers) are the working majority involved in the production of essential commodities. Although there is a clear separation between the first three castes, which are ritually and socioeconomically dominant (referred to as the twice-born), and the fourth laboring caste, which is

3. Mosse, *Saint in the Banyan Tree*, 96.
4. Jodhka, *Caste in Contemporary India*, 25.

ritually suspect and socioeconomically dominated (referred to as the once-born), they together form the constituents of the Hindu human community.[5]

In historical terms, it is unclear when and how these castes became part of the fabric of the social, political, economic, and religious life of India. Some claim that the notions of caste-based relations emerged sometime within the Aryan and Vedic eras (ca. 1500–500 BCE).[6] Several such scholars trace the concept of caste to the *Purusha* hymn in Rig Veda 10:90 that describes what appears to be the traditional Hindu human ontology. The four castes are said to have derived from different parts of *Purusha*—a cosmic being.[7] However one understands the relationship between Hindu Scripture and the emergence of the notions and practice of caste-based relations, it is likely that the Rig Veda (perhaps the oldest of the Vedas) might have provided a religious justification for the caste system in India.[8]

If we accept the general belief among some scholars that the Rig Veda was composed between ca. 1500 and 500 BCE, the caste system in Hinduism might have had its origins during this period.[9] But it is equally possible that caste-based relations preceded the written form of the Vedic tradition and also the Laws of Manu (*Manusmriti*), which were composed between ca. 1250 and 700 BCE. Manusmriti 8:410–418 describes the three upper castes (Brahmins, Kshatriyas, and Vaishyas) as "twice-born" (*dvija*)—they can participate in a religious initiation rite known as "second birth" or "spiritual birth" (*upanayana*) and also in other religious activities.[10] On the relationship between the Brahmins and Kshatriyas, the former holds a spiritual authority (priesthood) and the latter holds a military authority (kingship or royalty).[11] The lowest of the four castes, Shudras, are believed

---

5. Clarke et al., "Introduction," 4–5.

6. For a summary of the relevant arguments pertaining to the experience of Indian Dalits, see Massey, *Roots of Dalit History*, 1–31.

7. Duncan Forrester, for example, alludes to the theological anthropology of the Rig Veda to make the case for the Christian roots of Western egalitarianism. For Forrester, while Christian Scripture presents humanity's common origins and also explains distinctions between human beings as the consequence of the Fall, the Rig Veda presents such differences as "part of the original structure of things," which ought to be preserved. See Forrester, *Caste and Christianity*, 9.

8. Dumont, *Homo Hierarchicus*, 25, 68; Vijayakumar, "Historical Survey of Buddhism in India," 4.

9. Frykenberg, *Christianity in India*, 61. See Massey, *Downtrodden*, 12–13.

10. Dumont, *Homo Hierarchicus*, 67; see also Srinivas, *Religion and Society among the Coorgs*, 24.

11. Dumont, *Homo Hierarchicus*, 72.

to be "once-born" and slaves. While the Kshatriyas and Vaishyas are allowed to study "sacred texts, offer sacrifices, and give to the Brahmins," the Shudras are to "obey and serve without envy."[12] Unlike the people with castes, Dalits (formerly known as the "Untouchables") have largely been denied the rights to be fully human.[13]

Despite mixed reviews of the origins of the caste system, several Dalit theologians have construed caste relations as a foundation for their theologies. Some have accepted the *aboriginal theory*, which claims that Dalits are direct descendants of the *mula nivasi* ("the original settlers" or "indigenous people") of India.[14] According to this theory, around ca. 1500 BCE, Sanskrit-speaking (white) Aryans conquered and also colonized the original dwellers (Indus people) of Indus Valley.[15] Some scholars claim that the Aryan invasion was responsible for the destruction of the Indus civilization and also the introduction of the *Vedic civilization*—cultures, religious practices, and language (Sanskrit)—to the indigenous people.[16] To maintain their conquered territory and people, the Aryan invaders introduced social boundaries that eventually led to the subjugation and exclusion of the indigenous dwellers from the main economic activity of the time. In Rajkumar's words, they were assigned "unskilled, unproductive, lowly and menial jobs" and also were "treated with utter contempt."[17] Sadly, such dehumanizing view of Dalits is still prevalent in some parts of modern-day India.

The caste system is grounded in the concepts of *jāti* and *varna*.[18] M. N. Srinivas, however, argued that the real unit of the caste groups (including the untouchables) is better understood in terms of *jāti* rather than *varna*.[19] Srinivas defined *jāti* as "a very small endogamous group practicing

12. Dumont, *Homo Hierarchicus*, 68–69.

13. See Moffatt, *Untouchable Community in South India*; Massey, "Christianity to Be Renewed?," 27.

14. Massey, *Dalit Theology*, 26. See also Massey, *Downtrodden*, 12–15. M. E. Prabhakar also holds the aboriginal theory. See Prabhakar, "Search for a Dalit Theology," 40–41.

15. The Indus people produced what has been called the "Indus Valley civilization." See Massey, *Dalit Theology*, 39–44, 62. For archeological and historical studies on the Indus Valley Civilization, see Wheeler, *Civilizations of the Indus Valley and Beyond*; Gordon, *Prehistoric Background of Indian Culture*; Sankalia, *Prehistory and Protohistory in India and Pakistan*; Piggott, *Prehistoric India*.

16. Rapaka, *Dalit Pentecostalism*, 8.

17. Rajkumar, *Dalit Theology and Dalit Liberation*, 6.

18. Rajkumar, *Dalit Theology and Dalit Liberation*, 4.

19. Srinivas, *Religion and Society among the Coorgs*, 24. Srinivas prefers to speak of a fivefold division (including the so-called Untouchables) rather than a fourfold division of *jāti* (excluding the "Untouchables").

a traditional occupation and enjoying a certain amount of cultural, ritual, and juridical autonomy."[20] Birth is what defines one's lineage. The *varna* system, for Srinivas, is what "furnishes an all-India frame into which the myriad *jāti* in any single linguistic area can be fitted."[21] In other words, the *varna* system is a social arrangement of the different *jātis* in a common structure, albeit with some compromises and flexibility.[22] Louis Dumont approached the relationship of *jāti* and *varna* differently. He painstakingly differentiated between *jāti* (castes) and *varna* (colors or estates).[23] For him, the *varnas* (estates) are the traditional hierarchical rankings or ordering of society grounded in the notions of status and power.[24] The *varna* (estate) system, as he noted, has actually five categories (Brahmins, Kshatriyas, Vaishyas, Shudras, and the Untouchables) even though some Hindu texts insist there are only four.[25] Dumont conceded that both the *jāti* (caste) system and the *varna* (estate) system "culminate in Brahmins."[26] He postulated that while the caste system is grounded in the notion of impurity and purity, the *varna* system is primarily grounded in hierarchy and power. However, he noted that the notions of pure and impure are somewhat implicit in the *varna* system, particularly in the relationship between the Brahmins and the Kshatriyas.[27]

Some scholars that reject the aboriginal theory as a viable explanation of the origins of the caste system in India have proposed a *purity and pollution* theory as an alternative explanation.[28] Such scholars borrow heavily from Dumont's association of the caste (*jāti*) system with the notions of purity and impurity. According to the purity and pollution theorists, the caste system did not come into existence as a result of the subjugation of a conquered indigenous (Indus) people by foreign (Aryan) invaders. The caste system is rather a social construct that was originally enacted to regulate an "inherently untidy, disorderly, and chaotic" society.[29] In such social arrangements, the acts that violate social boundaries are believed to be the original causes of caste segregations in India. The Paraiyars of South

20. Srinivas, *Religion and Society among the Coorgs*, 24.
21. Srinivas, *Religion and Society among the Coorgs*, 24–25.
22. Srinivas, *Religion and Society among the Coorgs*, 25–66.
23. Dumont, *Homo Hierarchicus*, 72.
24. Dumont, *Homo Hierarchicus*, 72.
25. Dumont, *Homo Hierarchicus*, 67.
26. Dumont, *Homo Hierarchicus*, 73.
27. Dumont, *Homo Hierarchicus*, 74–75.
28. Rajkumar, *Dalit Theology and Dalit Liberation*, 7.
29. Rajkumar, *Dalit Theology and Dalit Liberation*, 7.

India and the Candalas of North India (seen as the descendants of a Shu-dra father and a Brahmina mother) are examples of communities that are traditionally believed to have arisen as a result of prohibited hypergamous marriages.[30] Dalit communities are believed to be the direct descendants of ancestors who transgressed social laws and boundaries. As a penalty for the breach of social laws and boundaries, Dalits have been sentenced to a state of permanent pollution and also destined for unflattering jobs, including removing or touching dead bodies (humans and animals).[31] Interestingly, Peniel Rajkumar, a proponent of the purity and pollution theory, argues that stories about Dalits ancestors' sexual transgressions of social boundaries are fabrications. Nonetheless, he insists that the social imagination of purity-pollution relations offers the best explanations for caste-based segregations in India.[32]

The ontological-social nexus of purity and pollution raises some questions about the issue of cause and effect. What if the polluted status and polluting capabilities ascribed to Dalits were not the consequence of breaching social laws? Do certain occupations pollute people? Or are some people (Dalits) inherently polluted and therefore by extension pollute the kind of jobs they do (e.g., scavenging)? Or are some occupations and people (Dalits) inherently polluted? How one answers these questions will have a significant impact on the discussions on how best to address the problems of caste-based relations in India. For instance, James Massey published an essay in 2003 in which he described three essential principles of the Indian caste system, namely graded inequality, fixed occupation, and fixed lineage.[33] These principles, for Massey, practically rule out any material altera-tion in the caste system. He also argues that the rigidity of the Indian caste system's social ordering impedes the establishment of "a just and humane society where all people enjoy equal rights and dignity."[34] Other scholars have offered a different assessment of the flexibility of the caste system.[35] For example, M. N. Srinivas concedes that boundary markers are absolutely fundamental to the caste system.[36] Yet he argues that some of the boundar-ies are crossable in some communities, especially among the lowest caste (Shudras). In 1952, Srinivas observed that the Coorgs of South India who

30. Rajkumar, *Dalit Theology and Dalit Liberation*, 17.

31. Rajkumar, *Dalit Theology and Dalit Liberation*, 18.

32. Rajkumar, *Dalit Theology and Dalit Liberation*, 19.

33. Massey, "Christianity to Be Renewed?," 37–38.

34. Massey, "Christianity to Be Renewed?," 39.

35. Srinivas, *Religion and Society among the Coorgs*, 30.

36. Srinivas, *Religion and Society among the Coorgs*, 26.

regarded themselves as Kshatriyas—the royal and military caste—allowed the Shudras to escape their traditional lowly place in the caste system and seek upward mobility through a process of "Sanskritization": the practice of adopting the way of life (beliefs and customs) of the Brahmins (the priestly caste).[37] Similarly, Surinder Jodhka has noted that some Dalit communities in rural Punjab are no longer prohibited from using public wells and living in close proximity to people with a caste status. However, in some areas they are prohibited from entering Hindu temples and participating in some religious rituals.[38] Jodhka also cautions against premature celebrations of the softening of caste-based relations because many Dalits continue to suffer degradation and marginalization.[39]

Though Article 17 of the Indian constitution (1950) prohibited the use of the term "untouchables" to describe Dalits, Jodhka's study shows that declaring a legal victory has not led to the abolition of caste-based stratifications and relations in many parts of India.[40] The word "untouchables," which has been largely abandoned, accentuates the traditional belief that Dalits are considered religiously and literally impure and therefore can pollute religious objects and people (from the four castes) by coming into direct or indirect contact with them. Peniel Rajkumar has noted that Dalits are believed to be capable of "polluting everything within the range of 74 feet."[41] To avoid polluting religious objects (e.g., a temple) and people, Dalits are required to "cover their mouth with a little pot when speaking with 'caste people,'" to live in separate communities situated outside of the main villages, and to announce their presence when entering a town in which caste people live by sounding an alarm in order to avoid the possibility of polluting them.[42]

Dalits' pollution is a serious religious matter. When pollution occurs, which may be as a result of physical contact or indirect contact (such as coming into contact with the shadows of Dalits or through cross-contamination—when the caste people who are contaminated come into contact with other people), purification rituals are required to cleanse the polluted.[43] These kinds of dehumanizing and degrading experiences of the Dalit

---

37. Srinivas, *Religion and Society among the Coorgs*, 30. Srinivas, who claims to have been the first to use the term "Sanskritization," prefers it to the term "Brahminization." See Srinivas, "Note on Sanskritization and Westernization," 481–96.

38. Jodhka, *Caste in Contemporary India*, 25–40.

39. Jodhka, *Caste in Contemporary India*, 48.

40. Jodhka, *Caste in Contemporary India*, 25.

41. Rajkumar, *Dalit Theology and Dalit Liberation*, 15.

42. Rajkumar, *Dalit Theology and Dalit Liberation*, 15–16.

43. Rajkumar, *Dalit Theology and Dalit Liberation*, 16.

communities in India have raised serious theological questions that Dalit Christians and theologians have not ignored. The questions concern human worth, dignity, and also Dalits' internalization of their lowly status as natural or divinely ordained.[44] I have chosen James Massey, a Dalit theologian, as a key interlocutor in my explorations of these questions and how they are addressed by Dalit Christian theologians.

James Massey's Theological Response to Dalits' Dehumanization, Oppression, and Liberation

James Massey was convinced that the Christian faith had something to say to the Indian caste system.[45] He embarked on the task of developing Dalit theology that was grounded in God's solidarity with and liberation of the oppressed.[46] I will explore Massey's theology, bringing him into conversation with the works of other Dalit theologians in order to highlight his unique theological contribution to Dalit theology.[47] In the following sections, I will discuss his theological method and also the content of his Dalit theology. I will attend to how he used Christian Scripture, church traditions, and the context of Indian Dalits to construct his theology.

44. On these issues, Massey writes, "because of the long history of oppression, Dalits have . . . lost their self-identity as full human beings, which they have now accepted 'as part of the natural order of things' or 'as privilege' and this is in a real sense the inner capacity of their being from which they need liberation or release and towards this end Dalit theology [should] lead them." Massey, *Dalit Theology*, 65–66.

45. Until his death in March 2015, Massey was the Director of the Center for Dalit/Subaltern Studies and Community Contextual Center in New Delhi. From 1985 to 1996, he served as the secretary of the Indian Society for Promoting Christian Knowledge (ISPCK). Massey was sort of a generalist: he wrote on several theological issues and translated the Bible into Panjabi. As an ordained priest, his work on Dalit theology displays the skills of someone who is a pastor at heart. Though he is fairly unknown to many theology students outside of India, Massey has contributed substantively to Dalit theological discourses. Arvind Nirmal (1936–95) may rightly be described as the "Father of Dalit theology" (technically "Shudra theology"); however, James Massey (1943–2015) was one of the earliest Dalit theologians that gave Dalit Christian theology its clear theological focus. Peniel Rajkumar rightly notes that James Massey was one of the "pioneers of Christian Dalit Theology." See Rajkumar, *Dalit Theology and Dalit Liberation*, 1.

46. Massey, "Christianity to Be Renewed?," 28.

47. For womanist or feminist Dalit theologians, the experience of Dalit women, who represent the most marginalized under the caste system, is the primary source and an important point of departure in theological exploration. See Anderson-Rajkumar, "Turning Bodies Inside Out," 202.

The Uses of Theological Sources in Massey's Theology

Christian Scripture plays a prominent role in Massey's theology. Unlike many Dalit theologians who trace the history of the term "dalit" to its Sanskrit roots, Massey explores its biblical roots, particularly its usage in the Old Testament.[48] He notes that the meanings of *dalit* in both Sanskrit and Hebrew languages retain its basic ideas: "to crack, split, be broken, or torn asunder, trodden down, scattered, crushed, [and] destroyed."[49] Focusing on its Hebrew usage, he contends that *dal* means much more than is captured by the English translation "poor." For him, "*dal* or *dalot* people are not only economically or physically poor or weak; they are also poor in their 'psychological ability,' and their being has been 'impaired' to such a state that they have become 'helpless.'"[50] He sees a correlation between the experiences of *Dalits* in ancient Israel and the experiences of Dalits in contemporary India: experiences of degradation, denigration, and exploitation. In India, however, the word *dalit* has acquired dual meanings. On one hand, *dalit* expresses the horrendous experience, plight, and pathos of Dalits, and on the other hand, Dalits themselves use the term to express their quest to reclaim their dignity from the caste system.[51] These dual meanings constitute the term "dalitness" as Massey imagines it. I will explore the idea of *dalitness* further when I discuss theological materials from the context of life of Indian Dalits. It is noteworthy at this point that Massey beckons Dalit theologians to explore the dalitness of the Dalit communities as an essential theological source.[52] In the meantime, I turn attention to the idea of liberation that is embedded in dalitness.

What does "liberation" really mean in the context of the oppressed? Massey locates his idea of liberation in Scripture, focusing on the role it played in oppressed communities of ancient Israel and also the role it might play in Indian Dalits' ongoing captivity and bondage to the caste system.[53] Also, he grounds his theological understanding of liberation in God's preferential attitude toward the poor. "The first thing to remember about Dalit theology," Massey writes, "is that, like other liberation theologies, it

48. Massey, *Towards Dalit Hermeneutics*, 1–34.

49. Massey, *Dalit Theology*, 25.

50. Massey, *Dalit Theology*, 19–20. Massey cites the following biblical passages to support the claim that "Dalit" people existed among the ancient Jewish people: Exod 30:15; Job 31:16; Ps 82:34.

51. Massey, *Dalit Theology*, 27.

52. Some theologians, like D. Manohar Chandra Prasad, argue that "Dalitness is the only source of Dalit theology." Prasad, "Dalit Theology," 167.

53. Massey, *Downtrodden*, 61.

is a theological expression born from the historical experience of the oppressed people and from their encounter with the God of the Bible, who
has always been biased toward the oppressed and the poor."[54] It seems that
three related realities—Dalit's historical captivity, God's preferential treatment of the oppressed, and Dalit's living encounter with this God of the
Bible who liberates the oppressed—provided Massey with a helpful framework to discuss liberation as a theological idea in his exploration of the
emancipation of Dalits from the oppressive caste system.

In addition to Scripture, Massey formulated his theology in dialogue
with the history of Christianity in India, particularly its theological heritage. In his assessment, Dalit theology arose partly because of the failures
of both Indian Christian theology and European missionary theology to
successfully address the questions posed to them by Dalit communities as
they attempted to understand their history and the dehumanizing effects of
their condition in light of the Christian faith.[55] Though he contrasts Dalit
theology with Brahmin Christian theology, he cautions against seeing Dalit
theology as a "'counter-theology' to European-constructed systematic theology or traditional Indian Christian theology."[56] For him, given that these
theologies were largely disinterested in the life, history, and experience of
the Dalits of India, Dalit theology cannot logically be described as what
counters them.[57] But what exactly are *European missionary theology* and
Indian Christian theology? In many of his writings, Massey used the expression "European missionary theology" to describe the forms of theologies
that European missionaries taught their Indian converts.[58] Examples of
such theologies are the pietistic theology of the missionaries trained in the
University of Halle and also Roman Catholic theology, which can be traced
back to Francis Xavier (1506–52) and Roberto de Nobili (1577–1656).
What was lacking in the theologies of many of the European missionaries
was a constructive engagement with the Indian caste system in light of a
biblical understanding of church as a new ecclesial community in which
social, racial, and ethnic barriers are to be abolished (Gal 3:28).[59] Some

54. Massey, *Downtrodden*, 61.

55. He writes, "The doers of Dalit theology, beside placing it in the past historical as
well as present Dalit context, also work on an assumption that the existing theologies,
which include old missionary theology and the present Indian Christian theology, are
irrelevant for the Dalits because they are neither based on their life experience nor do
they fulfill the needs of their life." Massey, *Dalit Theology*, 215.

56. Massey, *Downtrodden*, 62.

57. Massey, *Downtrodden*, 62.

58. Massey, *Dalit Theology*, 74–86.

59. Some of the earliest Western missionaries, according to Massey, used a

missionaries avoided the issue by creating separate communities such as "'mission compounds,' 'Christian colonies,' [and] 'Christian villages.'"[60] Others, such as the German Protestant pietistic missionaries, focused more on inward renewal of human beings and otherworldly affairs than *this* world's affairs.[61] These two main approaches adopted by European missionaries, for Massey, provided no useful and substantive theological contributions to the struggles of Dalits to gain freedom and liberation.

It is noteworthy that some historians and theologians do not share Massey's pessimistic account of missionaries' attitudes toward the caste system. For example, in his 1824 reply to Abbe Dubois's assessment of the state of affairs in India in regards to both Roman Catholic and Protestant missionaries' expeditions in the nineteenth century, James Hough wrote,

> We have seen that M. Dubois represents the Brahmins as inaccessible beings, and that "the barrier" between us and them is "impassable." Had he established Schools for the instruction of Youth, and conducted them upon liberal principles, he would have seen the Brahmins themselves crossing that barrier, and courting his acquaintance. One or two instances shall suffice, to prove that Protestant Missionary Schools are rapidly removing that "wall of partition," which has for ages separated the Brahmin from all other castes and descriptions of men.
>
> Boys of every caste are admitted into those schools. In Tinnevelly (and I believe the same practice is adopted everywhere else), we classed the Brahmin with the Soodra of equal attainments; and constantly have I seen them studying at the same desk, or standing up, side by side, to repeat their lessons. In one of our Schools, there were, at the time of my leaving the district, 4 Brahmins, 6 Soodras, 2 Mussulmans, 8 Roman Catholics, 1 Country-born, and 2 Pariars. One of those Brahmins, instead of leaving the school "as soon as he had attained the object" for which alone, as the Abbé Dubois asserts, they attend, continued there till he was upwards of twenty years of age: indeed, I left him in the school when I came away from the South. He seemed really to *love* the New Testament; and used to read it at home, notwithstanding the opposition of his family.[62]

---

disputation strategy, thinking they could covert Brahmins by showing them that Christianity was the true religion. See Massey, *Dr. B. R. Ambedkar*, 49.

60. Massey, *Dalit Theology*, 86.

61. Massey, "Christianity to Be Renewed?," 27. See also Massey, *Roots of Dalit History*, 62–72.

62. Hough, *Reply to the Letters of the Abbe Dubois*, 164.

Abbé Dubois's words indicate that some missionaries intentionally under-mined the caste system, which Massey appears to ignore. Unlike Massey, M. M. Thomas described three different responses of European missionar-ies to the caste system. First, some, operating on the "premise that the realm of religion is entirely separate from that of social structure and institutions" elected to leave the caste system undisturbed; Thomas described Roberto de Nobili as one example of such missionaries who were indifferent to the caste system.[63] Second, some missionaries, who held a somewhat opposite view to those who had an attitude of indifference to the caste system, considered "caste as an absolute religious and social evil of heathenism with which the Christian must radically break at the time of baptism."[64] Third, other mis-sionaries rejected the foregoing two views as inadequate, approached the complex issue of caste relations cautiously, albeit accommodated "it to a certain extent in church and society so as to give time for the ferment of the Christian fellowship to work within the caste system, redeeming it of its evils and finally revolutionizing it more radically."[65] Like M. M. Thomas, Duncan Forrester has argued that there were varying attitudes of European missionaries toward the Indian caste system, which largely depended on how they understood its intended function in India. For some who believed that the caste system performed nonreligious functions, it was to be left alone insofar as it did not impede Christian evangelism. But for many of those who construed the caste system as a religious phenomenon, it was to be dismantled.[66] Clearly, Massey's understanding of European missionaries' attitudes toward caste relations lacked nuance.

As stated earlier, Massey equally blamed "Indian Christian theol-ogy"—theologies produced by the upper caste Christians in dialogue with Hindu philosophical thoughts—for ignoring the struggles of Dalit com-munities.[67] Though such theologies might have been relevant to the needs of some educated upper-caste Christians, they overlooked Dalits' needs for liberation from oppression, poverty, suffering, injustice, illiteracy, and de-nial of identity.[68] Massey traces the origins of Indian Christian theology to Krishna Mohan Banerjea (1813–85) whose conversion to Christianity he attributes to the work of the Scottish Presbyterian missionary Alexander

63. Thomas, *Acknowledged Christ of the Indian Renaissance*, 260.

64. Thomas, *Acknowledged Christ of the Indian Renaissance*, 261.

65. Thomas, *Acknowledged Christ of the Indian Renaissance*, 261.

66. Forrester, *Caste and Christianity*, 6.

67. Massey, *Dalits in India*, 170–73.

68. Massey, "Need of a Dalit Theological Expression," 197–99. See also Massey, "In-gredients for a Dalit Theology," 58.

Duff (1806–78).[69] Banerjea was deeply influenced by the cultural and political movements in nineteenth-century India that aimed to accommodate the Hindu culture to the British imperialists' and colonialists' Western culture.[70] Obviously, not all Indian Christian theologians had a positive view of the Hindu culture and philosophical ideas. Several progenitors of Indian Christian theology, of course, made the case for continuity between the two religions. T. V. Philip has observed that Banerjea (who belonged to the Brahmin caste) was one of several Indian Christian thinkers in the nineteenth century who attempted to "establish a positive and creative relation between Christianity and Hinduism."[71] In *The Arian Witness*, Banerjea argued in favor of bringing together some ideas in Christian Scripture and in the Vedas.[72] In a lecture entitled "The Relation between Christianity and Hinduism," he also proposed the following theses:

> (1) That the fundamental principles of Christian doctrine in relation to salvation of the world find a remarkable counterpart in the Vedic principles of primitive Hinduism in relation to the destruction of sin, and the redemption of the sinner by the efficacy of Sacrifice, itself a figure of *Prajāpati*, the Lord and Savior of the Creation, who had given himself up as an offering for that purpose. (2) That the meaning of *Prajāpati*, an appellative variously described as a Purusha begotten in the beginning, as *Viswakarma* the creator of all, singularly coincides with the meaning of the name and offices of the historical reality of Jesus Christ, and that no other person than Jesus of Nazareth has ever appeared in the world claiming the character and position of the self-sacrificing *Prajāpati*, at the same time both moral and immortal.[73]

As the text above shows, Banerjea explored a form of Christology that was grounded in the Rig Veda. He associated Jesus Christ with the *Purusha* or the primal (cosmic) being in the Rig Veda. For Banerjea, Jesus was the fulfillment—the true *Prajāpati* or *Purusha*—of Vedic Hinduism. Jesus, he argued, was "the *Prajāpati*, the Purusha begotten before the worlds, who died that you might live, who by death hath vanquished death, and brought life and immortality to light through the Gospel."[74] Banerjea's goal was political as

---

69. Massey, *Dalit Theology*, 97. For biographical studies on the life and work of Krishna Mohan Banerjea, see Philip, *Krishna Mohan Banerjea*.

70. Satyavrata, *God Has Not Left Himself*, 92.

71. Philip, *Krishna Mohan Banerjea*, 1.

72. Banerjea, *Arian Witness*.

73. Banerjea, "Relation between Christianity and Hinduism," 181–82.

74. Banerjea, "Relation between Christianity and Hinduism," 200.

well as theological. Politically, Banerjea hoped that bringing Christianity (its Western versions, especially the version brought by British colonialists and missionaries) and Hinduism (the religion of the colonized) together would result in "a better understanding of the relation between the rulers and the ruled, between men of the West and men of the East."[75] Theologically, he aimed to show the rationality of Christianity and its value for understanding the true teaching of classical Hinduism, particularly the teaching about the *Purusha*.

For Arvind Nirmal, the fulfillment theory presented by Krishna Mohan Banerjea and other theologians did not adequately attend to the theological needs emanating from the pain, pathos, and history of Dalit communities.[76] Massey clearly shares Nirmal's assessment of Indian Christian theology.[77] Though he acknowledged that P. D. Devanandan and M. M. Thomas were representative of a few Indian theologians who took the living experience and history of Indians seriously in their theological writings, Massey insisted that they continued in the traditions of philosophical and theological discourses on Hinduism's relationship to Christianity.[78] It is possible that by focusing almost exclusively on the form of oppression that arose from the caste system of India but largely ignoring the form of oppression that arose from British colonization of India, Massey missed the opportunity of finding some allies among Indian Christian theologians whose works exposed the oppressive nature of Western colonization.[79]

Given the proximity between Indian Christian theology and some philosophical thoughts in Hinduism, which is largely responsible for the religious justification of caste systems in India, it is not surprising that many Dalit theologians have rejected Indian Christian theology because they judged it to be ineffective for addressing the struggles and sufferings of Dalit communities.[80] Perhaps in Massey's generalized assessment, he argued that Indian Christian theology is "completely irrelevant to the Dalit reality, because logically [and historically] it joins hands with the missionary or traditional European Christian theology in perpetuating the dalitness of the Dalits."[81] Massey looked for theological allies among

75. Banerjea, "Relation between Christianity and Hinduism," 182.

76. Nirmal, "Toward a Christian Dalit Theology," 29.

77. Massey, *Downtrodden*, 48–51.

78. Massey, *Roots of Dalit History*, 76.

79. Thomas, *Acknowledged Christ of the Indian Renaissance*, see especially ch. 9.

80. Bird, *M. M. Thomas and Dalit Theology*, 5–9.

81. Massey, *Dalit Theology*, 104. See also Massey, "Ingredients for a Dalit Theology," 58. Ironically Indian Christian theology and European missionary theology inspired Massey to formulate a theology that moved away from their theological goals but

theologians who explored the sufferings of oppressed communities. Drawing inspirations from other liberation theologians such as North American Black liberation theology, Latin American Liberation theology, and Korean Minjung theology, Massey focused on developing a theology that took seriously the theological questions that are contained in the daily life and struggles of Dalit communities.[82]

What sort of issues, which were embedded in the life situation of Dalits, functioned as theological data for Dalit theologians like Massey? The historical realities of Dalits' oppressed condition is central to Massey's Dalit theology. Knowing one's history can become liberative and can also "assist in a liberating process of self-discovery and visioning for the future, at both the individual and collective levels."[83] Two interrelated raw theological data that are embedded in the context of Dalit communities have contributed immensely to Massey's theology. The first is *dalitness*. The function of this term is double-edged, as I noted earlier. On one hand, it expresses the totality of the dehumanizing condition of Dalits that must be opposed and eradicated from their psyches (negative sense). On the other hand, dalitness can become the impetus for Dalits to draw incredible strength from their history to fight for their liberation and well-being in their *own* ways (positive sense).[84] In Massey's theology, *dalitness*, in its negative sense, is the undeserved and unwarranted condition that Dalits have been forced to endure for centuries.[85] He describes dalitness, in this sense, as India's "original sin."[86] He challenges theologians who desire to write theologies for Dalit communities not to ignore the history of the people who make up the communities, especially how they have internalized their state of dalitness. Dalits' perception of their history has partly propelled them into solidarity with those sympathetic to their quest for liberation from oppressive structures.[87] Massey insists that hearing the voices of Dalits themselves in their narration of their own history is as important as the content of the narration itself. As Dalits tell their own story of oppression and dehumanization, they participate in framing their quests for liberation and for

---

attended to the peculiar needs and experience of the Dalits of India. In other words, Indian Christian theology and European missionary theology largely functioned somewhat like a theological signpost that showed Massey things to avoid in his theological exploration.

82. Massey, *Downtrodden*, 51.

83. Webster, *Historiography of Christianity in India*, 223.

84. Massey, *Downtrodden*, 2.

85. Massey, *Dalit Theology*, 28.

86. Massey, *Towards Dalit Hermeneutics*, 19.

87. Massey, *Dalit Theology*, 217.

reclaiming their dignity.[88] The history of Dalits, for example, can serve as a *way of remembering* that will assist in bridging the gap between Dalits' past experiences and present experiences. Theologians, therefore, are to attend not only to Dalits' present experience but also to the past imagination of the non-humanity of Dalits that continues to shape how some of them view their identity and place in India.

The second raw theological data from the context of Dalit communities that have shaped Massey's theology may be subsumed under the term *sub-humanity*: a people lacking in certain qualities, rights, and capabilities that are inherent in Brahmins, Kshatriyas, Vaishyas, and Shudras. What does it mean for Dalits to live in a society that has traditionally treated them as less than human or as inferior human beings? The practice of untouchablity is a concrete expression of the Dalits' dehumanization. In a study conducted in the Punjab region, Surinder Jodhka notes that although untouchability is not strictly practiced in some areas, it continues to be enforced in many villages during festivals. He writes,

> Caste prejudice and untouchability were most pronounced at the village-level festivals and feasts. This kind of discrimination took various forms. Perhaps the most obvious occasion was during the serving of food. As with the *langar* in dominant-caste *gurdwaras*, Dalits would often be asked to wait until everyone else had eaten and left. Though not so pronounced, there were also reports of separate utensils being used for Dalits during village feasts.[89]

Implementing the code of impurity ritually enforces the lowly place of Dalits in India. As those whose so-called permanent function is to "remove impurity from the social world," Dalits are generally seen as perpetually impure partly because of the kind of work they do, such as scavenging, grave digging, and disposing of carcasses.[90] Paramjit Judge has noted that Dalit women in some cases suffer the most in terms of the humiliation that is associated with untouchability: "Among the numerous exclusions and discriminations the most horrifying in certain cases was that their women were not allowed to cover their breasts thus denying them the basic right to honorable living."[91]

Interestingly, Massey did not devote time to the notion of Dalits' impurity in his theology. Although, as I will show later, he devoted a great

88. Massey, *Dalit Theology*, 217.

89. Jodhka, *Caste in Contemporary India*, 40.

90. Deliege, "Replication and Consensus," 156.

91. Judge, "Between Exclusion and Exclusivity," 266.

deal of time to theological anthropology, he preferred to ground his theological reflections on Dalit's full humanity in other aspects of their dehumanizing experience.[92] In *Dalit Theology*, he made a casual reference to
"cleanliness and uncleanliness" of Dalits for the purposes of highlighting
the oppressive structure of the caste system.[93] It appears that Massey construed the social stigma and exclusion of impurity as stemming from the
ontological devaluation of Dalits. Peniel Rajkumar, however, has argued
that some Dalit theologies of liberation, which are grounded in scriptural
liberative motifs, especially the "Exodus paradigm of liberation," do not
quite get at the root cause of social stigma of Indian Dalits who are treated
as polluted and polluting human beings.[94] He argues that making a casual
reference to purity and pollution does a disservice to the project of Dalit
theology. For example, it renders Dalit theologies powerless in nudging
Indian Christians toward the task of dealing with the issue of discrimination in churches and the society at large.[95]

Rajkumar is very critical of the grounding of Dalit theology in the liberation of the people of Israel from the Egyptian captivity. For him, God's
liberative acts demonstrated in the Exodus narrative and Deuteronomy
creed (Deut 26:5–12) present the notions of divine "victimization" and "vic-
tor-hood" that are "incompatible with the experiences of Dalits."[96] He contends that the Exodus narrative is not value free and should be interrogated

92. Massey's interest in the Exodus motif could be because of Arvind Nirmal's influence on his theological work, which is thoroughly grounded in God's liberative acts.
He writes, "Christian Dalits in India also affirm their own experience. What I mean is
that as we should be aware of our historical consciousness, our roots, and our identity,
we should also be aware of our present Christian consciousness. We are not just Dalits.
We are Christian Dalits. Something has happened to us. Our status has changed. Our
exodus from Hinduism—which was imposed on us—to Christianity, or rather to Jesus
Christ, is a value experience—a liberating experience . . . Our exodus to him enabled us
to recognize our dalitness, the dalitness of Jesus of Nazareth, and also the dalitness of
his Father and our Father—our God; in our exodus to Jesus Christ, we have had a liberating experience. Although we have not reached our ultimate goal, we are confident
that the Jesus of Palestine or the more immediate Jesus of India is in the midst of the
liberation struggle of the Dalits of India. A Christian Dalit theology, therefore, should
also be doxological in character. Our struggle is not over as yet, but we ought to be
thankful that it is undergirded by our experience and our own exodus hope." Nirmal,
"Toward a Christian Dalit Theology," 34–35. Dalit theology, for Nirmal, should be an
attempt to sing two genres of theological song. On one hand, it should be a theology of
lament and protest. On the other hand, it should be a song of hope, understood as an
already not-yet reality.

93. Massey, *Dalit Theology*, 109.

94. Rajkumar, *Dalit Theology and Dalit Liberation*, 59–61.

95. Rajkumar, *Dalit Theology and Dalit Liberation*, 60.

96. Rajkumar, *Dalit Theology and Dalit Liberation*, 61–62.

from the perspective of the Canaanites: "The image of God which emerges from the Deuteronomy and Exodus paradigms is highly estranged from the Dalit images of God and Goddesses and is more in continuity with the images of the Hindu Brahminic 'weapon Gods.'"[97] The warring Yahweh that commanded the annihilation of the Canaanites seems to be on the side of the Aryans, if one accepts the Aryan invasion theory, as Massey does.[98] Rajkumar also calls into question the theological value of a dominant God or people of God for confronting the notions of pollution and purity. In place of the Exodus liberative motif, Rajkumar proposes the synoptic Gospels' healing stories of Jesus as the most appropriate point of departure for Dalit theology:

> Notions of purity and pollution furnish substantial common ground between the twenty-first-century Indian caste context and the context of the synoptic healing stories, which is suggestive of heuristic compatibility . . . Those afflicted in one or other symbolic bodily zones, as well as those possessed or affected by a malevolent spirit, lacked symbolic bodily integrity, which further pointed to deficient purity, wholeness and holiness, which makes it easy to co-opt all the taxonomies [of illness] under the taxonomy of purity and impurity. The categorical construction of taxonomies points out that issues of purity and pollution were integral to illness. We can now say that, in light of these findings, it can be said that notions of purity and pollution constitute the overarching paradigm and common intersecting arena of the social-cultural matrices of [twenty-first-century] Indian society and those of first century Judaism. This makes cross-cultural hermeneutic application a plausible enterprise.[99]

How, then, do the healing stories, which signal an impurity-purity nexus, offer a better prospect for tackling the idea that Dalits are polluted and polluting? Taking as an example the healing of lepers who were considered both polluted and polluting and therefore suffered discrimination, Rajkumar argues that the healing stories model for Dalit theologians how to construct theologies that address the discrimination against Dalits on the basis of their impurity.[100] One theological problem with Rajkumar's proposal is that it could imply that Dalits are actually impure and require healing, like the lepers. Obviously, the idea of pollution is socially constructed and lacks any

---

97. Rajkumar, *Dalit Theology and Dalit Liberation*, 63.

98. Rajkumar, *Dalit Theology and Dalit Liberation*, 64.

99. Rajkumar, *Dalit Theology and Dalit Liberation*, 79–80.

100. Rajkumar, *Dalit Theology and Dalit Liberation*, 115.

ontological value: Dalits are not inherently ill or impure. Rajkumar, how-ever, seems to focus on the discriminatory social order that equated physical (or medical) illness with social or religious impurity. "The image of Jesus which emerges in the [healing] stories," Rajkumar says, "is an image of Jesus enraged at the oppressive forces which marginalizes the man" who had lep-rosy.[101] As I noted earlier, Massey opted to pursue the dignity of Dalits not from their so-called state of pollution but rather by exploring the dehuman-izing anthropology that deprives them of their true humanity and dignity. His theological objective and vision are embedded in his understanding of the tasks of Dalit theology that I discuss below.

General Tasks of Dalit Christian Theology

When the word "dalit" is used as a prefix to a theology, it functions as a com-pass directing theologians to attend to the particular history, life situation, and culture of Dalit communities.[102] But for what purpose should Dalit theology be constructed? To discern Massey's response to this question, I will attend to what he considered the main tasks of Dalit theology. There is no textual evidence that he outlined these tasks in their order of importance. They are rather interlocking tasks that should be understood complementarily and not as mutually exclusive. I will describe the tasks briefly, highlighting how Massey expressed them in some of his writings.

Conscientization task: In this context, "conscientization" is the act of reawaking in Dalits their inherent worth as human beings. Here is one example of Arvind Nirmal's influence on Massey's theology. For Nirmal, "the historical Dalit consciousness is the primary datum of a Christian Dalit theology. The question of Dalit consciousness is really the question of Dalit identity, the question of our roots."[103] Nirmal sees Dalit conscious-ness as a creed analogous to Christian creeds such as the Nicene Creed and the Apostles' Creed.[104] If creeds are terse confessions of faith that ought to govern how a community is to think, act, and live theologically, Dalit consciousness, for Nirmal, should govern the project of Dalit theology.[105] Massey seems to agree. His emphasis on the history of Dalits has given a

---

101. Rajkumar, *Dalit Theology and Dalit Liberation*, 122.
102. Massey, *Dalit Theology*, 215.
103. Nirmal, "Toward a Christian Dalit Theology," 32.
104. Nirmal, "Toward a Christian Dalit Theology," 32.
105. Nirmal, "Toward a Christian Dalit Theology," 33.

clear focus on the role conscientization can play in Dalit theology.[106] He believed that Dalit theology

> can help in raising the consciousness of the Dalits to the fact that they are remnants of a casteless community, based upon a divinely established principle of equality (as against the caste-based divided communities, which is the handiwork of human beings).[107]

Dalit theology ought to confront the internalization of the state of oppression, lowly caste, dehumanization, and marginalization. Theologians should not see this task merely as an intellectual exercise but also as an exercise in getting Dalits to recognize their dalitness (i.e., its negative sense) and to proceed to reject it as contrary to God's will.[108]

A positive value of the presumed Dalits' state of non-caste is the opportunity it creates for Dalits to see themselves as the "the original casteless human community, which God created in the beginning, based on the principle of equality."[109] It can also bring them together as a community with a common experience.[110] Conscientization can help to protect Dalits against the temptation to internalize and accept a dehumanizing condition. It can also create an opportunity for a healthier way of remembering: the choice to remember an oppressor without seeking retaliation or following the path of the oppressor. For instance, engaging in this form of theological conscientization will help immunize Dalits against adopting an oppressive mindset when they move upward in life or escape from their lowly place.[111]

Conscientization, which has taken different forms in both religious and nonreligious groups, has spurred on many Dalits to become religiously, theologically, and socially aware of the need to actively protest against their dehumanized condition and also to seek liberation from forms of oppression. To cite an example, while some Dalits have opted not to sever ties with Hinduism but rather have sought ideas of social transformation within its structures, others have chosen *conversion* as a means to express their protest against the justification of caste-based discriminations with the Vedas and Manusmriti. Unlike Bhimrao Babasaheb Ramji Ambedkar (1891–1956) who blamed Hinduism and the Vedas as the root causes of the awful conditions of Dalits, those who chose to retain Hinduism as their religion pushed

---

106. Massey, *Dalits in India*, 121–29.
107. Massey, *Dalit Theology*, 223.
108. Massey, *Downtrodden*, 79.
109. Massey, *Downtrodden*, 79.
110. Massey, *Downtrodden*, 79.
111. Massey, *Downtrodden*, 82.

for the reformation of Hinduism or the escape of one's lowly status through the process of Sanskritization.[112] Those who opted to abandon Hinduism for other religious traditions, like Ambedkar, preferred to challenge the caste system from outside the walls of Hindu religious beliefs.

The mass conversion of Hindu Dalits to other religions in the twentieth century, which was partly occasioned by the decision of Ambedkar to publicly renounce Hinduism in October 1956, was a form of religio-political protest against the inhumane condition of Dalit communities.[113] There were, of course, earlier examples of mass conversions of people of low castes to Christianity such as the conversion of the *Paravar* or Fishermen caste in the early 1500s.[114] Duncan Forrester notes that between "1535 and 1537 about 20,000 people, practically the whole caste, were baptized," even though there were no structures in place to disciple them in the Christian ways of life. In 1542, Francis Xavier also "baptized several thousand children and started some rudimentary instruction of converts in Tamil."[115] Large-scale conversions of Hindu Dalits and the lowest caste groups to other religions resurfaced with a new vigor in the late 1860s.[116] Though the mass conversions phenomena did not immediately change the oppressed condition of Dalits, they created the paths for sustained literary, political, and religious protests against the inhumane condition of people of lowest castes and people without caste (Dalits).[117] As public displays of dissent and protest, the mass conversions planted the seed of liberation in the consciousness of many Dalits that later germinated and blossomed into the struggles to regain Dalits' full humanity, dignity, and rights.

Jeremiad task: For Massey, Dalit theologians are to issue a prophetic indictment for the pain, pathos, and suffering of Dalit communities. The

---

112. Rajkumar, "Diversity and Dialectics of Dalit Dissent," 58–59.

113. Massey, *Downtrodden*, 42. For a helpful discussion on Ambedkar's reasons for abandoning Hinduism, see Massey, *Dr. B. R. Ambedkar*, 24–42. Regarding Ambedkar's renunciation of Hinduism and acceptance of Buddhism on October 14, 1956, W. R. Vijayakumar wrote: "On the day of his conversion, Ambedkar founded the Bharathiya Buddha Mahasabha (Buddhist Society of India) with the object of propagating the Dhamma, especially among the untouchables. On the day following the conversion he made a speech and explained why he chose a religion which was very difficult to follow. He concluded his speech thus: 'This conversion has given me enormous satisfaction and pleasure unimaginable. I feel as if I have been liberated from hell.' When asked about the motive behind the conversion movement, Ambedkar replied, 'We are making efforts to reach manhood.'" Vijayakumar, "Historical Survey of Buddhism in India," 31.

114. Forrester, *Caste and Christianity*, 14.

115. Forrester, *Caste and Christianity*, 14.

116. Forrester, *Caste and Christianity*, 69.

117. Massey, *Downtrodden*, 42–45.

scope of the indictment should not be restricted to the religious and theological spheres but should also extend to the social, economic, and political
arenas.[118] Dalit theology also should be a form of lamentation designed to
warn non-Dalits who oppress Dalits that they have equally lost their own
humanity. "The role of Dalit theology," Massey writes, is to make non-Dalits
"conscious about the suffering and pain of the Dalits and also about their
own non-humanity, which allows them to treat the Dalits oppressively."[119]
Massey learned from M. M. Thomas that theology ought be a living activity in which theologians intentionally immerse themselves in the actual
environment of people's lives.[120] Once theologians recognize this task, they
will, like some Hebrew prophets, declare God's word in the sharpest possible voice that calls into question the attitudes and actions that cause or
sustain oppression in the world. Theologians, of course, should not deliver
prophetic warnings against oppression or call for repentance from a safe
distance. On the contrary, they should participate in the actual experience
of the oppressed. Massey considered the Hebrew prophet Jeremiah a model
of such endeavor. He described Jeremiah as a preacher that fully identified
and had direct experience of the suffering of his people (Jer 12:3–4). He
notes that Jeremiah's laments are the direct proof of his personal sufferings along with his community (Jer 11:18–23; 12:1–6; 15:10–21; 17:4–8;
18:18–23; 20:7–13, 14–18).[121]

   Pastoral task: Citing Judges 6:11–18, Massey argues that Dalit Christian leaders can learn from Gideon's dialogue with the angel of the LORD
and also from the encouragement Gideon received from the angel. Massey
observes that many Indian churches use negative or discouraging words
that do more harm than good in terms of helping Dalits to seek their full
humanity and liberation from all forms of oppression.[122] Conversely, he
argues, "any pastor who intends to work among the weaker and oppressed
communities needs to take note of the approach and pastoral methodology
that the divine messenger had adopted in the case of Gideon."[123] One way
of bridging the gap between theological edifices and pastoral care in the
context of Dalit Christianity is to write in Dalits' vernaculars.[124] Writing in

118. For discussions on the nature of jeremiad rhetoric in a non-Indian context, see
Kaveny, *Prophecy Without Contempt*.

119. Massey, *Dalit Theology*, 223–24.

120. Massey, "Christianity to Be Renewed?," 25–26.

121. Massey, *Dalit Theology*, 195.

122. Massey, *Dalit Theology*, 184.

123. Massey, *Dalit Theology*, 184.

124. Massey, "Ingredients for a Dalit Theology," 60–61.

the vernaculars would not only be useful in producing original theological works but also would be valuable in making Dalit Christian theologies accessible to the local readers (Dalits) who need them the most.[125] Using Dalits' vernaculars—language (both written and oral) and thought—to formulate the theologies that are designed for their communities can aid Dalit Christians to *own* such theologies by identifying, critiquing, and appropriating them. Grasping fully Christian theological beliefs and ideas about the inherent worth of all human beings, which is made possible by the vernaculars, can become a powerful asset in Dalits' fight for their dignity, value, and worth as human beings in Indian society.

Praxis of Solidarity task: To be in solidarity with the oppressed is to make their burden of oppression one's own. Recognizing the danger of doing theologies that lack the impetus for social action, Massey contends that Dalit theology should act as a spur to social action. "Dalit theology," he writes, "has to enable the ordinary Christians to take active part in the struggle of Dalits."[126] Against the common view among some Christian communities that it is unchristian to join any struggle or movement for the liberation of Dalit communities, Massey argues it is *Christian* to participate in both religious and nonreligious movements for the liberation of Dalits who are being crushed under the weight of the caste system. Christian "solidarity" in the context of Dalits' history and experience, according to Massey, should be understood in light of "Divine solidarity"—God's identification with humanity in the mystery of the Incarnation.[127] He writes:

> God Himself first has shown His solidarity with human beings in history. The Bible writers, in order to concretize God's action of solidarity, picked up a case history of a nation, namely, Israel, who with time became a slave nation in Egypt. But God saw their suffering and oppression, which they had from the hands of their oppressors, Pharaohs of Egypt, and He decided to help them through Moses (Exodus 1:8–14; 2:23–25). While commissioning Moses, He said, "I have witnessed the misery of my people in Egypt and have heard them crying out because of their oppressors. I know they are suffering and have come down to rescue them from the power of the Egyptians . . ." (Exodus 3:7, 8). Here we see God not only offering His solidarity with the oppressed in words or in ideas, but in actions also shows that He

125. For Massey, it is better to write Dalit theologies in the vernaculars of Dalits and subsequently (if needed) translate them into foreign languages for "international consumption." Massey, "Ingredients for a Dalit Theology," 61.

126. Massey, *Dalit Theology*, 2.

127. Massey, *Dalit Theology*, 224.

"came down to rescue them," which means He became part of their struggle. His action also shows that He took a definite side of the oppressed against the oppressors, which was not [merely] a religious action, but . . . more of a political act [that] included even economic and social dimensions also.[128]

The deliverance motif in the book of Exodus clearly drives Massey's imagination of God's act of siding with the oppressed. This divine act of solidarity with the oppressed signals God's willingness to engage in all areas of life (social, economic, political, and religious) of the people of Israel who suffered under the Egyptian oppressive structures. Divine solidarity with humanity in the mystery of the Incarnation is a radical act that makes God a *Dalit*—the poor, oppressed, and marginalized. God's remedy for the oppression and suffering of the people of Israel was not merely to lecture human beings on how bad they have behaved but rather to identify with them "by becoming human" and by "becoming a part of human history."[129] Therefore, the Incarnation is the summary and climax of God's act of solidarity with humanity, particularly with the poor and oppressed—the Dalits of this world.[130]

Liberative task: This task focuses on the role that Dalit theology can play in promoting the liberation of Dalits and all who are oppressed.[131] Anderson Jeremiah, for example, argues that Dalits' ongoing dehumanizing experience requires reframing christological questions about Jesus's personhood and message in order to examine his significance for liberative actions that will enable Dalits to "move toward an emancipated life."[132] Some Dalit theologians have rejected an uncritical acceptance of Latin American liberation theology as a model for doing theology in India. Arvind P. Nirmal is one such theologian. He argued that the forms of Latin American liberation theology, which adopted "a Marxist analysis of socioeconomic realties—the haves and the have-nots," were inadequate for dealing with

128. Massey, *Dalit Theology*, 218–19.

129. Massey, *Dalit Theology*, 219.

130. Massey, *Dalit Theology*, 219. Elsewhere Massey wrote: "The climax of God's solidarity with human beings, particularly the oppressed people of this world, we find in His incarnational act. The summary of this act of God we find in John 1:14. Here we find through the act of incarnation God not only identifying Himself with human beings, he also fully becomes a part of human history by making 'his home among us' . . . [This] model of solidarity, which we find in the historical incarnational act of God, indeed puts forward a challenge to us as Dalit Christians to follow, so that our common experiences . . . should become the basis of an authentic Dalit theology." Massey, *Roots of Dalit History*, 86.

131. Massey, *Dalit Theology*, 224.

132. Jeremiah, "Exploring New Facets of Dalit Christology," 151.

the reality of caste-based relations in India.[133] For Nirmal, Dalit theology should be "counter-theology": it should be distinguishable from the predominant Indian Christian theology that is "essentially Brahmanic in character" and from other liberation theologies that are written from a non-Dalit context.[134] Nirmal's goal is to ensure that the theologies written from the perspectives of Dalits' sufferings and pathos are not "assimilated and finally conquered" by other theologies.[135]

Massey, unlike Nirmal, is more open to learn from and identify with liberation theologies of Latin America and elsewhere. He writes,

> Concerning Dalit theology, the one most important thing we should remember is, like its other sister liberation theologies, it is a theological expression, which has taken birth, on one side, from the historical experience of oppressed people, who address themselves by the name "Dalit," and, on the other side, their encounter with the God of the Bible, who has always been biased towards the oppressed and historically poor.[136]

Massey's words indicate his affinity with Latin American liberation theology. The claim that the "God of the Bible . . . has always been biased towards the oppressed and historically poor" echoes the idea of the preferential option for the poor, which was central to some of the theological arguments of Latin American liberation theologians such as Gustavo Gutiérrez. Like Nirmal, however, Massey concedes that liberation theologies of North America (Black liberation theology), Latin America, and South Africa have their unique histories. Dalit theology equally has its distinct history that other liberation theologies do not share.[137] Given that theologians should attend to the particularity of their own communities' history, Dalit theologians ought to ground their *liberation* theologies in the actual history and life situations of Dalits, while being open to learning from the liberation theologies constructed *from* and *for* different historical contexts.[138]

I explore below Massey's "theological anthropology"—theological reflection on what it means to be human in light of the traditional Christian belief that human beings are God's image bearers. The five tasks described above provide a useful context for understanding his theological anthropology.

133. Nirmal, "Dialogue with Dalit Literature," 64.
134. Nirmal, "Dialogue with Dalit Literature," 76.
135. Nirmal, "Dialogue with Dalit Literature," 76.
136. Massey, *Dalit Theology*, 219–220.
137. Massey, *Dalit Theology*, 220–221.
138. Massey, *Dalit Theology*, 221.

Theological Anthropology

It may be futile to seek an overarching theme in Massey's Dalit theology because he wrote on several theological subjects. Nevertheless, one can discern in his theological writings unrelenting efforts to reimagine and also reassert the full humanity of Dalits in light of the biblical teaching of God's creation of a casteless human race. Almost all of Massey's theological discussions on Dalits' history, experience, social location, and life situation seem to culminate in or point in the direction of theological anthropology. At the heart of his theological anthropology is the repudiation of the belief that Dalits are "no-people"—that is, counterfeit human beings or sub-human beings. Within the first few pages of *Downtrodden*, Massey argues: "Dalit people are those who, on the basis of caste distinctions, have been considered 'outcastes' because the architects of the system did not see fit to include them in the graded fourfold caste structure of Indian society." Massey goes on to argue that on the basis of this exclusion Dalits "have been made to bear extreme forms of disadvantage and oppression which virtually reduced them to a state of being 'no-people.'"[139]

Dalits' dehumanization raises an essential theological anthropology question: What does it mean to be fully human in light of the Christian idea of *imago Dei* (image of God)? This is a question that invites Dalit Christians to read Genesis texts that speak about the inherent ontological worth of all human beings because God made them in God's own image (1:26–27). For Massey, one of the services Christian theology can render to Dalits is to provide them with the "assurance that they are fully human in the sight of God."[140] It should also aid Dalits in their efforts to rescue, recover, and redeem their full humanity. Since many Dalits, for centuries, have been forced into accepting (and consequently have internalized) a sub-human status, theologians are to be persistent in retelling the story of Dalits and the schemes of their oppressors. They can help Dalit communities to rediscover their full human identity by embracing the truth "that there was a time when they had all their rights and were 'normal human beings.'"[141] As the casteless ones, Dalits are the true representatives of God's original intention for the equality of human beings.[142]

After commenting briefly on the different names given to Dalits by non-Dalits, Massey argues, by choosing the term *dalit* as the primary form

139. Massey, *Downtrodden*, 1–2.

140. Massey, *Downtrodden*, 49.

141. Massey, *Downtrodden*, 78.

142. Massey, *Downtrodden*, 79.

of self-identification, Dalits show their willingness to accept the state of *dalitness* as the first step they have taken toward their liberation.[143] However, using the underserving status of counterfeit human beings or sub-humans, traditionally ascribed to Dalits, as a relevant theological data should inspire theologians to pursue vigorously the goal of realizing Dalits' "full human-ness" as the "ideal of the *Imago Dei*, the image of God in us."[144] Reclaiming and reasserting the full humanity of Dalits, of course, is an enormous task given their long history of oppression. Massey notes that one of the difficult tasks of theologians who desire to reclaim Dalits' full humanity is to get Dalits themselves to reject the belief that their dehumanized condition is "a part of the natural order of things," which is not to be obstructed or seen as a privilege which should be embraced wholeheartedly.[145]

Massey locates his theological anthropology within the sphere of scriptural liberative motifs. For him, two related divine acts of intervention in human history provide the impetus for constructing Dalit theological anthropology that aims to promote the full humanity of Dalits and all op-pressed people.[146] The two divine acts are: first, "God is on the side of the oppressed"; second, "God liberates the oppressed."[147] For Massey, three biblical figures—Moses, Gideon, and Jesus—shed light on these two divine acts. Moses showed that God had a deep interest in the enslavement of the oppressed and was unwavering in seeking their deliverance. The life of Moses also revealed that God partners with human beings in God's acts of liberation.[148] Regarding Gideon, who initially doubted his ability to lead God's people, Massey notes that he represents Dalits' lack of confidence in undertaking the enormous task of liberating themselves as an oppressed community (Judg 6:15). He writes, "The Hebrew expression '*ha-dal*' means 'dalit' by the use of which Gideon confesses his own and his community's situation, and would say, 'I am a Dalit, how can I undertake such a great responsibility?'"[149] Dalits, like Gideon, should unashamedly express their lowly place before God and also be open to God's empowerment as they

---

143. Massey, *Downtrodden*, 3. It is likely that Massey borrowed the language of "no people" from Arvind Nirmal who argued that for far too long many Indians have been subjugated to a status of "no people" and "no human." This status of *no-human*, for Nirmal, should become a part Dalits' "theological affirmation or confession." Nirmal, "Toward a Christian Dalit Theology," 34.

144. Nirmal, "Toward a Christian Dalit Theology," 34.

145. Massey, *Roots of Dalit History*, 53.

146. Massey, *Dalit Theology*, 177.

147. Massey, *Dalit Theology*, 177.

148. Massey, *Dalit Theology*, 177–78.

149. Massey, *Dalit Theology*, 183.

seek their liberation.[150] They should draw strength and encouragement from God's commitment to the cause of the oppressed. As in the case of Moses, another theological lesson Dalits can learn from Gideon's experience is that God partners with humanity to bring about liberation and freedom to oppressed communities. Unlike Moses and Gideon, Jesus sheds a new light on the lengths God is willing to go in order to partner with humanity in the project of liberating the oppressed. The incarnational Christology of Massey presents Jesus—God incarnate—as one whose liberative work surpasses other deliverers and liberators.[151] God's choice of a lowly incarnate state, for Massey, shows that God identifies with the marginalized: "In him [Jesus], we meet God as a full human being" and also the "one who came to us as the poorest of the poor (in real sense of a Dalit)."[152] Arvind Nirmal had a similar view:

> Dalitness is best symbolized by the cross. On the cross, he was the broken, the crushed, the split, the torn, [and] the driven-asunder man—the Dalit in the fullest possible meaning of that term. "My God, my God, why has hast thou forsaken me?" he cries aloud from the cross. The Son of God feels that he is God-forsaken. That feeling of being God-forsaken is at the heart of our dalit experiences and dalit consciousness in India. It is the dalitness of the divinity and humanity that the cross of Jesus symbolizes.[153]

The divine *kenosis* (self-emptying) is God's *yes* to humans' cry for liberation from the oppressive forces that dehumanize God's image bearers. The divine *kenosis*, however, was a sacrificial act that exposed Jesus to all sorts of rejection and abuses.[154] By means of his entire life (including the cross and resurrection), Jesus enacted a community of God's people that is called to the work of liberation through the empowerment of the Holy Spirit.[155] If Jesus's liberative (or salvific) work extends to all humanity, the new community he has called into existence should proclaim the good news of liberation both to the oppressed and their oppressors:

> The Nazareth Manifesto of Jesus [see Luke 4:16–21] envisions the transformation of the whole human society, which includes . . . liberation for the dominant and oppressive group of people

150. Massey, *Dalit Theology*, 183–84.

151. Massey, *Dalit Theology*, 187.

152. Massey, *Dalit Theology*, 187.

153. Nirmal, "Towards a Christian Dalit Theology," 39.

154. Massey, *Dalit Theology*, 189.

155. Massey, *Dalit Theology*, 190–91.

who had become captive and blind to the various structures [they created].[156]

To conclude this chapter, Massey has made some lasting and substantive contributions to Dalit theology. I can only hope that I have given him well-deserved attention. His focus on reclaiming and reasserting the full humanity of all Dalits has given Dalit theologians an important foundation for exploring new theological ways to tackle the ongoing suffering of many Dalits who continue to be treated as counterfeit human beings in some parts of India. I will, however, highlight one area of weakness in his corpus of writing on Dalit theology, namely, his reluctance to interact with Dalit womanist and feminist theologians. Massey made a passing statement in his 2013 essay, where he identified "feminist theology" as one of the four contextual liberation theologies in India.[157] Surprisingly, in his theological commentary on Jesus's interaction with the Samaritan woman (John 4), whom Massey calls an "untouchable," he quickly moved to the common experience of all Dalits without attending to what the experience of the woman might say about Dalit women and their peculiar experience. For Massey, "the whole point of this story is that Jesus showed his disciples how there is need to reverse the existing caste or race or gender-based social order."[158]

Massey's lack of sustained interactions with Dalit female theologians or with the plight of Dalit women is particularly striking given that in India Dalit women have suffered dehumanization in some cases more than Dalit men. The following penetrating words of the Women's Organization for Liberation and Development highlight poetically the plight of Dalit women (WOLD):

We shall break the class oppression
That thrives on women's labor.
If we don't, we'll have to spend
All our lives in useless tears.

Hunger pangs drive us to toil every day;
We slave all day for a handful of gruel.
O, the merciless masters chase us on the one side,
And our starving children wail on the other side.

---

156. Massey, *Dalit Theology*, 209.
157. Massey, "Christianity to Be Renewed?," 52.
158. Massey, "Dalits in India," 29–30.

O, the torments of our drunken husbands on the one hand,
The persecution of our creditors on the other hand.
"What is right, to live or to die?"
Is the nagging question burning our hearts.

Having borne unlimited number of children,
We have become victims of earth's displeasure,
So we'll cast our burdens upon the Lord
And dare to stand up and fight for release![159]

As Shalini Mulackal has observed, many Dalit women experienced three forms of oppression due to their caste, class, and gender.[160] For Mulackal, these forms of oppression pose serious theological questions to Dalit theologians and all theologians that take seriously the liberative motif in Christian Scripture. Also, she argues that Christian theological anthropology, unlike the Vedic anthropology, should be grounded in the equality and dignity of all persons. "Both man and woman," Mulackal says, "bring God's touch to the world. Therefore anything that goes against this God-given dignity of woman needs to be countered at all costs."[161] Mulackal's theological anthropology allows us to see an important area of theology that could have benefited Massey's theology.

In the next chapter, I turn attention to African Christianity, using Kwame Bediako as a key interlocutor. Like Massey, Bediako is preoccupied with the idea of identity and its role in theological discourse. Unlike Massey, Bediako is focused on the role the pre-Christian traditions of Africa should play in constructing Christian theology *for* African Christianity. Bediako's theology is more in tune with the project of Indian Christian theology that sought a creative way to bring Christianity and Hinduism into dialogue. He adopted the presupposition of "gap and fulfillment" to argue for continuity between African indigenous religions and Christianity.[162]

159. Women's Organization for Liberation and Development (WOLD) Group, "Dalit Women," 168.

160. Mulackal, "Women," 155.

161. Mulackal, "Women," 170.

162. Ezigbo, *Re-imagining African Christologies*, 26–35, 76–78.

4

Indigenous Culture and the Project of African Theology

African theology, as a project of sub-Saharan African Christianity, warrants a look in two directions. First, it requires a theologian to explore the clash of cultures that ensued, with devastating consequences, as European explorers, colonizers, and missionaries attempted to impose their cultures on African communities. Numerous theological treatises on the impact of European Christianity on Africa communities have emerged as African theologians examine both the positive and negative outcomes of this clash. Second, the project of African theology demands a careful examination of the current theological issues that condition the life of Christian communities in Africa as they appropriate Christian beliefs and practices in their context. Theologians should avoid the temptation of interpreting such current issues primarily from Africa's encounter with Western colonization and imperialism. Though Western colonialism and imperialism remain a useful context for understanding Christianity in sub-Saharan Africa, they may not prove useful in understanding some issues Christian communities face in post-colonial Africa. These two directions, which the project of African theology nudges theologians to explore, highlight two themes that are central to the discussions I undertake in this chapter. The first theme is the considerable influence that African indigenous cultures exert on the practice of the Christian faith in many African communities. The second theme is the emergence of Jesus's person, work, and significance as a pivotal theological issue in the discourse on African theology. I begin first by summarizing the main issues and their historical contexts.

Theological Case: Theological Value of Africa's Indigenous Cultures to Christianity

Summary of the Issues

- Christianity's seeming inflexibility and lack of openness to learn from and also be informed by the indigenous cultures of Africa, especially in the imagination of the Christian message.

- The analogous relationship of Jesus's mediatory work to African ancestors' mediatory work.

Historical Background

Should the indigenous cultures of Africa contribute to the content of the Christian message that is designed for African communities? From an astonishing early period, sub-Saharan theologians have aimed to provide substantive answers to this question. At the core of the question is how best to construct a viable relationship between Africa's indigenous cultures (beliefs, customs, practices, and worldviews) and the Christian faith, a foreign religion that might appear hostile to traditional African religions. The task of constructing such a relationship burdened many Christian leaders in the 1700s and 1800s who raised questions about the nature, utility, and adequacy of the forms of European Christianity that were exported from Europe to sub-Saharan Africa. They were the forerunners of what is now called *African theology*—the theology that is designed to address African Christians' spiritual quests and theological needs. Some of the Christian leaders opted to reform the mission-founded churches from outside of the ecclesiastical walls of such churches. Others chose to reform the mission-founded churches from within their ecclesiastical traditions. However, both those who chose to reform the mission-founded churches from within their traditions such as the Nigerian Bishop, Samuel Ajayi Crowther (ca. 1806–91), and those who opted to reform and critique the mission-founded churches by establishing parallel ecclesial communities such as the Congolese prophetess, Vita Kimpa (ca. 1684–1706), and the Liberian prophet, William Wade Harris (ca. 1860–1929), laid the foundations for African theology.[1]

The quests for ecclesiastical reforms noted above were occasioned by many factors, several of which concerned the need to develop theologies that were, on one hand, effective for addressing the spiritual needs of African

---

1. See Tienou, "Indigenous African Christian theologies," 73–77; Parratt, *Reinventing Christianity*, 1–12.

Christians and, on the other hand, faithful to the genius of the Christian faith. For example, in the mid-nineteenth century, the Niger Missions expeditions (1841–91), which were launched from Sierra Leone and spearheaded by African missionaries such as Samuel Ajayi Crowther, pressed for a contextualized Christianity that took African languages and cultures seriously in formulating Christian worship and expressing doctrines. The catalyst for such adventurous contextual thinking is Henry Venn's ideas of a "Native Pastorate": an African church that is governed by three principles—self-support, self-governance, and self-propagation.[2] The outcomes of the so-called native pastorate were deeply marred by disagreements between some European missionaries of the Church Missionary Society (CMS) and African priests.[3] Other internal disputes and controversies led to two disparate paths to create a *native African church*: the establishment of churches that paralleled the mission-founded churches and the restructuring of the mission-founded churches so that they become in tune with the life situations of Africans.[4] These two ways of creating a native African church, along with some theological controversies they evoked, laid the foundations for lively contextual theological activities in the twentieth century.[5] I will briefly

2. In an 1842 document drafted to make the case for the Foruah Bay College's building project, which was signed by Henry Venn and other officials, a native church and African pastorate were described as an effective way to ensure the lasting presence of the Christian faith in West Africa. The documents states: "(1) It has afforded additional and very painful proofs of the baneful influence of the climate of West Africa on European constitutions: so much so, that all parties are agreed, that to benefit Africa extensively, by imparting to her our religious and social blessings, Africans themselves must be the principal agents. (2) The important and cheering fact has been established, that both Chiefs and people are willing to receive instruction from Black Men, even [if] such as they know to have been in a state of slavery; and that such Black Men, trained in the Schools and Institutions of the Society of Sierra Leone, are capable of acceptably imparting it." See Warren, *To Apply the Gospel*, 60–61.

3. For discussions on the Niger Missions expeditions, see Ajayi, *Christian Missions in Nigeria 1841–1891*; Walls, *Missionary Movement in Christian History*, 102–18; Sanneh, *Translating the Message*, 130–56; Hanciles, "Anatomy of an Experiment," 63–82.

4. See Ayandele, *Holy Johnson, Pioneer of African Nationalism, 1836–1917*; Walls, *Cross-Cultural Process in Christian History*, 155–64; Sanneh, *Translating the Message*, 143–46.

5. The British historian of Christianity, Andrew F. Walls, and the Gambian historian and scholar of religion, Lamin Sanneh, have shown that the expansion of contextualized versions of Christianity in many parts of Africa, Asia, and Latin America exculpated Christianity from the charge of being a Western religion. The flourishing of Christianity in these continents have equally weakened the hope in some Western quarters that religion would soon disappear as a force to be reckoned with in the public square. For both Walls and Sanneh, Christianity is translatable: it is inherently capable of genuine contextualization. Sanneh locates the translatability of Christian religion in its global missions' impetus: "Through the drama and trauma of Roman imperial repression in

describe such contextual theological activities, focusing on those that contributed to the project of African theology.

The impetus for African theology can be traced back to two conferences held in the mid-1950s. The first conference took place in Ghana in 1955 and the second conference was held in Paris in 1956. Papers presented at the conference in Ghana, which focused on the concerns and ideas of mainly Ghanaian scholars, theologians, and church leaders, were published under the title *Christianity and African Cultures.*[6] The proceedings of the conference in Paris in 1956, whose attendees were African Christian leaders from the French-speaking regions of Africa, were published under the title *Des Pretres Noirs s'interrogent.*[7] These conferences exposed the dangers of Westerners' marginalization of Africans in the church and also derogatory attitudes toward African cultures. They also revealed the resolve of African Christians to confront Western colonialism, imperialism, and the negative outcomes of missionary expeditions with the insights and ideas they learned from African nationalist and *négritude* movements.[8] As African political elites pushed for the independence of African nations from Western colonization and imperial rule, several African Christian leaders fought for the freedom of African Christianity from the teachings and practices of foreign missionaries that stifled the rise of African theology.[9] One such Christian leader was the Ghanaian anthropologist Kofi Abrefa Busia (1913–78). He challenged theologians to confront the identity crisis

Palestine the fledging Christian religion embarked on its world errand deeply conscious of its claim that it was a religion for all time and for the whole world, and not just for one time, place, and people." Sanneh, *Disciples of All of Nations*, 3. Cultural matrix, particularly language, is an effective factor in the expansion of Christianity. Given that Christianity does not endorse any language as particularly sacred, it is only natural that vernaculars, as evidenced in the task of bible translation, functioned "as the appointed and indispensable means God chooses to bring into existence communities of faith." Sanneh, "Significance of the Translation Principle," 35. Like Sanneh, Andrew Walls has explored the translatability of Christianity in several of his writings. Walls argues that the decision of the Jerusalem council (Acts 15) to rule against proselytism paved the way for Gentile Christian communities to discern new (non-Jewish) theological questions and answers that informed the understanding of Christian living. Walls writes, "The new Christians were not proselytes, following the converted cultural pattern of earlier believers; they were converts, needing, under the guidance of the Holy Spirit, to turn the ways of their own societies toward Christ." Walls, "Rise of Global Theologies," 24–25.

6. Christian Council of the Gold Coast, *Christianity and African Culture.*

7. Kinkupu et al., *Des prêtres noirs s'interrogent.*

8. Parratt, *Reinventing Christianity*, 13–24.

9. Dickson, *Theology in Africa*, 122.

in African Christianity, which ensued as Christians struggled to relate the Christian faith with traditional African worldviews.[10]

Many theologians clearly heard Busia's challenge to them. Interestingly, while some embraced Busia's challenge as a positive thing, others worried about the potential dangers of such an endeavor to the credibility of the Christian faith. Elsewhere, I described three main pathways that some African theologians have followed in their explorations of traditional African religions' relationship to Christianity.[11] The Nigerian Evangelical theologian Byang Kato represented theologians who adopted the "destructionist presupposition": the idea that Christianity and traditional African religions are essentially at war.[12] For Kato, traditional African religions are "man-made," but Christianity derives from Jesus Christ who is truly God.[13] Theologians who attempted to find common ground between Christianity and traditional African religions, in Kato's judgment, are bound to end up with a dangerous form of syncretism. He argued that African theology propagated by theologians such as John Mbiti and J. K. Agbeti was in effect "a funeral march of Biblical Christianity and a heralding of syncretism and universalism."[14] Though Kato's concerns are noteworthy, however, in seeking the preservation of the gospel from cultural corruption, he failed to see that all expressions of the Christian faith have deep cultural accents. Bediako rightly argued that Kato's theological hermeneutics was deeply misguided insofar as he only envisioned the biblical text as the solution to theological problems generated in African context but did not acknowledge the role that Africa's context could play in helping African Christians to grasp fully the teaching of the Bible.[15] The second path that some

10. Busia, "African Worldview," 1; Busia, "Ancestor Worship, Libation, Stools, Festival," 23.

11. Ezigbo, *Re-imagining African Christologies*, 35–42; Mbiti, "Christianity and Traditional Religions in Africa," 150–56.

12. Ezigbo, *Re-magining African Christologies*, 35–42. In the twentieth century, some African theologians, particularly those in the sub-Saharan region, engaged in extended polemic against their fellow African theologians who were open to use concepts from the traditional religions of Africa to express the Christian gospel message. The polemics were useful, at least in some sense: like theologians in the early Church era, those African theologians were able to work out their understanding of Christian identity in dialogue with African cultures, history, and experience. The theologians showed that when Christianity enters into a new culture, its adherents must undertake the complicated task of expressing their faith as they "come to terms with the various facets" of the new culture. Bediako, *Theology and Identity*, 16.

13. Kato, *Theological Pitfalls in Africa*, 17.

14. Kato, *Theological Pitfalls in Africa*, 55.

15. Bediako, *Theology and Identity*, 407.

African theologians have followed in their theological explorations is grounded in the "gap and fulfillment" presupposition.[16] In this theological pathway, Jesus and Christianity (though not understood interchangeably) are said to fulfill the aspirations of traditional African religions. The third pathway is grounded in the "reconstructionist presupposition."[17] Rather than simply (or uncritically) construing Christianity as fulfilling or perfecting traditional African religions, theologians should see both Jesus and Christianity as possessing the capabilities and the skills to discern useful ideas from the traditional cultures of Africa.

These three broad paths to contextualized theologies that are designed for African communities, which many African theologians have adopted, highlight the complexity of the task of working out an adequate relationship between African indigenous cultures and Christianity. Some female theologians' criticisms of the oppressive nature of some aspects of Africa's cultural practices further accentuate the complexity of the task. The voices of such female theologians have become a reminder to all African theologians not to focus only on external forces that are disrupting the Christian experience of African converts. They have nudged African Christians to examine internal factors—African cultures and ecclesial cultures—that dehumanized women. African male theologians needed to hear, in the words of Mercy Oduyoye, that when "women read the Bible, they often hear what is unheard by men."[18] Interestingly, before the founding of the Circle of Concerned African Women Theologians in 1989, some female theologians were asking penetrating theological questions about the kind of theology that African male theologians fed the churches in Africa. In 1977, for example, Zoe-Obianga made the following observation about women's experience which displays the form of subjection they suffer:

> Women have to face those obstacles that come from . . . those
> who accuse us of being revolutionaries, dangerous subversives.
> Our commitment is viewed as provocative and often causes us
> to be abused or scorned to a discouraging degree.[19]

One may ask: Was Jesus presented in the Christologies of African male theologians interested in liberating Africans from Western colonization but aloof to the dehumanizing experience of African women? Was the Jesus of the male theologians disinterested in the concerns of women who

16. Ezigbo, *Re-imagining African Christologies*, 26–35.

17. Ezigbo, *Re-imagining African Christologies*, 42–46.

18. Oduyoye, "Feminist Theology in an African Perspective," 167.

19. Zoe-Obianga, "Role of Women in Present-Day Africa," 145.

were denied pastoral leadership in the mission-founded churches?[20] For Zoe-Obianga, African theologians who write in the area of Christology should show that "commitment to Christ requires the liberation of African women."[21] Theologians should also take up the responsibility of demonstrating to all African women that they "will no longer be slaves: not of uncomprehending and intransigent husbands and brothers, nor of a retrogressive society, nor of alienating church structures. They are freed by their faith that opens all possible horizons to them."[22]

Male and female theologians who understood the need to develop theologies for African Christianity that would answer the actual questions of African Christians have carried the weight of the project of African theology. Kwame Bediako, whose writings I examine in the remainder of this chapter, has made unique contributions to African theology, particularly in the area of indigenous African cultures' relationship to African Christianity.

Kwame Bediako's Theological Response to the Issue of African Indigenous Cultures-Christianity Relations

A few weeks after engaging in an emotional conversation about the future of African theology with Kwame Bediako (1945–2008) at Liverpool Hope University, I got the sad news that he passed away. Professor Bediako in some ways attended the 2008 Conference on World Christianity, which was organized by Liverpool Hope University in honor of Andrew F. Walls, with the intent to say his farewell to friends and colleagues. Walls, who invited me to the conference, introduced me to Bediako. As our conversation progressed, Bediako said to me: "I am battling a serious illness. I don't know how long I will live." The news of his passing, therefore, was not entirely surprising to me (Bediako died on June 10, 2008). Yet, the terrible shock his death gave me has in some ways created a memorial in my heart for a theologian whose theological writings I deeply admire. The theological work of sub-Saharan African theologians who were Bediako's peers pales by comparison to his impressive constructive writings on African theology. Andrew Walls rightly observed that Bediako "labored so that generations of scholars, confident equally of their Christian and their African identity, might be formed in Africa . . ."[23] I count myself as one such scholar.[24] Bediako's unwavering commitment to

20. Zoe-Obianga, "Role of Women in Present-Day Africa," 146–47.

21. Zoe-Obianga, "Role of Women in Present-Day Africa," 148.

22. Zoe-Obianga, "Role of Women in Present-Day Africa," 148.

23. Walls, "Kwame Bediako and Christian Scholarship in Africa," 188.

24. The theological work of Bediako has shaped my theological life. To name a

African theology impelled him to start the Akrofi-Christaller Institute for Theology, Mission, and Culture (ACI), an "institution where devotion to scholarship and understanding of cultures of Africa would be pursued in a setting of Christian worship, discipleship, and mission."[25] In 2009, I visited the ACI located in Akropong-Akuapem, Ghana. I wished Bediako had not departed so soon so as to continue our conversation about the future of African theology. What follows is my attempt to articulate some of Bediako's theological insights that are pertinent to the project of African theology.

Bediako stood on the shoulders of other impressive African theologians. Building on the theological foundations laid by theologians such as the Nigerian theologian E. Bolaji Idowu and the Kenyan theologian John S. Mbiti, Bediako strenuously demonstrated that identity construction ought to be at the center of theological discussions on the indigenous religious beliefs of Africa and their usefulness for African Christianity.[26] The role that the traditional cultures of Africa should play in the imagination of African Christian identity and gospel-culture relations were the primary focus of Bediako's second doctoral dissertation, which he completed in 1983 at the University of Aberdeen under the guidance of Andrew Walls. In 1992, Regnum Books published the dissertation under the title *Theology and Identity*.[27] In the preface to the book, Bediako wrote:

> From quite early in my Christian conversion experience, I have felt the need to seek a clarification for myself of how the abiding Gospel of Jesus Christ related to the inescapable issues and questions which arise from the Christian's cultural existence in the world, and how this relationship is achieved without injury to the integrity of the Gospel.[28]

Here, Bediako outlines the central issues that underlie his discussions on vernacular theologizing, identity construction, and ancestor Christology. I will discuss these themes, focusing on how Bediako understood them and their place in the project of Africa theology.

---

few areas in which our interests intersect: we both have been shaped by the friendship and tutelage of Andrew F. Walls; we share concerns about the relevance of theologies intended for Africans that ignore the existential needs of Africa; also we are christocentric in our theological approaches.

25. Walls, "Kwame Bediako and Christian Scholarship in Africa," 188.
26. Bediako, "Roots of African Theology," 59.
27. Bediako, *Theology and Identity*.
28. Bediako, *Theology and Identity*, xi.

Vernacular Theologizing

For those familiar with the writings of Bediako, the pursuit of the role of the vernacular (mother tongue) in formulating Christian theology conditioned his understandings of the relationship between the gospel and culture, the nature of theological research, how to express the Christian faith in Africa, and how to assess the contribution of African Christian theologies to global Christianity. He construed the vernacular as what is authentic, original, and essential to a community. It is a community's language, which is ingrained in culture, thought, beliefs, and way of life. For Bediako, theology ought to be the product of the vernacular and not merely expressed in it. His point, of course, is that the context of a community, which includes the vernacular, is an important *locus theologicus*.

At the core of his theological method is what may be characterized as *vernacular theologizing*—the act and "principle of interpreting a religion through the language in which the faith is experienced and expressed."[29] This way of doing theology prompted him to reject the German missionary Dietrich Westermann's desire for Christianity to obliterate the pre-Christian religious traditions.[30] As we will see later, Bediako was convinced that "the pre-Christian religious roots of Africa [is] analogous to the achievement of the early Hellenistic Christian theologians, who . . . claimed the best in their cultural and intellectual heritage of the gospel."[31] In some ways he followed in their footsteps in recognizing the importance of some non-Christian religious and philosophical ideas for formulating and expressing the Christian faith.[32] He was equally shaped by contemporary Christian thinkers, three of whom—Andrew F. Walls, John S. Mbiti, and Vincent Mulago—are noteworthy.

From Andrew Walls, Bediako learned that the shifting of the center of Christianity's gravity (both in terms of its population growth and influence on local cultures) from the Western world to other parts of the world was underway.[33] He also learned from Walls that Africa, especially sub-Saharan Africa, will have a major say in the expansion of Christianity across the world

29. Bediako, *Christianity in Africa*, 210.

30. Bediako, "Roots of African Theology," 58. See Westermann, *Africa and Christianity*.

31. Bediako, "Roots of African Theology," 64.

32. As Stephanie Lowery rightly notes, Bediako showed that "modern African intellectuals are not alone in their argument that African religio-cultures deserve more attention and appreciation." Lowery, *Identity and Ecclesiology*, 64.

33. Walls, "Towards Understanding Africa's Place in Christianity," 180–89.

and that African Christians' contribution to Christian theology might not (and need not) conform to the patterns of Western theologies. Walls wrote:

> The fact remains Christian scholarship is not going to be a luxury for Africa, but a necessity. Its domestic task will be formidable. Already we can see the urgent tasks of formulating a Christian understanding of the state in a form the West has never known, of the Christian in local communities, of the Christian revolutionary movements, of the nature of Christian marriage (only gradually do we realize how European cultural factors have molded, as well as being molded by, the African "traditional" Christian pattern), the restatement of the faith in African categories.[34]

Walls made this observation in the late 1970s. In retrospect, his was a prophetic voice that has in some substantive ways come to fulfillment. Interestingly, his observation was partly based on his study of African Christianity and also some works of African theologians such as E. Bolaji Idowu. For example, in 1969 Idowu appealed to African theologians to

> seek to discover in what way the Christian faith could best be presented, interpreted, and inculcated in Africa so that Africans would hear God in Jesus Christ addressing Himself immediately to them in their own native situation and particular circumstances.[35]

Walls' guidance most likely led Bediako to fully appreciate Mbiti's work on African indigenous religions and also to see them "as *praeparatio evangelica*."[36] If the pre-Christian tradition of Africa prepared the way for the arrival of the Christian faith, it made no theological sense either to discard or obliterate it under the guise of preserving the purity of the Christian gospel. Mbiti was indeed one of the earliest African religion scholars that highlighted the need to explore in depth how the vernacular is directly linked to the penetration of the Christian gospel in the tropical Africa. In 1965, Mbiti published an essay in which he observed that for "most people in tropical Africa, an African language is still the mother tongue, and forms the psychological background for their thinking and understanding."[37] Therefore, he argued, "Great emphasis should be given to the use of African languages in communicating the Gospel, and in making Christian concepts assimilated

---

34. Walls, "Towards Understanding Africa's Place in Christianity," 184.

35. Idowu, "Introduction," 16.

36. Bediako, "Roots of African Theology," 60.

37. Mbiti, "Ways and Means of Communicating the Gospel," 331.

in the life of the Church."[38] Mbiti's understanding of the role of the mother tongue moves beyond merely seeking equivalent words (vocabulary) in African languages that express biblical concepts. The vernacular, for him, should be understood in a nuanced way that recognized how cultures govern and inform the language-game.[39] Language is not neutral; it is shaped by the cultures of the community that produces, adopts, and uses it. For Mbiti, "The Gospel has to sink into the thinking process, attitude, and the vocabulary of the people, if it is to make its lasting impact upon the life of the whole person and the whole community."[40] Clearly, Bediako learned from Mbiti that the vernacular plays an essential role in the ways Africans understood and expressed the Christian faith they inherited from Western missionaries. The idea of Christianity's translatability, which Bediako utilized in making the case for the theological value of the vernacular for formulating Christian theology, was equally present in Mbiti's writings.[41]

Vincent Mulago is another African theologian that helped Bediako to sharpen his understanding of the identity issues that have haunted many Christian communities in sub-Saharan Africa since the time of European colonization and missionary work in the continent. Bediako benefited from Mulago's extensive theological discussion on Christian identity, which is grounded in the belief that the Christian gospel does not "build on emptiness" or *tabula rasa* but rather on the fertile soil of indigenous religions.[42] Focusing on the Bantu people, Mulago argued that there is continuity between some religious aspirations of the Bantu indigenous religion and Christianity. Mulago, however, was wary of a superficial discussion on the relationship between the Bantu indigenous religion and Christianity that lacked a robust understanding of the differences of both religions. For him, African theologians "must aim at preserving not only their ancestral past but at being authentic Christians, faithful to their origins and to the Church."[43] They should learn from the concept of vital participation in community as

38. Mbiti, "Ways and Means of Communicating the Gospel," 331.

39. In this context, the term "culture" refers to the "complex whole which includes knowledge, belief, art, morals, law, custom and any other capabilities and habits acquired by a [a person] as a member of a society." See Taylor, *Primitive Culture*, 1.

40. Mbiti, "Ways and Means of Communicating the Gospel," 331.

41. Mbiti wrote: "Christianity is a universal and cosmic faith. . . . Our duty now is to localize the universality and cosmicity. Europe and America have Westernized it, the Orthodox Churches have Easternized it; here in Africa we must Africanize it. It belongs to the very nature of Christianity to be subject to localization; otherwise its universality and cosmicity become meaningless." Mbiti, "Christianity and Traditional Religions in Africa," 145–46.

42. Bediako, *Theology and Identity*, 350.

43. Mulago, "Christianisme et culture africaine," 326.

construed in Africa's indigenous religions. *Vital participation*, for him, offers a way of imagining the relationship between the notion of community of interrelated persons in Africa's indigenous religions and in Christianity. He writes, "The desire of the Bantu for contact with each other and union through symbols is achieved in the sacrament of the Church which make it possible for us to merge our lives with that of Christ."[44] At the heart of Mulago's theology is the attempt to resolve the tension of being truly *African* and truly *Christian* at the same time. In Bediako's view, Mulago's concepts of *union vitale* and participation are important assets to African theology and theologians.[45] Bediako's insistence on retaining the memory of Africa's pre-Christian and pre-Islamic cultures in the theological reflections on African Christian identity is clearly shaped by Mulago's insights into the complexity of identity imagination and construction.[46]

In order to grasp and also fully appreciate Bediako's contribution to the fields of African theology and contextual theology, we must set his writings in the context of some African theologians' protest against some forms of Western theologies on the grounds that they did not see any positive use of African traditional religious beliefs for formulating Christian theology. Consequently many of the theologians judged several aspects of such Western theologies to be inadequate for African Christianity. They also challenged and protested against any attempts to impose such Western theologies (either by missionaries or their protégés) upon African Christians. Though Bediako shared some of the sentiments of these theologians, he insisted on the need to develop theologies that moved beyond merely protesting against Western theologies. To accomplish this task, he argued that such theologies should be grounded both in African primal or indigenous culture and the Christian gospel.[47] For instance, in *Theology and Identity*, he explored theological clarifications for "how the abiding Gospel of Jesus Christ relates to the inescapable issues and questions which arise from the Christian's cultural existence in the world, and how this relationship is achieved without injury to the integrity of the Gospel."[48] The pursuit of such theological clarifications led him to engage

44. Mulago, "Christianisme et culture africaine," 327–28.

45. Bediako, *Theology and Identity*, 374.

46. Bediako, *Theology and Identity*, 237, 375.

47. As Gillian Bediako has noted, the term "primal" when attached to the term "religion" highlights "in a positive light, the religious traditions of indigenous people around the world and down through the ages who were formerly despised in Europe and the West generally as 'primitive, superstitious, and even demonic.'" Bediako, "Christianity in Interaction with the Primal Religions," 182.

48. Bediako, *Theology and Identity*, xi. For Bediako, the quest to define the boundary

in sustained discussions on the issues of identity construction, especially in relation to African Christians and African primal cultures. Before examining Bediako's discussion on identity construction, a brief assessment of his *vernacular theologizing* is in order.

One strength of Bediako's vernacular theologizing is that it brings into focus the natural mode of Christianity's subsistence. Christianity, as a translatable and translating religion, can take on new forms of expression when it encounters a new context. This way of understanding the nature of Christianity was especially useful in the eras when African theologians were preoccupied with the task of showing that Christianity is not a Western religion.[49] Another strength is that vernacular theologizing relativizes the sacredness of any form of Christianity's expression in terms of liturgy and theology. When, for example, a particular Western theology is understood as the most original, authentic, and archetypal Christian theology, it is not really theology itself that is often in view but rather the now-outdated notion that Europeans are ontologically superior to Africans. Vernacular theologizing was useful for the project of reclaiming the authenticity of Africans, African indigenous traditions, and African Christianity in the context of Westerners' derogatory view of Africa. It was equally of great importance in halting the project of Europeanization or Westernization of Africans in the nineteenth century and twentieth century under the guise of Christian evangelism or civilization. Mercy Amba Oduyoye rightly noted in the late 1970s that in order for Christianity to be a living faith in Africa, theologians must accelerate their task of bringing Christianity and "African culture" into meaningful interactions. Such interactions, for Oduyoye, can help African Christianity "escape being a fossilized form of nineteenth-century European Christianity."[50] Finally, vernacular theologizing has spurred on some theologians to vehemently reject such derogatory view of Africans and their cultures. Many now boldly explore some uniquely African thoughts that are

---

and form of "Christian identity" was central to some theologies of the second-century theologians such as Tatian, Tertullian, Justin Martyr, and Clement of Alexandria and also the twentieth-century sub-Saharan African theologians such as E. Bolaji Idowu, John S. Mbiti, Mulago Musharahamina, and Byang H. Kato who aimed to work out the relationship between Christianity and other religious and cultural traditions. This quest, however, could not be successfully satisfied without taking seriously the culture and history of a theologian. While the second-century theologians imagined the Christian faith in light of the Greco-Roman Hellenistic culture in which they lived, the twentieth-century theologians sought to imagine the Christian faith in light of Western colonization of Africa, Western missionary expeditions in Africa, and the primal religions of Africa.

49. Bediako, *Christianity in Africa*, 123.

50. Oduyoye, "Value of African Religious Beliefs and Practices," 110.

useful for formulating befitting theologies to the life situations of African Christians. One example is the idea of ancestorship, which has provided a beneficial environment for African christological discourse. As we will see later, Bediako took full advantage of the idea of the ancestral cult in Africa to formulate his ancestor Christology.

Bediako's version of vernacular theology and theologizing is not without some weaknesses. First, it could lead to an unhealthy nostalgia: the constant quest or longing for a return to the so-called "pre-Christian tradition" of Africa. It is not entirely clear if one can successfully recover a pristine condition of pre-Christian traditions of Africa. Though seeking the pre-Christian (and pre-Islam) religious traditions is not *de facto* wrong, it is fraught with misguided assumptions. Pristine primal or indigenous African traditions (values, cultures, religions, and beliefs) might no longer be accessible. In this century, even in the twentieth century when Bediako first proposed his idea of vernacular theology, the primal religious beliefs have been heavily disrupted by the advent of Christianity, Islam, and Western civilizations. Also, the indigenous traditions of Africa are dynamic: they are open to change (and have actually changed), adapting new forms and meanings as they encounter new ideas.[51]

Second, vernacular theologizing, at least in Bediako's model, might not be robust enough to adequately address the contemporary needs of African Christians who now live in the "Christian era" (juxtaposed with a pre-Christian era of Africa). As I noted earlier, Bediako's preoccupation with the pre-Christian tradition of Africa was undoubtedly useful during and in the immediate aftermath of Western missionary enterprise in sub-Saharan Africa. However, given that Europeanization of Christianity may no longer be the pivotal issue in twenty-first-century Africa, which is now a major center of Christianity, one wonders whether seeking a pre-Christian tradition is really relevant in this era. Contextual theologians are to discern theological materials (questions and thoughts) in the context of life of contemporary African Christian communities rather than longing for a return to a pre-Christian era of Africa. I am not, of course, suggesting that all African Christian communities are completely immunized against the colonial mentality. My point is rather that theologians ought to address the theological problems or needs of their own era. A nostalgic longing for a pre-Christian tradition of Africa can distract theologians from focusing on the theological questions and issues of present-day African Christians. Unless looking toward the pre-Christian and pre-Islam tradition of Africa can

51. Bediako concedes that African traditional beliefs are evolving. See Bediako, *Christianity in Africa*, 212.

contribute substantively to the theological solutions for present-day issues that confront African Christians, it should not be a focal point of contemporary African theology.

Third, it is also not entirely clear if pre-Christian African thoughts and ideas would prove to be the best vehicles for conveying or explaining some Christian beliefs to present-day African Christian communities. Identity construction is an act of negotiation: a community's act of rethinking its life in the complex matrix of its past (what it *was*), its present (what it *is*) and its future (what it is to *become*). Although the past of a community should not be ignored, it should not stifle the opportunity to identify and use new concepts to formulate theology. Proposing, for example, that Jesus is an ancestor in ways that are analogous to ancestors in the African indigenous worldview may not be as useful to African Christians who do not know or care much about the cult of ancestors.[52] I will return to explore this claim further in my assessment of Bediako's ancestor Christology. In the meantime I will attend to Bediako's discussion on identity issues in African Christianity.

Christian Identity and the African Context

In what follows I explore the concept of identity construction in Bediako's theology, particularly its implications for African Christianity. For Bediako, that some African Christians returned to the resources of traditional African religions when faced with some personal life challenges (such as infertility and poor health) rather than relying solely on Christianity's resources is symptomatic of a serious identity crisis. In his view, many African Christians are drawn into the taxing life of negotiating their identity as individuals who are simultaneously *African* (by birth or culture) and *Christian* (by birth or faith confession). In the spirit of vernacular theologizing, Bediako proposes *vernacular Christianity* as a possible solution to the problem of identity crisis in African Christianity.

Identity imagination or construction is a human phenomenon. It emerges naturally as people become aware of their own distinctives and of their neighbors' features and distinctives. Self-identification—how a community chooses to name itself in terms of ethos, beliefs, practices, history, and so on—is sometimes an act of negotiation. This act of negotiation can be done proactively or defensively depending on the community's circumstances and needs. For example, a community can switch to a defensive mode when it genuinely feels that its identity is under severe threats or that the boundaries that mark out its distinctives are breached or compromised

52. Bediako, *Christianity in Africa*, 210.

either by internal or external factors. In this case, the community is pressured to reinforce or reestablish its unique characteristics and features. Whether such reinforcement is to be designed as a buffer to prevent outside factors from penetrating the comfort of *insiders* (members of a community) or rather to stop them from acquiescing to the demands of external factors, can become a muted point in real-life situations. However, how the boundaries are reinforced or reestablished will require the art of irenic negotiation to avoid the devastating strategy of a purification process that would result in genocide, as Rwanda experienced in 1994. The Rwanda genocide, which in some ways was stoked by an unresolved identity dispute between two major ethnic groups, Hutus and Tutsis, should serve as a perspicuous reminder of how the joy of those who wear the invisible clothes of identity might be tempered by the lasting and disorienting stench of death.

Is Christian identity a matter of hermeneutics or theological imagination? According to Kwame Bediako, it is both:

> [The] question of identity with its significance for the development of theological self-consciousness constitutes a shared presumption of the formative phase of Hellenistic Christian thought in the second century AD on the one hand, and the early flowering of Christian theology in the post-missionary Church in twentieth-century Africa on the other. According to this argument, the question of identity constitutes a "hermeneutical key" which, by granting access to the kind of concerns exhibited by Christian writers in the two contexts, leads to a deeper understanding of the modern situation in particular, and shows how the modern context manifests features which are identifiable elsewhere in Christian history.[53]

When African Christians ask theological questions (sometimes expressed in songs, prayers, and literature), it is likely, if they are asking as *Africans*, they do so from the context of their life. Answering such questions in a manner that does not take seriously their context may lead to identity problems, especially when such answers are borrowed from foreign theological repertoire. Bediako partly blames the identity crisis of African Christians on Western missionaries, particularly those who acted in accordance with the predominant belief that Europeans were ontologically superior to Africans.[54] Although Bediako concedes that such a derogatory view

53. Bediako, *Theology and Identity*, 426–27.

54. Bediako argues, "Instead of producing a real meeting at the specific level of religious apprehension and theology, the missionary enterprise produced what can be called an African identity problem . . . Therefore, the well-known 'quest for an African theology' by [African] theologians must be understood as a quest for a framework in

of Africans did not originate with the missionary movement, he notes that when missionaries "treated Africa and Africans as savage, ignorant and superstitious, they were very often expressing something of this general European *Afrikaanschauung*."[55]

Bediako construed identity crisis in African Christianity as an invitation to theologians to shoulder the responsibility of showing that "the African experience of the Christian faith can be fully coherent with the religious quests in African life."[56] What, then, is the solution to the identity problem of African Christianity?[57] Bediako proposes two interrelated responses: Christianizing the pre-Christian traditions (religion, culture, and language) of Africa and Africanizing the Christian experience of Africans. By *Christianizing* the pre-Christian traditions of Africa, he means "making room in the African experience of religious powers for Christ and the salvation he brings."[58] By *Africanizing* the Christian experience of Africans, he means "employing Christian tools" to mend the "torn fabric of African identity" with the intent to bring about "a fuller and unfettered African humanity and personality."[59] Also, it means formulating African Christianity in ways that address meaningfully fundamental issues in African Christianity, which include identity crises and the negative impacts of some Western theologies on African Christianity.[60] Bediako steers away from E. Bolaji Idowu's indigenization model in his proposals for how to deal with identity crises in African Christianity because it might not allow for a lively interaction between the Christian faith and African cultures.[61] Indigenization seems to suggest a one-way street in which a theologian is tasked with safely transplanting the Christian faith (of biblical and Western origins) to Africa.[62]

---

which African Christian identity could inhere, in terms meaningful also for the demands of African integrity; for without such integrity African Christian theology would be impossible. If it is correct to link this vital theological quest with Africa's missionary past, it is not surprising that some ask whether the missionary enterprise itself did not proceed on inadequate theological premises." Bediako, "Biblical Christologies," 88.

55. Bediako, *Christianity in Africa*, 5–6.

56. Bediako, *Christianity in Africa*, 60.

57. The issue of identity has preoccupied as well as perturbed many African theologians. This is a complex issue that requires attending to what it means to be "African" and "Christian." As I have argued elsewhere, several factors inform and shape Africans' theological discussions on what constitutes the identity of Africans who are Christians. See Ezigbo, "African Christian or Christian African?," 664–82.

58. Bediako, *Christianity in Africa*, 5.

59. Bediako, *Christianity in Africa*, 5.

60. Bediako, *Christianity in Africa*, 5.

61. Bediako, *Christianity in Africa*, 117.

62. Bediako, "Epilogue," 249.

For Bediako, the vernacular is the most effective means for implementing the two processes of Christianizing the pre-Christian traditions of Africa and Africanizing the Christian experience of Africans. The role of vernacular in accomplishing these dual tasks should not come as a surprise because the Christian faith is "culturally infinitely translatable."[63] The event of the Pentecost (Acts 2), Bediako argues, is a historical evidence which shows that divine speeches occur in the vernacular and also warrant both vernacular theologizing and Christianity:

> The ability to hear in one's own language and to express in one's own language one's response to the message which one receives, must lie at the heart of all authentic religious encounter with the divine realm. Language itself becomes, then, not merely a social or psychological phenomenon, but a theological one as well. Though every human language has its limitations in this connection, yet it is through language, and for each person, through their mother tongue, that the Spirit of God speaks to convey divine communication at its deepest to the human community. The significance of Pentecost, therefore, has to do with more than answering to the chaos of Babel and restoring harmony between God and humanity, and between human beings. Its deeper significance is that God speaks to men and women—always in the vernacular. Divine communication is never in a scared, esoteric, hermetic language; rather it is such that "all of us hear . . . in our own languages . . . the words of God" [Acts 2:11].[64]

Since Christianity does not ascribe a sacred status to any particular language, it is reasonable to see the vernacular as an important tool to express the Christian faith in ways that draw resources from the cultures of Christian communities throughout the world. As Bediako observes, "The existence of vernacular Bibles not only facilitates access to the particular communities speaking those languages, but also creates the likelihood that the hearers of the Word in their own languages will make their own responses to it and on their own terms."[65] To say that Christianity is translatable by means of the vernacular is to claim that it has a universal appeal: the Christian faith can feel well at home in all cultures of the world. Therefore, to Bediako, proposing that Christianity is "a non-Western religion" does not mean that Western Christianity has become irrelevant to Christians in other parts of the world. Rather, it means that Christianity has a universal outlook in its

63. Bediako, *Christianity in Africa*, 61.
64. Bediako, *Christianity in Africa*, 60.
65. Bediako, *Christianity in Africa*, 62.

DNA and evangelization culture. He writes, "Translatability is also another way of saying universality. Hence the translatability of the Christian religion signifies its fundamental relevance and accessibility to persons in any culture within which the Christian faith is transmitted and assimilated."[66] As a translatable religion, Christianity is inherently capable of contextuality: it can be formulated, interpreted, appropriated, and expressed in different cultural contexts.[67] Also Christianity's translatability, for Bediako, makes it "capable of subverting any cultural possessiveness of the Faith in the process of its transmission."[68] This understanding of Christianity's translatability has a profound impact on Bediako's theology, especially on his Christology. He argues that the doctrine of the Incarnation is a supreme example that God's Word (*Logos*) occurs in the realm of human vernacular.[69]

One offshoot of Bediako's vernacular theology (and theologizing) is vernacular Christianity. As I explore his conception of vernacular Christianity and its value for Africans, it is important to bear in mind that his goal is to provide a theological justification for promoting in Africa a form of Christianity that is thoroughly grounded in the primal religious thoughts, cultures, history, and experience of Africans. He believes that the expansion of Christianity in Africa is directly linked to the use of vernacular in the formulation and expression of Christian faith in the continent.[70] For instance, in his comparison of the modes of expression of Christianity and Islam in Africa, he contends that they differ in the level of importance they ascribe to the original languages of their Scriptures. While in Islam the Arabic texts of the Qur'an are esteemed highly above the non-Arabic translations, Christians do not have any reverential status for Aramaic, Hebrew, and Koine Greek—the original languages of Christian Scripture.[71] One of the main reasons for the differences in attitude toward the original languages of the Qur'an and the Bible, as Mona Siddiqui has noted, is because Scripture and prophecy "are inextricably tied to divine communication" in Islam—Muslims come to see God principally through the Prophet Muhammad and the Qur'an, whereas in Christianity, "Scripture and prophecy play a secondary role"—Christians come to see God principally through Jesus Christ, God incarnate.[72] The pivotal theological point here is that by rejecting the notion

66. Bediako, *Christianity in Africa*, 109.
67. Bediako, "Epilogue," 244.
68. Bediako, *Christianity in Africa*, 110.
69. Bediako, *Christianity in Africa*, 110.
70. Bediako, *Christianity in Africa*, 62.
71. Bediako, *Christianity in Africa*, 109.
72. Siddiqui, *Christians, Muslims, and Jesus*, 8.

of a sacred scriptural language Christianity makes every translation of its Bible "substantially and equally the Word of God."[73] The African theologian, therefore, is tasked with giving a positive assessment of the "African pre-Christian religious heritage," viewing it as a relevant "preparation for the Gospel in Africa" and also as the "substratum for the idiom and existential experience of Christianity in African life."[74]

Bediako's idea of a *vernacular Christianity*—a form of Christianity that is understood, expressed, and appropriated in the local language, thought, experience, history, and culture of a community—presents a distinctive color of Christianity in Africa.[75] This form of Christianity intentionally (and sometimes unintentionally) assumes many cultural manifestations or incarnations.[76] In some ways, to speak of African Christianity is to identify or highlight the form of Christianity that has taken up the idiom, beliefs, values, and thought of African cultures. One belief that has shaped some of Bediako's theological work is the close interactions of the spirit and human worlds in the worldview of many African communities.[77] On the nature of the spirit world, he notes that it is a world of "disturbed power, perhaps even of fragmented power; it is as much a universe of conflict as the rest of the fallen world in that it is a world not of one Center, God, but many centers."[78] It is also a world that upholds the "unity and multiplicity of the Transcendent."[79] The understanding of the spirit world and the impact of this world on the human world shape the practice of the Christian life in Africa. Many African Christians live daily in response to the spirit world. Therefore, any Christian theology that does not account for the place of the spirit world and how human beings are to navigate it will hardly interest most Christians.[80]

The spirt world's relationship with the human world holds an important place in Bediako's imagination of vernacular Christianity. In his thinking, African Instituted Churches (AICs) are the best examples of

73. Bediako, *Christianity in Africa*, 62.

74. Bediako, *Christianity in Africa*, 76, 82–83.

75. John Mbiti shares the same estimation of the role of the vernacular in the expression and expansion of Christian faith in Africa. See Mbiti, "Ways and Means of Communicating the Gospel," 329–50. For a historical analysis of the idea of Christianity's translatability, see Sanneh, *Translating the Message*.

76. Bediako, *Christianity in Africa*, 16, 109.

77. Bediako, *Christianity in Africa*, 97.

78. Bediako, *Christianity in Africa*, 100.

79. Bediako, *Christianity in Africa*, 100.

80. For further discussions, see Ezigbo, *Re-imagining African Christologies*, especially ch. 6.

vernacular Christianity. AICs may be described as the churches that are founded by Africans to meet African perennial and peculiar needs. They emphasize the spiritual calling of their leaders: prophets, prophetesses, and healers who "underwent a resurrection experience" and have returned with a "new message of repentance, of giving up witchcraft, and believing in the God of the Bible."[81] The earliest founders of AICs, such as Garrick Braide, Joseph Babalola, and Joseph Kimbangu, to name just a few, were somewhat the forerunners of African Christian theology. They created Christian movements that flourished among Africans and in many cases expanded in defiance of Western missionaries' protest and condemnation. Unsurprisingly, AICs were criticized by many Western missionaries and some of their protégés. As Andrew Walls observed, "In mission or 'mainline' church circles the new churches were commonly regarded as 'sects' or 'cults' or as a syncretistic Cave of Adullam, frustrated ambition in league with polygamy, adultery, superstition, and ignorance."[82] The derogatory attitudes of the mission-founded churches, especially Evangelical churches, toward AICs have continued to this day. Many of these churches see AICs as mission fields ripe for Christian evangelism and conversion. Interestingly, some members of the mission-founded churches attend AICs as a last resort to address their spiritual and physical needs.[83]

In the remainder of this chapter, I will discuss Bediako's attempt to formulate a Christology that is grounded in his vernacular theologizing and vernacular Christianity. I will focus on his ancestor Christology, which is his major contribution to the discourse on the identity, person, and significance of Jesus Christ.

Ancestor Christology

Bediako's preferred African term for Jesus of Nazareth is *ancestor*:

> We need to read the Scriptures with Akan traditional piety well in view, in order to arrive at an understanding of Christ that deals with the perceived reality of ancestors. We need also to make the biblical assumption that Jesus Christ is not a stranger to our heritage, starting from the universality of Jesus Christ rather than from his particularity as a Jew, and affirming that the Incarnation was the incarnation of the Savior of all people, of all nations and of all times . . . We hold on to his incarnation as

81. Oduro et al., *Mission in an African Way*, 61.
82. Walls, "Building to Last," 4.
83. Oduro et al., *Mission in an African Way*, 6–7.

a Jew because by faith in him, we too share the divine promises given to the patriarchs and through the history of ancient Israel (Ephesians 2:11–22).[84]

In 1998, Bediako published an article entitled "Doctrine of Christ and the Significance of Vernacular Terminology" in which he argued for the christological value of the concept of ancestor for formulating Christologies that are intended for African Christians.[85] Bediako's line of christological questioning in the article reveals his conviction that theological and biblical exegesis must move beyond establishing the meanings in Hebrew, Aramaic, and Greek languages to the complex task of formulating theologies that are grounded in biblical teaching with "all possible languages in which biblical faith is received, mediated, and expressed."[86] For example, he asked "whether the experience of the reality and actuality of Jesus as intended in Christian affirmation can inhabit the Akan world of *'Nana'* [ancestor] in the same way that it could inhabit the Greek word of *'Logos'*?"[87] Vernacular theologizing, Bediako argues, is required to successfully answer this question insofar as this way of doing theology requires "discerning and recognizing what is happening creatively in the context as people encounter, live out, and attempt to express their experience of the reality and actuality of Jesus Christ."[88] The context of the community in which people learn about the Christian faith will undoubtedly shape how they experience the ministry, life, and teaching of Jesus Christ.[89] It also should be expected that the languages, thoughts, concepts, and ideas that originate from the context of Christian communities would shape how they formulate and express their understandings of Jesus's person, work, and significance.

By pursuing an ancestor Christology model, Bediako stands in the tradition of other African theologians who understood the identity and functions of ancestors, as construed in many traditional African societies, as a useful matrix to formulate their Christologies.[90] To cite some examples, the Congolese theologian and ethicist Benezet Bujo in *African Theology in*

---

84. Bediako, *Jesus and the Gospel in Africa*, 24.

85. Bediako, "Doctrine of Christ," 110–11.

86. Bediako, "Doctrine of Christ," 110.

87. Bediako, "Doctrine of Christ," 110.

88. Bediako, "Doctrine of Christ," 110.

89. Bediako wrote that the "mother tongues and new idioms are crucial for gaining fresh insights into the doctrine of Christ." Bediako, "Doctrine of Christ," 111.

90. I have discussed elsewhere the different ways in which African theologians use the concept of ancestor to formulate their Christologies. See Ezgbo, *Re-imagining African Christologies*, 71–80.

Its Social Context made the following observation about the christological value of the concept of ancestor for Christology:

> Could not the recognition of the place which the ancestors and elders occupy in the life of Africans stimulate theologians to construct something new? In particular, could we not use this cultural phenomenon to find a new "Messianic" title for Jesus Christ and work out a new theological way of speaking of him? I would like to suggest that such a new way of speaking would be to give Jesus the title of "Ancestor Par Excellence," that is, of "Proto-Ancestor."[91]

But who can qualify as an ancestor and why is the work of ancestors analogous to the work of Jesus Christ? In many sub-Saharan African traditional communities, ancestors generally are seen as the "living dead," to borrow John Mbiti's words. They are believed to be *dead* because they are no longer visibly present with the members of their families and communities that are alive.[92] They are also believed to be *living* in two senses. First, they are kept alive in the memory of their surviving family members and kindred through rituals, ceremonies, and festivals. As Mbiti has noted, ancestors are believed to have the powers to "visit their surviving relatives in dreams, or visions, or even openly, and make their wishes known."[93] Second, they are believed to have the powers to bless or punish members of their living family and kindred through drought, illness, misfortunes, and many other ways. The traditional African notion of ancestral veneration speaks to the inherent communality of the traditional African anthropology. It also underscores Africans' idea of communal identity. The centrality of living in communion with one's ancestors was important enough to some Africans who rejected Western missionaries' eschatology that suggested or implied that African Christians would be separated eternally from their good ancestors who died without hearing about Jesus.[94]

Several theologians find ancestral mediation to be a useful framework for bringing traditional African religions and Christianity into a theological dialogue. Bediako is obviously one such theologian. Ancestral mediation,

91. Bujo, *African Theology in Its Social Context*, 78–79.

92. Mbiti, *Introduction to Africa Religion*, 77.

93. Mbiti, *Introduction to Africa Religion*, 78.

94. Mbefo, *Christian Theology and African Heritage*, 10. Those Africans would not have found Byang Kato's soteriology helpful: "The Biblical answer to the question concerning those who died before hearing the gospel seems to be that they go to hell. There is no clear basis for optimism in this case. No one deserves to be saved in any case. So the question of God's partiality does not arise." Kato, *Theological Pitfalls in Africa*, 181.

to Bediako, offers great opportunities for "filling out some dimensions of spiritual experience and historical consciousness which are inherent in the Christian religion."[95] Bediako might have been influenced by John Mbiti's nuanced fulfilment theory. Mbiti wrote:

> The task of fulfilment does not mean saying only yes; it also says no. In order to preserve, it may be necessary to prune as well; and traditional African religions need a lot of pruning if their best values are to be preserved and taken up in Christianity. Christian fulfilment means, in effect, a universalizing act, and what cannot measure up to that height is not worth fulfilling. Only Christianity has the legal credentials to pass the right judgement on traditional religiosity; and unless Christianity does that in Africa, it will find itself wrapped up in a lot of religiosity not unlike the type that our Lord pronounced "dead" in Phariseeism and Judaism. Even religiosity can become dead, and not only dead but rotten. We must give Christianity the opportunity and freedom to remove deadness and rottenness from our traditional religiosity.[96]

Clearly, Mbiti privileges Christianity over traditional African religions. One wonders who his audience really is. Would adherents of the traditional religions be receptive to his assessment in the same way Christians would? Why does Christianity have the "legal credentials to pass judgement on [African] traditional religiosity"? Why does he deny traditional African religions the so-called legal credentials to judge Christianity? Why Christianity and not Jesus? Is Christianity immune to the kind of "dead" religiosity that Mbiti describes? Mbiti's version of fulfilment theory, like Bediako's, is grounded in the belief that traditional African religions are *praeparatio evangelica* (preparation for the Gospel).[97] The fulfilment model creates a fertile ground in which the traditional African belief about the mediatory role ancestors play in their communities can be compared to the mediatory work of Jesus.[98] In such comparison, Jesus typically emerges as a

95. Bediako, *Christianity in Africa*, 212.

96. Mbiti, "Christianity and Traditional Religions in Africa," 153.

97. Mbiti, "Christianity and Traditional Religions in Africa," 147–50.

98. For a recent discussion on ancestor Christology, see Luka, *Jesus Christ as Ancestor*. Several African theologians have rejected the kind of fulfillment model espoused by Mbiti and Bediako. Byang Kato, an ardent critic of Mbiti, argued against the fulfillment theory: "Animistic worship is no proof that man is trying to worship God. It, however, shows man's awareness of the existence of the Supreme Being and man's rebellion against that God. It also shows the deep search for the Reality in spite of the unconscious flight from Him. Only Jesus Christ can meet this thirst, not by filling up the measure of idolatry but by transformation." Kato, *Theological Pitfalls in Africa*, 114.

superior being: he is believed to be greater than African ancestors both in terms of his ontology (being) and works. Bediako, for example, argues that Jesus displaces Africans' "natural ancestors" and replaces them because he is the "Supreme Ancestor" that mediates between God and humanity.[99] For him, Jesus is the one who completely fulfills Africans' aspirations for blessings from the spirit realm: "Once Jesus comes, the ancestors are cut off as means of blessing and we lay our power-lines differently."[100]

If African natural ancestors were not "rivals of Jesus," as Bediako claims, why, then, wouldn't Jesus work with and through them to disseminate God's blessings to Africans? Why would Jesus need to displace and replace them as mediators in order to satisfy Africans' longings for a healthy relationship between the human realm and the spirit realm? Bediako's responses to these questions can be subsumed under three main claims: (a) that the traditional African beliefs in ancestors, their identity, and their function are only provisionary theological guides; (b) that the ancestors are merely human, unlike Jesus who is God incarnate; and (c) that the traditional belief in ancestral mediation is in fact a myth. On the provisionary theological role, Bediako argues that God's salvific work in and through Jesus Christ was anticipated and prefigured in Africans' quests and responses to the Transcendent, which are embedded in the ancestral cult.[101] His figural reading of the traditional African ancestral cult allows him to link the Jewish ancestors, particularly Abraham, to Africans through the salvific work of Jesus Christ.[102] Regarding the finitude of African natural ancestors and the infinitude of God incarnate, he says: "Because ancestors, even in their realm of spirit existence, remain in African understanding essentially human just like ourselves, they cannot therefore ultimately be rivals of Christ in Christian consciousness."[103] Another area in which Jesus displays his superiority over the ancestors is in the defeat of the power of death by rising from the dead.[104] On the claim that the traditional belief in ancestral mediation is a

---

99. Bediako, *Christianity in Africa*, 217.

100. Bediako, *Christianity in Africa*, 217.

101. Bediako, *Christianity in Africa*, 224–25.

102. Bediako writes, "The relevance of the Old Testament for understanding the place of ancestors stems . . . from the fundamental theological affirmations that in Christ, and through faith-union with Christ in the Gospel, we become 'the seed of Abraham and heirs according to the promise . . . ' In Christ, then, we receive 'an adoptive past' through our 'Abrahamic link,' thus connecting our past with the entire past of the people of God." Bediako, *Christianity in Africa*, 227.

103. Bediako, *Christianity in Africa*, 217–18. See also Bediako, *Jesus as the Gospel in Africa*, 31.

104. Bediako, *Jesus as the Gospel in Africa*, 31.

myth, he argues that the central issue is Jesus's functional superiority over African ancestors. He writes,

> Strictly speaking, the cult of ancestors, from the intellectual point of view, belongs to the category of myth, ancestors being the product of the myth-making imagination of the community. To characterize the cult of ancestors as "myth" is not to say that the cult is unworthy of serious attention. The term stresses the functional value of the cult of ancestors. For myth is sacred, enshrining and expressing the most valued elements of community's self-understanding.[105]

For Bediako, once the ancestral mediation is understood as a myth, it becomes clear how Jesus Christ effectively fulfills the aspirations of the traditional African communities in regards to ancestral mediatorial functions.[106] It is noteworthy that by describing the ancestral mediation of African ancestors as a myth, Bediako equally paved the way to dismiss it and also to present Jesus as "the only real and true Ancestor and Source of life for all mankind, fulfilling and transcending the benefits believed to be bestowed by lineage ancestors."[107]

Bediako's ancestor Christology has shown the necessity and utility of constitutive contextual theologizing, which requires using theological materials from the cultures of Africa to construct Christian theologies. He has demonstrated a genuine attempt to formulate a Christian understanding of Jesus Christ with the ideas, thoughts, and aspirations that are presented in African ancestral veneration and mediation.

Communities in sub-Saharan Africa that have retained the cultural beliefs about the mediatorial roles of ancestors can benefit from Bediako's ancestor Christology notwithstanding its problems. To name some of the problems, he comes dangerously close to the "destructionist presupposition" that promotes discontinuity between traditional African religions and Christianity, which he vehemently opposes as can be seen in his critical assessment of Byang Kato's theological writings.[108] If, as Bediako claims, the traditional African belief in ancestral mediation is a "myth" and that Jesus replaces African ancestors, it implies that Christianity and its teaching about Jesus Christ are superior to traditional African religions and its teaching about ancestors. It is difficult to see how adherents of traditional African religions will not see

105. Bediako, *Jesus as the Gospel in Africa*, 30.

106. Bediako, *Jesus as the Gospel in Africa*, 30.

107. Bediako, *Jesus as the Gospel in Africa*, 31.

108. Bediako, *Christianity in Africa*, 216. See also Bediako, *Theology and Identity*, 386–425.

Christianity as a foreign invader that seeks to eliminate one of their essential religious beliefs. To be clear, when African theologians such as Bediako and Uchenna Ezeh make a case for the ancestor Christology model, they are only saying that Jesus is analogous to African ancestors, particularly in terms of mediatorial functions.[109] To use the classical Greek Christian christological terminology, Jesus is *homoiousion* (of similar substance) and not *homoousion* (of the same substance) with African ancestors.

Another problem with Bediako's ancestor Christology concerns the validity of comparing Jesus with African ancestors. Theologians who propose an ancestor Christology for African Christianity must shoulder the responsibility of demonstrating how Jesus would have qualified for the position of an ancestor in Africa if African elders found him guilty of transgressing the laws and customs of ancestors. As I have argued elsewhere, Jesus could not have qualified as an African ancestor.[110] When understood from the perspective of the custodians of Jewish traditions (priests, scribes, and rabbis), Jesus was deservedly punished for violating many Jewish traditions (Matt 12:1–13; Luke 23:13–25; John 10:22–33). Therefore, proposing that Jesus is an ancestor or the chief ancestor raises serious theological problems despite its perceived usefulness to African Christians.

One other area that merits serious theological reflections for the theologians that propose African ancestral mediation as a useful theological material for constructing Christologies is the issue of discipleship. People who become ancestors in many traditional societies of Africa must be judged to be the true disciples of the customs, ethos, and laws that are believed to be inextricably rooted in the foundations of their societies. Ancestral mediation, therefore, is not primarily a matter of a well-established system of beliefs but rather about praxis—a manner of living that is in conformity with the lifestyle modelled by ancestors, who are the custodians of their societies' customs, ethos, and values. In a totally different context, Latin American liberation theologians have repositioned praxis as a central theme in both theological reflection and the Christian life. These issues are taken up in the next chapter.

109. See Ezeh, *Jesus Christ the Ancestor*.
110. Ezigbo, "Jesus as God's Communicative and Hermeneutical Act," 51.

5

The Poor in Latin American Liberation Theology

A major argument of this book is that doing theology contextually awakens in a theologian the need to attend properly to the actual context of a community.[1] In Latin America, a major center of Christianity in this present era, *poverty*—lacking in basic necessities of life such as food, shelter, and healthcare—is a pivotal issue that confronts many communities. Several Latin American theologians have construed poverty and the plight of the poor as constituting a major theological problem that cannot be successfully ignored in serious reflections on Christianity and its utility on the continent. I examine this theological problem, using Gustavo Gutiérrez as a primary interlocutor. I begin, however, by summarizing the theological problem and a survey of its historical background.

Theological Case: The Problem of Poverty and God's Preferential Love for the Poor

Summary of the Issues

- The usefulness of the Christian view of God as inherently love, and therefore, a loving being, to the poor in Latin America.

- Theological exploration of the practical implications of the life of Jesus, a poor Galilean (and according to the traditional Christian creedal teaching, God incarnate) for confronting the plight of the poor and promoting their liberation.

1. Gustavo Gutiérrez rightly argues that we "cannot separate the theological task from the Christian community and from the world in which it is found. Theology is an expression of the consciousness, which a Christian community has of its faith in a given moment of history." Gutiérrez, "Faith as Freedom," 26.

Historical Background

In the beginning of liberation theology, there were deaths—physical death and cultural death. The poor in Latin America largely experienced such deaths in the late 1960s and early 1970s. For the Roman Catholic priest and theologian Gustavo Gutiérrez, "cultural death" refers to the repression of the poor and the efforts to liberate them from their deplorable conditions. The poor faced existential threats from "increased exposure to pathogens" and from decreased access to services.[2] Some experienced physical death due to hunger, malnutrition, and curable sickness.[3] In Gutiérrez's view, the developmentalist policies, which impelled some developed countries to invest in underdeveloped countries, failed to tackle adequately the root causes of the massive scale of poverty in Latin American countries.[4] The real issue was not the lack of job opportunities, but rather the complex situation in which human dignity and freedom were denied:

> The true face of Latin America is emerging in all its naked ugliness. It is not simply or primarily a question of low educational standards, a limited economy, an unsatisfactory legal system, or inadequate legal institutions. What we are faced with is a situation that takes no account of the dignity of human beings, or their most elemental needs, that does not provide for their biological survival, or their basic right to be free and autonomous. Poverty, injustice, alienation, and the exploitation of human beings by other human beings combine to form a situation that the Medellín conference did not hesitate to condemn as "institutionalized violence."[5]

A notable outcome of the developmentalist policies, which may well be an unintended consequence, is the dependency of Latin American countries on the more developed countries. Western capitalism, in Gutiérrez's assessment, is gravely implicated in the unfavorable conditions of the underdeveloped countries. He writes,

> The underdevelopment of the poor countries, as an overall social fact, appears in its true light: as the historical by-product of the development of other countries. The dynamics of the capitalist economy lead to the establishment of a center and

2. Farmer, "Health, Healing, and Social Justice," 200.

3. Gutiérrez, *We Drink from Our Own Wells*, 9–10. See also Gutiérrez, *Truth Shall Make You Free*, 9–10.

4. Gutiérrez, *Theology of Liberation*, 49–51.

5. Gutiérrez, *Power of the Poor in History*, 28.

a periphery, simultaneously generating progress and growing wealth for the few and social imbalances, political tensions, and poverty for many.[6]

One can hear Karl Marx's critique of capitalism in the background. Gutiérrez clearly adopts Marx's social analysis and hermeneutics. I will return later in this chapter to attend to Gutiérrez's use of Marxian thought. Here, I merely intend to highlight the context and assumptions that moved Gutiérrez to favor the concept of "liberation" over "development." For him, rising above the external domination of capitalist countries and the internal domination of the elites that control national power structures require "a social revolution" that aims to "radically and qualitatively change the conditions" of the oppressed.[7]

Religious ways of thinking and responding to the deplorable conditions of people in the lower sectors of Latin American countries preceded the liberation theology movements.[8] In some ways the *comunidades eclesiales de base* (the base ecclesial communities), which arose in the late 1950s, created the path for liberation theology movements to flourish in many parts of Latin America.[9] Informal theologies of the base ecclesial communities, which experimented with contextual ideas of reading Scripture in light of the Roman Catholic tradition and the experience of Latin Americans, were replete with the ideas of liberation. Such communities emerged as the laity in Latin America, beginning in Brazil, welcomed the pastoral responsibilities given to lay catechists by the Roman Catholic Church.[10] Gradually,

6. Gutiérrez, *Theology of Liberation*, 51.

7. Gutiérrez, *Theology of Liberation*, 54.

8. In a paper he presented in 1976 at the first conference organized by African, Asian, and Latin American theologians to explore common theological issues and concerns, which was held at Dar es Salaam, Tanzania, Gutiérrez made the following comments: "The years 1965–1968 were decisive for the popular movement in Latin America and for the Christian participation in that movement. Liberation theology struck deep roots in those years, and we cannot understand what happened at Medellín Episcopal Conference without reference to the life of Christian communities at that time." See Gutiérrez, "Two Theological Perspectives," 246.

9. The emergence of the base ecclesial communities may be traced back to the training of lay people in Brazil, many of whom led small Christian communities in rural areas with no direct access to the ordained priests. One of the factors that occasioned the training for the lay people was the growing influence of Protestantism in Brazil. In response, the first training center for lay people who would become catechists was inaugurated at Barra do Pirai (present-day Rio de Janeiro) in 1958 under the directives of Bishop Don Agnelo Rossi. The catechists led their communities "two or three times a week, for the purposes of reading the Bible, praying together, and singing hymns." See Dawson, *Birth and Impact of the Base Ecclesial Community*, 55.

10. Boff, *Ecclesiogenesis*, 2–3.

but unwaveringly, base communities read Scripture and evaluated church tradition in the light of their own life situations.

Rethinking whose rights it is to read and interpret the Bible (priest-lay catechist dynamics) and decide a church's structure was one of the consequences of the decision of the Roman Catholic Church to give more responsibility to the laity in order to address the shortage of priests in Latin America. The base ecclesial communities, which were the offshoots of the decision, raised questions about the hierarchical structures that promoted inequalities in the church. As Leonardo Boff observes,

> Christian life in the basic communities is characterized by the absence of alienating structures, by direct relationships, by reciprocity, by a deep communion, by mutual assistance, by communality of gospel ideals, by equality among members. The specific characteristics of society are absent here: rigid rules; hierarchies; prescribed relationships in a framework of a distinction of functions, qualities, and titles.[11]

These communities had other notable characteristics. The numerical size of each community, which is typically between twenty and fifty people, makes it possible for members to engage in direct relationships, to ruminate on their common faith, and to share in their joys and sufferings. The Second General Conference of Latin American Bishops (Puebla) commended the base ecclesial communities for their effective work in evangelization and also for promoting liberation and development in Latin America.[12]

Though some ideas of liberative praxis were present in the theologies of the base ecclesial communities, constructive and detailed reflection on liberation as a theological hermeneutic began with professional theologians. Some of them participated in the Conferences of Latin American Bishops that took place in the 1900s. Between 1955 and 1979, Latin American Roman Catholic bishops held three episcopal conferences that highlighted the quest of some church leaders to articulate the identity of Roman Catholics and forms of Catholicism in Latin America. The first of these conferences was held in Rio de Janerio, Brazil, in 1955 and resulted in the founding of *Consejo Episcopal Latinoamericano* (CELAM).[13] The Second and Third Episcopal Conferences of Latin American bishops have had more influence on the writings of liberation theologians. The Second General Conference was held in Medellín, Colombia, in 1968, and the Third

11. Boff, *Ecclesiogenesis*, 4.

12. Third General Conference of Latin American Bishops, "Pastoral Overview of the Reality That Is Latin America," I.3.96, in *Puebla*, 47–48.

13. Gott, "Introduction," 10–13.

General Conference was held in Puebla, Mexico, in 1979. These conferences, which were both pastoral and theological in focus, prompted some Christian leaders in Latin America, especially Roman Catholic priests, to assess "with a pastoral eye some of the aspects of the present sociocultural context in which the church is carrying out its mission, and also the pastoral reality that confronts evangelization as it is operative today and as it moves into the future."[14] To effectively do evangelism, priests are to "know the Latin American people in their historical context and their varied circumstances."[15] This was a call to do theology contextually.

The official documents of the Medellín conference covered a vast range of topics, including theology, pastoral exhortations, and analyses of the education, economic, and social structures of Latin America. The documents espoused three themes that are of great value to the project of Latin American liberation theology. First is the call for the churches of Latin America to understand the signs of the times. A church's evangelization should be in "harmony with the 'signs of the times.' It cannot be outside time or history. In fact, 'the signs of the times' . . . constitute a 'theological situation' and a mandate from God."[16] Second, the church should be open to self-criticism as it opposes the socioeconomic and political structures that impoverish people. It should oppose "institutionalized violence"—the type of violence that is grounded in exploitative and repressive social order—and seek the transformation of Latin America with the intent to bring about a more just society:

> As the Christian believes in the productiveness of peace in order to achieve justice, he also believes that justice is a prerequisite for peace. He recognizes that in many instances Latin America finds itself faced with a situation of injustice that can be called institutionalized violence, when, because of a structural deficiency of industry and agriculture, of national and international economy, of cultural and political life, "whole towns lack necessities, live in such dependency as hinders all initiative and responsibility as well as every possibility for cultural promotion and participation in social and political life," thus violating

14. Third General Conference of Latin American Bishops, "Pastoral Overview of the Reality That Is Latin America," I.1, in *Puebla*, 37.

15. Third General Conference of Latin American Bishops, "Pastoral Overview of the Reality That Is Latin America," I.1.3, in *Puebla*, 37.

16. Second General Council of Latin American Bishops, "Pastoral Concern for the Elites," 7.II.13, in *Church in the Present-Day Transformation of Latin America*, 132.

fundamental rights. This situation demands all-embracing, cou-
rageous, urgent and profoundly renovating transformations.[17]

Third, the church should be in solidarity with the poor by giving
priority to their situations. It should follow in the footsteps of Jesus Christ
who demonstrated his special love for the poor by providing for them, by
critiquing the social and religious structures that oppressed them, and by
living in poverty in solidarity with them. The church should recognize that
Jesus's mission "centered on advising the poor of their liberation."[18] It should
equally attend to the dignity of the poor and explore ways that can empower
them to pursue liberation from oppressive structures.[19]

The organizers of the Third Episcopal Conference (Puebla, 1979) were
not as supportive to liberation theologians as the organizers of the Medellín
conference (1968). Arthur McGovern names the Colombian-born Bishop
Alfonso Lopez Trujillo, who became the general-secretary of CELAM in
1972, as the chief antagonist that was partly responsible for the unfavorable
view of liberation theology and liberation theologians in the mid-1970s.
According to McGovern, prior to the Puebla conference, "Bishop Lopez
Trujillo did indeed try to select delegates and to promote a document that
would clamp down on the liberation movement."[20] Though Bishop Trujillo
did not succeed in clamping down on the project of liberation theology, his
unfavorable view of it most likely was responsible for the weakened "socioeconomic analyses and the theological perspectives enunciated at Puebla,"
which "lacked the forcefulness of Medellín."[21] Yet despite the measured support for the project of liberation theologians by the organizers of the Puebla
conference, its official documents made the case for the preferential option
for the poor.[22] It is within this historical context that Gustavo Gutiérrez
embarked on a sustained theological response to the plight and liberation
of the poor in Latin America.

17. Second General Council of Latin American Bishops, "Peace," 2.II.16, in *Church
in the Present-Day Transformation of Latin America*, 78.

18. Second General Council of Latin American Bishops, "Poverty of the Church,"
14.II.7, in *Church in the Present-Day Transformation of Latin America*, 215.

19. Second General Council of Latin American Bishops, "Poverty of the Church,"
14.III.11, in *Church in the Present-Day Transformation of Latin America*, 217.

20. McGovern, *Liberation Theology and Its Critics*, 14.

21. McGovern, *Liberation Theology and Its Critics*, 14.

22. "A Missionary Church Serving Evangelization in Latin America," IV.1.1134–
1253, in Third General Conference of Latin American Bishops, *Puebla*, 178–91.

Gustavo Gutiérrez's Theological Response
to the Plight of the Poor

The esteemed Peruvian theologian Gustavo Gutiérrez was one of the key progenitors of Latin American liberation theology. Born into a poor Amerindian (Quechua) family in Peru, Gutiérrez endured not only poverty but also the burden of belonging to a marginalized group.[23] Evidently, when Gutiérrez writes about the poor, the oppressed, and the marginalized, he does so not merely from his cognitive grasp of economic and theological analyses of the situation of the poor but also from his personal experience.[24] Living among and also serving the poor in Peru after his return from studies in Europe only deepened his struggles to make sense of the Christian faith by attempting to understand it from the perspective of the poor. Interestingly, his European theological education did not adequately prepare him for the theological questions embodied by the life of the marginalized sectors of his Peruvian society.[25] He was convinced that the poor confront the church with a quizzical face:

> How can we thank God for the gift of life when the reality around us is one of premature and unjustly inflicted death? How can we express joy at knowing ourselves to be loved by the Father when we see the suffering of our brothers and sisters? How can we sing the [the Lord's song] when the suffering of an entire people chokes the sound in our throats?[26]

23. Brown, *Gustavo Gutiérrez*, 21–22.

24. Robert McAffee Brown has noted that Gutiérrez's theology was "born in the midst of his sharing in the struggle of oppressed peoples to achieve liberation. Where they come from, what their grievances are, why the received theologies are inadequate for them, all influence the theology that grows out of that ongoing struggle." Brown, *Gustavo Gutiérrez*, 21.

25. In 1959, Gutiérrez completed his masters of theology degree at the Catholic University of Lyons (also known as the Catholic Institute of Theology). In an unorthodox academic tradition, Gutiérrez applied and received a doctorate degree in theology from the Catholic University of Lyons on May 29, 1985, on the basis of his published works and contributions to theological discourse. Christian Duquoc, the director of the dissertation, made the following comments in his opening remarks during Gutiérrez's doctoral defense: "The theology being done in Latin America has shown the extent to which Western theology has failed to take into account the evil effects of a success [of Western societies]." By "evil effects," Duquoc meant the situation of the poor and "the rupture hidden in success of society like the European." The text of the discussions can be found in Gutiérrez, *Truth Shall Make You Free*, 1–52.

26. Gutiérrez, *We Drink from Our Own Wells*, 7.

Against several odds, including poverty and illness, Gustavo has emerged as one of the major proponents of Latin American liberation theology.[27] Though he had to wait until September of 2013 to be (unofficially) invited to the Vatican by Pope Francis, the Vatican pontificate apparently signaled the necessity of recognizing him as a key Latin American Roman Catholic intellectual and theologian.[28] Gutiérrez's theological work has given a spur to different theological conversations around the world, especially those that emphasize human liberation from oppressive structures. He credits grassroots theological questions and reflections of Latin American Christians for the discovery of "liberation" as a central Christian theological solution to material poverty.[29] His unique contribution to the discipline of Christian theology is the positioning of the church as a prophetic interlocutor that actively engages in liberative praxis with the aim to empower the poor to seek liberation from oppression. As a prophetic interlocutor, the church should constantly discern the signs of the times and also should call the attention of Christians and nations to the experience of the poor—the marginalized victims of oppressive structures and social injustice. As the interlocutor that engages in liberative praxis, the church should embody the liberation of the poor through the practices of identifying with them and also by opposing oppressive structures that cause poverty.

Gutiérrez is rightly regarded as one the most influential liberation theologians. Leonardo Boff puts him on equal par with other "creators of an epistemological break" such as Aquinas, Luther, Descartes, Kant, Hegel, and Rahner.[30] But what exactly is the nature of Gutiérrez's intellectual break with the theological paradigms that preceded him? For Boff, it is Gutiérrez's location of his theology beyond the old theological approaches that were preoccupied with the rationality and systemization of Christian beliefs. Although he did not totally disregard the old theological approaches, he

27. Gutiérrez was bedridden because of osteomyelitis when he was twelve years old and was only able to overcome the stronghold of the illness when he was eighteen. See Nickoloff, "Introduction," 2.

28. Yardley and Romero, "Pope's Focus on Poor Revives Scorned Theology."

29. He wrote: "For many Christians active involvement in popular liberation struggles has created a wholly new way of living, celebrating, and communicating their faith. Poor or rich, they have deliberately and explicitly identified with the oppressed in our continent. They have come to that commitment by different paths, determined by class origin and personal philosophy, and have broken with their pasts in different ways. This is the major fact in the recent life of the Christian community in Latin America. It is the source and matrix of the effort at theological clarification that led to theology of liberation, which can only be understood in relation to liberation practice." Gutiérrez, "Two Theological Perspectives," 227.

30. Boff, "Originality of the Theology of Liberation," 38.

brought historical praxis to the center of his theological method. An under-lying principle driving his discussion on the church's *historical praxis*—its particular form of action—is theologizing from the perspective and also for the interest of the oppressed.[31] Boff observes that in "doing so [Gutiérrez] has inaugurated forever a new way of doing theology, from the transform-ing action, from within the action, as a critique of and in support of this action for liberation."[32] Focusing specifically on the Latin American context, Gutiérrez sees the task of a Christian theologian as engaging in a critical reflection that ought to be "the fruit of a confrontation between the Word accepted in faith and historical praxis."[33]

Several voices—religious, economic, and theological—guided Gutiér-rez's theological reflections on the questions that the poor address to the Christian faith.[34] One such voice was the Spanish historian and missionary Bartolomé de Las Casas (1484–1566). Gutiérrez describes him as a "fierce champion of the equality of all humans" and as one who concretized the idea of salvation in Christ by linking it to the establishment of social justice.[35] He also contends that Bartolomé de Las Casas should be seen as a precursor of the notion of God's preferential option for the poor, a concept that is central to his theological reflections on the poor and poverty. He writes, "The poor are God's favorite persons because, says Las Casas, 'of the least and most forgotten, God has an altogether fresh and vivid memory.' This preference for the poor, marginalized, and downtrodden, then, ought to be a norm of life for the Christian."[36] Gutiérrez equally engaged and learned from Peru-vian poets and social critics whose writings provided great insights into the life of the marginalized. One such poet is César Vallejo (1892–1938). In *The God of Life*, he acknowledges the impact of Vallejo on his theological read-ing of the book of Job. He writes,

> Shortly before his death, [César] Vallejo dictated these dramatic and trust-filled lines to his wife Georgette: "Whatever be the cause I must defend before God after death, I myself have a defender: God." In the language of the Bible he had a *goel* [de-fender]. This was a God whose fleeting presence he had felt at certain moments of his life. On this occasion, in a decisive hour

31. Boff, "Originality of the Theology of Liberation," 39.
32. Boff, "Originality of the Theology of Liberation," 39.
33. Gutiérrez, *Theology of Liberation*, 47.
34. See Gutiérrez, *On Job*, xiv–xvii.
35. Gutiérrez, "Indian," xv, xviii.
36. Gutiérrez, "Indian," xx.

of his life, he sees this God at his side as he faces the judgment that his life has merited from the same God.[37]

Gutiérrez sees in Vallejo's perception of God a similar imagination of God's role in human life, the life of the poor in particular, in Job's understanding of God (Job 19:25–27).

Gutiérrez borrowed from and also engaged the theological ideas of the official documents of both the Medellín and Puebla episcopal conferences. The publication of his groundbreaking work, *Teología de la liberación* (*A Theology of Liberation*), in 1971 brought the ideas of liberation of theology into the consciousness of many Christian theological communities around the world.[38] In the introduction of the first edition of *A Theology of Liberation*, Gutiérrez describes the goal of the book as

> an attempt at reflection, based on the gospel and the experiences
> of men and women committed to the process of liberation in the
> oppressed and exploited land of Latin America. It is a theologi-
> cal reflection born of the experience of shared efforts to abolish
> the current unjust situation and to build a different society, freer
> and more human.[39]

In this book and his subsequent publications, he explored theological rationales and warrants for bringing the Christian faith into the public discourse on social justice. His vision for a just society and the role of theology, Christian theology in particular, in the construction of such society will be the focus of the remainder of this chapter. I will begin with his theological method.

Theological Method

At the heart of Gutiérrez's theology is an exegesis of a society in order to discern its social ills and also an exegesis of Christian Scriptures and eccle-sial traditions with the intent to discern the form of spirituality that ought to inform Christians' response to the social ills of a society. His theological method is deeply informed by his understanding of the condition of the poor, the sociocultural structures that have perpetuated poverty in Latin America and the Caribbean, and the role that Christian theology can play in overcoming poverty. In *We Drink from Our Own Wells*, he argues that

37. Gutiérrez, *God of Life*, 158.

38. Orbis books published an English translation in 1973 under the title: *A Theology of Liberation*.

39. Gutiérrez, *Theology of Liberation*, xiii.

doing Christian theology requires two, albeit related, stages: (1) deliberating on the life of Christian communities in light of their faith in God and (2) articulating and expressing the content of the life of faith.[40] For him, the reflection on the experience of following Jesus Christ in discipleship constitutes the central theme of any solid theology. Therefore, in theological reflections, the communities of Jesus's disciples are to be made aware that they are under the movement of the Holy Spirit, who calls upon them to proclaim the good news: "The Lord is risen! Death and injustice are not the final word of history. Christianity is a message of life, a message based on the gratuitous love of the Father for us."[41]

For Gutiérrez, the impetus for Christian theology arises as believers attempt to understand the Christian faith in light of their life situation. Therefore, a theological outline or "pre-understanding of the faith" is in all Christians insofar as they seek to live their lives in a manner that conforms to the Christian faith.[42] Given that theological outlines are present in Christians, theologians are to exegete the life situations of Christian communities with the intent to access such outlines and also to use them as the foundations of their theologies. "Foundation" is not merely a starting point, but rather "the soil in which theological reflection stubbornly and permanently sinks its roots and from which it derives its strength."[43] As I argued in chapter 1, the context—i.e., the history, culture, and contemporary state of affairs—of a Christian community performs essential tasks in the formation of Christian theology. For example, it provides the raw materials or "outlines," to use Gutiérrez's word, with which theologians can construct refined theological products—Christian theological messages that address theological questions embedded in the life situation of Christians. A theological product should not be merely a result of reflections on the life situation of a community but also a result of participating in the struggles of the community for liberation.[44] Theological activity, therefore, should bring together reflection and praxis—active participation in society, especially in transforming the social structures that impoverish and dehumanize people. The crucial methodological framework espoused by Gutiérrez is that theological activity

---

40. Gutiérrez, *We Drink from Our Own Wells*, 136.

41. Gutiérrez, *We Drink from Our Own Wells*, 1.

42. Gutiérrez, *Theology of Liberation*, 3

43. Gutiérrez, *Theology of Liberation*, 3.

44. "Theology must be a critical reflection on humankind, on basic human principles. Only with this approach will theology be a serious discourse, aware of itself, in full possession of its conceptual elements." Gutiérrez, *Theology of Liberation*, 9.

should not be "simple affirmations . . . of truths, but of a commitment, an overall attitude, and particular posture toward life."[45]

As noted earlier, liberation theology, which played a key part in the Latin American liberation movements in the late 1960s, began as grassroots theological reflection on the struggles and exploitations of many Latin Americans. Gutiérrez has argued that without the grassroots theological reflections of the common people and also the "populist movement and its historical praxis of liberation," liberation theology as an academic exercise might not have arisen.[46] The ways in which Latin American Christians, especially the laity, attempted to make sense of their Christian faith in light of their situations, became an important theological well from which academic theologians drew inspirations and insights. Given that history "is the concrete locale of human encounter" with the Triune God, in Gutiérrez's view, it is expedient to reinterpret human history from the standpoint of the hopes and struggles of the "losers" (the marginalized) and not from the perspectives of the "winners" (the rulers and the powerful) of this world.[47] He argued that the church's commitment to the world's and people's wellness ought to be the privileged *locus theologicus* of Christian theology.[48] In his reflection on Job 16:2–6, he argued against doing theology that does not grapple with the real-life situations of people. For him, Job 16:2–6 is a "rejection of a way of theologizing that does not take account of concrete situations, of the sufferings and hopes of human beings."[49]

Liberation theology is in a sense the pursuit of a *theological hyphen* that would help Christians to effectively bring into dialogical communication two seemly conflicting states of affairs; namely, God's gratuitous love for humanity and the dehumanizing condition of the poor (those who are materially or economically poor) in Latin America. Gutiérrez makes this point in *On Job*:

> How are we to talk about a God who is revealed as love in a situation characterized by poverty and oppression? How are we to proclaim the God of life to men and women who die prematurely and unjustly? How are we to acknowledge that God makes us a free gift of life and justice when we have before us the suffering of the innocent? What words are we to use in telling those who are not even regarded as persons that they are

45. Gutiérrez, *Theology of Liberation*, 6.
46. Gutiérrez, "Two Theological Perspectives," 240.
47. Gutiérrez, "Two Theological Perspectives," 248.
48. Gutiérrez, *Theology of Liberation*, 9.
49. Gutiérrez, *On Job*, 29.

the daughters and sons of God? These are key questions being asked in the theology that has been forming in Latin America and in other places throughout the world where the situation is the same.[50]

The questions that Gutiérrez raises here, which arose from the situation of the poor, are deeply theological and therefore merit the attention of Christian theologians. As a contextual theologian, Gutiérrez pressed these questions and also the contexts of Latin America of his day for some theological materials with which to construct his theology. For example, the critique of a deed-consequence principle in the book of Job, the theme of the suffering of the innocent, and the celebration of a "disinterested religion . . . as true religion" have shaped Gutiérrez's imagination of how to speak and relate to God in the context of unjust and underserved suffering.[51] He also drew upon theological materials from Scripture and church traditions. I will, however, begin with the theological materials he extracted from the context of Latin Americans.

Theological Materials from the Latin American Context

I will discuss two major theological materials embedded in the experience of the poor that can be discerned in Gutiérrez's theological writings. These are the irruption of the poor and the use of Marxian hermeneutics to exegete the social condition of Latin American poverty.

Irruption of the Poor

The expression "irruption of the poor" in Latin American liberation theologies, especially in Gutiérrez's theology, refers to the idea of coming to terms with or realizing one's condition. It is the poor's awareness of their unjust condition and the need to fight for their liberation and freedom from oppressive institutions. In his words, the *irruption of the poor* "means that those who until now were 'absent' from history are gradually becoming 'present' in it."[52] This form of irruption was already building up before the late 1960s when theologians started to engage in constructive theological reflection on the situation (suffering and pathos) of the poor and the need for their liberation. However, they seized the opportunity and the

50. Gutiérrez, *On Job*, xiv.

51. See Gutiérrez, *On Job*, 5–30.

52. Gutiérrez, *Truth Shall Make You Free*, 8.

theological insights these provided. For instance, some were inspired to develop theological critiques of some aspects of the life and teaching of the church that were unhelpful to the needs of the poor. "When the wretched of the earth awake," contends Gutiérrez, "their first challenge is not to religion but to the social, economic, and political order oppressing them and to the ideology supporting it."[53]

In Gutiérrez's assessment, the majority of poor Latin Americans in the 1960s and 1970s preferred "social revolution" to "reform" as the most viable path to their liberation from dependence "on external powers and domination by internal minorities" that "typify the social structures of Latin America."[54] Convinced that in the final analysis poverty means "death," he argued that the irruption of the poor, which has brought into sharp focus the life and pathos of the poor, prompted important theological questions. Among the many theological questions that the irruption of the poor raises are: How does the God that Christians call a loving father and creator view the poor of this world? How is Christian theology relevant to the experience of the poor of Latin America who are largely the victims of oppressive structures? What does a life destined to death as a result of poverty say about God's love for humanity? He challenged theologians to answer these questions in a manner that displays the good news the Christian faith promises to the world. For example, if the irruption of the poor raised questions about the worthiness of the life of the poor facing death due to malnutrition or curable diseases, Christian theologians should show how the Christian gospel promotes human life and flourishing.[55] For him, the life of the poor, which is an embodiment of non-love, exclusion, and denial of social rights, challenges Christians to reflect deeply on what it means to say to poor people: "God loves you."[56] They are to show how the irruption of the

53. Gutiérrez, "Two Theological Perspectives," 240.

54. Gutiérrez, "Two Theological Perspectives," 240. To Gutiérrez, liberation from oppressive structures requires "a social revolution, which will radically and qualitatively change the conditions" in which the oppressed live. See Gutiérrez, *Theology of Liberation*, 54, 59. The Argentine theologian Jose Bonino shares the same view of the role of revolution in Latin Americans' protest against unjust social systems. He writes, "as a Latin American Christian I am convinced—with many other Latin Americans who have tried to understand the situation of our people and to place it in the world perspective—that revolutionary action aimed at changing the basic economic, political, social and cultural structures and conditions of life is imperative today." See Bonino, *Christians and Marxists*, 7–8.

55. Gutiérrez, "Expanding the View," 6. See also Gutiérrez, *We Drink from Our Own Wells*, 28.

56. Gutiérrez, "Saying and Showing to the Poor," 27.

poor "means a genuine irruption of God" in the lives of poor people.[57] The poor experience God through their suffering, joy, doubts, and hopes. Yet their expendable life raised questions about God's gift of life.

The phenomenon of the irruption of the poor gradually nudged many Latin American liberation theologians to develop theologies that are rooted in actual human history.[58] Attending to human history opened new opportunities for them to begin to imagine the God of the Bible as the being that orientates the world in the direction of justice and the establishment of just societies.[59] Many began to respond to poverty and to the situation of the poor in ways that were grounded in Jesus's life as a poor Galilean and his commitment to the poor. For Gutiérrez, Jesus's answer to the condition of the poor consisted of liberating words and acts. He writes,

> When Jesus made human beings see and walk and hear and, in short, gave them life, he was giving an example for that time and a mandate to the Christian community throughout history. This is what is meant by "remembering the poor," and it is something we should be "eager to do" (Gal 2:10). There is no authentic evangelization that is not accompanied by action in behalf of the poor.[60]

In other words, Jesus's act of healing gave "full meaning to the good news for the poor" and constituted a summon to his followers to be the witnesses to God's care for the lives of the poor.[61]

It is noteworthy that Gutiérrez aimed to construct a theology that passed the test of Christian orthodoxy (right doctrines and beliefs) and the test of Christian orthopraxy (right deeds and actions).[62] These dual tasks, which he viewed as a theological dyad, compelled him to pursue concrete actions that are appropriate in terms of their fidelity to the Christian faith and the actuals needs of the poor. For him, Christian theology, and consequently Christian theologians, should clarify for followers of Jesus Christ that the Easter message ("the Lord is risen!") is a witness to God's declaration that "death and injustice are not the final word of history" and also that God's love for all people is most vividly expressed in the liberation of the poor.[63] In their theological undertakings, Christians are to embrace

57. Gutiérrez, *We Drink from Our Own Wells*, xix.

58. Gutiérrez, *Power of the Poor in History*, 7.

59. Gutiérrez, *Power of the Poor in History*, 7.

60. Gutiérrez, *We Drink from Our Own Wells*, 43–44.

61. Gutiérrez, *We Drink from Our Own Wells*, 44–45.

62. Gutiérrez, *We Drink from Our Own Wells*, xviii.

63. Gutiérrez, *We Drink from Our Own Wells*, 1.

the "critique that comes from practice—the following of Jesus."[64] And, for him, the act of following Jesus requires that Christians "walk with and be in commitment to the poor" since in doing so they will "experience an encounter with the Lord who is simultaneously revealed and hidden in the faces of the poor (Matt 25:31–46)."[65]

The phenomenon of irruption of the poor did not only raise questions about Christian discipleship but also questions about God's attitude toward the poor. In his response to God's attitude towards the poor, Gutiérrez contends that the irruption of the poor should become, methodologically speaking, a theological hermeneutical lens. Using the irruption of the poor as a theological lens, of course, required a new way of doing theology that would push a theologian to make the life situation of the poor a theological workshop. Adopting such theological hermeneutics implies that Christian theologians should become both what might be described as *armchair theologians* and *fieldwork theologians*. As fieldwork theologians, they are to become exegetes of the present-day context of a society, particularly the complex structures that are responsible for poverty. As armchair theologians, they are to become attentive exegetes of Scripture, church tradition, and relevant theological literature.

Returning to the issue of God's attitude toward to the poor, it will be helpful to recall that one of the unique contributions of Gutiérrez to the field of contextual theology is the repositioning of Christian practice in the center of theological reflections, instead of having it at the margins or construing it as an afterthought.[66] Such repositioning of Christian practice (spirituality) in the center of theological reflection implies that theologians are to make the life situation of Christians the arena in which Christian theology (critical reflection on the Christian faith) is constantly worked out. But how does this way of understanding the place of Christian practice in theological reflections relate to his thinking on God's attitude toward the poor? Commenting on the nature of Christian spirituality or discipleship vis-à-vis the poor, he argues that Christians are to embody God's preferential love for the poor of this world by empowering them to seek liberation from the forces that create and perpetuate poverty. In his view, framing the relationship of the situation of the poor and Christian theology in a manner

---

64. Gutiérrez, *We Drink from Our Own Wells*, 51.

65. Gutiérrez, *We Drink from Our Own Wells*, 38.

66. Reflecting on the question "Who do you say that I am," which Jesus posed to his disciples at Caesarea Philippi (Mark 8), Gutiérrez argues: "[W]e cannot give a merely theoretical or theological answer. What answers it, in the final analysis, is our life, our personal history, our manner of living of the gospel." Gutiérrez, *We Drink from Our Own Wells*, 51.

in which Christian spirituality (the practice of following Jesus's way of life) takes a center stage opens the door for a robust understanding of the role of the church in fighting against poverty. He argues that Christian "spirituality" should not be viewed as the concern of the "dispossessed and marginalized" and those who support the question for liberation. Also, Christian spirituality should not be restricted to individual piety.[67] On the contrary, Christian spirituality concerns the practice of liberation, that is, the process of giving life to the poor who are facing death as a result of malnutrition, curable diseases, and dehumanizing conditions.

The life of the poor, for Gutiérrez, constitutes a "restless gospel—restless and threatening to the big and the powerful of the world."[68] His theological imagination vis-à-vis the poor of Latin America aimed to empower Latin Americans to undertake the related tasks of speaking about the liberation of the poor and acting in ways that bring about the liberation of the poor. He pressed for answers—theological answers—to the question: How can we say to the poor that God is a loving father? Given his conviction that Christianity's evangelical mandate—to proclaim God as good news to all people—is incompatible with the existence of unjust structures, he contends that the church must "break its ties with an unjust social order" even if it means risking the church's freedom to live out its faith publicly without interference from the custodians of unjust political structures.[69] In his view, the church in Latin America (the Roman Catholic Church, in particular) was complicit in the presence of poverty, either "by its links with the established order" or "by silence regarding the evils this order implies"; identifying this is an important step in identifying with the situation of the poor.[70] He challenged the church to rethink its relationship with the political orders and its attitude toward the poor. In order to successfully engage in such acts of rethinking, he asserted that church should gain knowledge about the situation of the poor, a task that would require Latin American Christians to use available intellectual (theological and non-theological) resources available to them for examining the different causes of poverty in the continent. As we will see in the next section, Karl Marx's discussion on the poor in the context of a capitalist society and also Marxists' discourse on the situation of the poor provided a helpful intellectual resource to many liberation theologians for assessing the causes of poverty in Latin America. Gutiérrez dialogued with Marxists in his exploration of how best to reread

67. Gutiérrez, *We Drink from Our Own Wells*, 13–16.
68. Gutiérrez, "Response," 184. See also Gutiérrez, *Power of the Poor in History*, 37.
69. Gutiérrez, *Theology of Liberation*, 61, 72, 81.
70. Gutiérrez, *Theology of Liberation*, 63.

and reappropriate biblical texts that discuss the situation of the poor and God's concern for the poor. I unpack this claim below.

Marxian Hermeneutics: Exploitative Systems
as the Prime Cause of Poverty

For Gutiérrez, Europe's industrial revolutions produced bourgeois societies. The bourgeoisie were both agents and beneficiaries of the industrial revolution, especially the dominance that was occasioned by the exploitation of Europe's working class and the poor.[71] Realizing that their condition was not primarily the result of laziness but rather a result of exploitative structures, the poor increasingly sought to liberate themselves from such structures.[72] The exploitative socioeconomic structures raised theological questions insofar as they dehumanized the image bearers of God. Borrowing some ideas from Marxism, although not uncritically, Gutiérrez sets out in most of his theological writings to make the case that the condition of the poor in Latin America, when understood as a social problem, is not the result of personal mistakes but rather the result of oppressive social and cultural structures.

What role did Marxian thoughts on poverty play in Latin American liberation theology? Marxism's relation to Latin American liberation theology should be understood within the matrix of the life situation of the Latin American poor who inspired several liberation theologians. In Gutiérrez's words,

> theology does in fact find itself in direct and fruitful confrontation with Marxism, and it is to a large extent due to Marxism's influence that theological thought, searching for its own sources, has begun to reflect on the meaning of the transformation of this world and human action in history.[73]

Bringing Christian theology into dialogic communication with Marxism, especially its critical analysis of the socioeconomic and political structures that gravely impact the working class, helped liberation theologians to focus attention on the transformation of the world. In *The Truth Shall Make You Free*, Gutiérrez hints at his intent to explore the relationship between social sciences and the Christian faith: to study "social reality for the purposes of a better understanding, in the light given by [Christian] faith, of the challenge and possibilities that this reality presents to the church in

---

71. Gutiérrez, "Two Theological Perspectives," 231.
72. Gutiérrez, *We Drink from Our Own Wells*, 20.
73. Gutiérrez, *Theology of Liberation*, 8.

its work of evangelization."[74] The context he provides here is useful for understanding his use of Marxian thought; namely, to undertake the necessary task of "social analysis in order to understand [the Latin American] situation—not in order to use [such] analysis in the study of matters more strictly theological."[75] In other words, drawing resources from the field of social sciences, particularly the resources that pertain to the assessment of the social condition of a society, is useful to theologians who aim to express the Christian faith concretely in real life.

There is no attempt by Gutiérrez to accept Marxism as a judge of the Christian faith. Rather he draws upon the work of Karl Marx and some Marxian scholars with the intent to analyze the social and economic conditions that caused massive scale poverty in Latin America. He writes,

> At no time, either explicitly or implicitly, have I suggested a dialogue with Marxism with a view to a possible "synthesis" or to accepting one aspect while leaving others aside. Such undertakings were indeed frequent during those years in Europe . . . and were beginning to be frequent in Latin American circles. Such was not my own intention, for my pastoral practice imposed needs of a quite different kind.[76]

As Andrew Levine has observed, Marxism's "remedy" for poverty "consists in overcoming capitalism by instituting an economic order based on social ownership and forms of economic coordination that avoid the deleterious consequences of market arrangements or, or at least, of markets 'as we know them.'"[77] Gutiérrez clearly favors socialism over capitalism not because the former is immune to exploitative structures but rather because the latter was the key culprit in the exploitation of the working class in Latin America.[78] Naming the United States of America as the most powerful capitalist nation, Gutiérrez blames capitalism as the major factor in the oppressive economic structures that were responsible for the debilitating conditions of the working class in Latin America.[79]

Since Gutiérrez named the United States of America as one of the culprits in the form of poverty that arises from capitalism, I would like to say a few words about the grip of neoliberal economics and political theory on

74. Gutiérrez, *Truth Shall Make You Free*, 58

75. Gutiérrez, *Truth Shall Make You Free*, 58.

76. Gutiérrez, *Truth Shall Make You Free*, 63. For some helpful discussions on Latin American Christianity and Marxism, see Bonino, *Christians and Marxists*.

77. Levin, "Marxism and Poverty," 262.

78. See Gutiérrez, *Theology of Liberation*, 54, 64–67.

79. Gutiérrez, *Theology of Liberation*, 54.

American socioeconomic life, and the challenge it poses to Christianity.[80] Neoliberal economics promote capital arrangements and the mechanisms for servicing and safeguarding them, which are geared toward amassing profits and wealth. The 2008 catastrophic financial crisis has done very little to curb the surge of neoliberal economic policies of many countries, including the United States of America. The crisis, however, unleashed intense debates on the morality of certain business practices and policies.[81] For some American Christians, a neoliberal economic system is biblically warranted. For instance, in *The Poverty of Nations*, Wayne Grudem and Barry Asmus argued that the free-market economic system is grounded in Christianity's moral teaching. Though they concede the presence of some bad players in the free-market economic game, they argue that it tends "to discourage and punish wrong behavior and [tends] to encourage and reward virtuous behavior, and does these things better than other economic systems" available.[82] Conversely, Cynthia Moe-Lobeda has noted that although a neoliberal economy generates "growth" (increasing national income, wealth, production, and consumption), it deceptively conceals or minimizes its devastating exploitative tendencies.[83] An example of such exploitative tendencies is embodied by some workers who are overburdened with a larger number of tasks because of their employers' quests for cheap labor and excessive profits. Neoliberalism, especially its "model of economic globalization," for her, "disables moral agency—the capacity to embody active love," which entails creating "economically sustainable, socially just, and compassionate communities."[84] Kathryn Tanner has a harsher criticism of finance-dominated capitalism, an essential feature of the neoliberal economic system. "The general mechanisms employed by Christianity to assure wholehearted commitment to God," writes Tanner, "run radically contrary . . . to those

80. I adopt David Harvey's description of neoliberalism as "a theory of political and economic practices that proposes that human well-being can best be advanced by liberating individual entrepreneurial freedoms and skills within an institutional framework characterized by strong private property rights, free markets, and free trade. The role of the state is to create and preserve an institutional framework appropriate to such practices. The state has to guarantee, for example, the quality and integrity of money . . . State interventions (once created) must be kept to a bare minimum because, according to the theory, the state cannot possibly possess enough information to second-guess market signals (prices) and because powerful interest groups will inevitably distort and bias state interventions (particularly in democracies) for their own benefit." Harvey, *Brief History of Neoliberalism*, 3.

81. Braedley and Luxton, "Competing Philosophies," 4.

82. Grudem and Asmus, *Poverty of Nations*, 187–88.

83. Moe-Lobeda, *Healing a Broken World*, 48.

84. Moe-Lobeda, *Healing a Broken World*, 46.

used by finance-dominated capitalism to induce total compliance."[85] Gutiérrez would most likely agree with the criticisms marshalled by Moe-Lobeda
and Tanner against the destructive aspects of capitalism. In his view, capitalism creates "a situation of dependency" that forces the developing countries
to be "kept in a condition of neocolonialism."[86] Though Gutiérrez does not
explicitly discuss the relationship between "socialism" and "social revolution"—he clearly prefers the latter to the former—he sees both as a concrete
critique of the capitalist system.

Beyond the theological materials he discerned in the context of
Latin America, Gutiérrez also drew upon theological materials that he
discerned in Christian Scripture. I examine some of these theological materials below. He used the materials to construct his theological solutions
to the exploitative structures that Marxism helped him to identify in the
Latin American context.

Theological Materials from Scripture

Christian Scripture is replete with discussions about the poor. Two broad
categories of the poor can be discerned in both the Old Testament (Hebrew
Bible) and the New Testament. We may describe these two categories as the
poor in spirit and the *poor in body*. Broadly, the poor in spirit may be understood in two different ways. Negatively, it may refer to the people who
are spiritually bankrupt. They are people who are spiritually unhealthy.
They could be people who do not have a relationship with God through
Jesus Christ (John 3:18) or Jesus's disciples who are not living faithfully
in conformity to his teaching (John 15:1–17; Rom 12:1–2). Some might
have got into this condition because of experiencing hardships that are the
result of poverty and oppressive structures.[87] According to Mark Powell,
Jesus's announcement of divine blessing upon the "poor in spirit" points
to "eschatological reversals for the unfortunate and eschatological rewards
for the virtuous."[88] Positively, the poor in spirit refers to people who are
spiritually humble and recognize their vulnerability, finitude, and sinful-
ness before God (Matt 5:3; Jas 2:5).[89]

---

85. Tanner, *Christianity and the New Spirit of Capitalism*, 87.

86. Gutiérrez, *Theology of Liberation*, 64–65.

87. Powell, "Matthew's Beatitudes," 460–69; Smith, "'Blessed Are the Poor in (Holy)
Spirit'?," 389–96.

88. Powell, "Matthew's Beatitudes," 460.

89. For discussions on the phrase "Poor in Spirit," see Simonetti, *Matthew 1–13*,
79–81; Barbu, "Poor in Spirit and Our Life in Christ," 261–74.

The poor in body are people who lack basic material ingredients for a quality life (such as sources of income, food, and shelter) that they rightly deserve as human beings and creatures in the image of God (see Deut 15:4, 7, 11; 24:12; Job 5:15; 2 Sam 22:28; Ps 72:13; 107:41; Job 24:9; Prov 22:22; Isa 26:6; Hab 3:14; Matt 5:3; 19:21; 26:9; Luke 6:20; Jas 2:5–6; Rev 13:15). The Hebrew terms *ebyon, ani,* and *dal,* and the Greek term *ptochos,* when understood collectively, describe the horrendous experiences of the poor: dehumanization, exploitation, marginalization, dispossession of resources and income (e.g., land), and denial of protection against the actions of oppressors. Gutiérrez's theology of liberation clearly focuses on the poor in body. He describes them (in the Latin American context) as the victims of "death," which is as a result of starvation, curable illnesses, and oppressive structures.[90] He writes, "I am talking about the real poverty in which vast majorities of human beings live, and not about the idealized poverty that we sometimes excogitate for our own pastoral, theological, and spiritual purposes."[91] To him, the situation of poverty in Latin America was clearly an affront to God (a loving father of the world) and conflicted with the kingdom or reign of God that Jesus proclaimed.[92]

How are biblical ideas of poverty to be successfully brought into the discourses on poverty, the sufferings of the poor, and the liberation of the poor? In *The Power of the Poor in History,* Gutiérrez challenged Christians to approach the Bible from four related hermeneutical angles.[93] First, they are to read the Bible from a "christological" lens. This means seeing Jesus as the "fulfillment of the promise of the Father" and also as the one who functions as a bridge between the Old Testament and the New Testament. Second, Christians are to read the Bible "in faith" because they constitute the community of Christ's followers who commit to his way of life as the "Lord of history." Third, they are to read the Bible from a "historical" perspective, focusing on God's liberative activity because God acts and reveals Godself in human history. Fourth, they are to read the Bible from a "militant" viewpoint because, as followers of Jesus Christ, they are to participate in the liberation of the sectors of human society that suffer injustice and marginalization. These four related hermeneutical frameworks, for him, can help theologians to discern theological materials in the Bible. He constructed his own liberation theology with the theological materials he harnessed from both the Hebrew Bible and the New Testament. I will highlight three such

90. Gutiérrez, *We Drink from Our Own Wells,* 9–10.
91. Gutiérrez, *We Drink from Our Own Wells,* 16.
92. Gutiérrez, *We Drink from Our Own Wells,* 10.
93. Gutiérrez, *Power of the Poor in History,* 4.

theological materials; namely, the role that human freedom and liberation play in God's salvific activity in the world, God's preferential love for the poor, and the role of the church in making God's kingdom visible in this world by attending to the needs of the poor.

Human Freedom and Liberation as the Essence of Salvation

Once the Christian idea of salvation is rescued from the captivity of metaphysics—an abstract reflection on God's salvific work in the world—a new door opens for construing it as God's act of healing the world of its spiritual and social ills in which human beings are summoned to participate. The terms "spiritual" and "social" are used here broadly to highlight the continuum of God-human relations (vertical) and the relationship between human beings (horizontal) in the Christian imagination of God's salvation. Christians, as Jesus's disciples, are to embody his teaching on God's salvific healing— social and spiritual—that he proclaimed and practiced. For Gutiérrez, liberation is an essential component of this salvific healing: "Liberation is an all-embracing process that leaves no dimension of human life untouched, because when all is said and done it expresses the saving action of God in history."[94] The context of Gutiérrez's liberation theology—the horrendous situation of poor Latin Americans and the different, inadequate attempts to solve it—requires Christians to practice liberation continually as they confront poverty.[95] They are to act in ways that show concretely that God is the giver of life by practicing the act of *liberation*—giving of life—to the poor whose condition in most cases leads to death.[96]

The practice of liberation exposes the weakness of a dichotomous understanding of prayer and action, the inadequacy of being indifferent to physical pains and the experience of the poor under the guise of spirituality, and the weakness of a futuristic understanding of God's restoration of the world.[97] However, the practice of liberation is a costly endeavor: "The present-day Latin American experience of martyrdom bids us all turn back to one of the major sources of all spirituality: the blood-stained experience of the early Christian community, which was so weak in the face of the imperial power of that day."[98] Also, the practice of liberation entails paying special attention to the poor because they are "the privileged ones in God's

94. Gutiérrez, *We Drink from Our Own Wells*, 2.
95. Gutiérrez, *We Drink from Our Own Wells*, 2–3.
96. Gutiérrez, *We Drink from Our Own Wells*, 7.
97. Gutiérrez, *We Drink from Our Own Wells*, 19–22.
98. Gutiérrez, *We Drink from Our Own Wells*, 23.

kingdom."[99] Jesus models for his disciples how to practice liberation with respect to the poor. By alleviating the "suffering of *some* of the poor" during his earthly ministry, Jesus shows that the "promise of the good news of the reign of God is being proclaimed to *all* the poor of history. It is a proclamation through liberating words and liberating actions."[100]

Gutiérrez partly relied on God's liberative act in Exodus for insights into God's concerns for the oppressed and also the necessity of empowering the oppressed to break away from their oppressors. God (Yahweh) raised a liberator (Moses) to set free the people of Israel from the deplorable condition of slavery in Egypt.[101] In 1975, Gutiérrez published an essay that highlighted human freedom as a theme that is present in the Christian conscience.[102] *Human freedom*, in this context, is grounded in Christ's love that compels his disciples to serve others (Gal 5:1, 13).[103] Therefore, the liberation of the poor in Latin America proposed by liberation theologians, argues Gutiérrez, should not be restricted to the quest to overcome "economic, social, and political dependence."[104] It should rather be broadened to include the quest for a "new humanity" in which all people are set free "from all servitude" and also are empowered to be the "artisans" of their own destiny.[105] Drawing insights from the writings of Brazilian social critic Paulo Freire (1921–97), Gutiérrez argues that the oppressed are to take up the task of their liberation in order for it to be authentic. The task of the allies of the oppressed should not be to become their voice—the primary agent of liberation. On the contrary, the allies of the oppressed should seek to nudge them toward transcending a naïve awareness to attain a critical awareness, which entails both rejecting their condition as their fate and discovering their own voice in the fight against oppressive systems.[106] There is a correlation between what Gutiérrez sees as the pathway to the liberation that is befitting to the poor in Latin America and the form of liberation that James Massey deems useful to the Dalits of India. Both Gutiérrez and Massey are in agreement that empowering the oppressed to seek their liberation from oppressive conditions and structures is important for preserving their inherent dignity as human beings.

99. Gutiérrez, *We Drink from Our Own Wells*, 9.
100. Gutiérrez, *We Drink from Our Own Wells*, 43.
101. Gutiérrez, *We Drink from Our Own Wells*, 74.
102. Gutiérrez, "Faith as Freedom," 25.
103. Gutiérrez, "Faith as Freedom," 26.
104. Gutiérrez, *Theology of Liberation*, 56.
105. Gutiérrez, *Theology of Liberation*, 56.
106. Gutiérrez, *Theology of Liberation*, 57. See Freire, *Pedagogy of the Oppressed*.

Human freedom, which ought to be grounded in liberation, requires expanding the Christian idea of salvation by moving beyond the traditional notion of converting non-Christians or focusing on the solution to sin "in virtue of a salvation to be attained" in the afterlife.[107] The works of individuals such as Karl Rahner paved the way for many Roman Catholic theologians to revisit the ecclesio-centric understanding of salvation that restricted the salvific blessings to the members of the church alone.[108] Vatican II's *Nostra Aetate*, *Lumen Gentium*, and *Gaudium et spes* also nudged some theologians to discern divine activity in the non-Christian religions.[109] For liberation theologians, the emphasis should be on rediscovering the connection between the sectors of human society that are being crushed under the weight of poverty and also God's salvific act in the life and work of Jesus. Gutiérrez argued persistently that the Christian idea of God's salvation has historical consequences:

> Christ is the truth, a truth that sets us free. The liberation he
> gives is an integral one that embraces all dimensions of human
> existence and brings us to full communion with God and one an-
> other. This liberation is therefore one that begins within history,
> which thus becomes a way to a fullness that lies beyond it.[110]

To Gutiérrez, one way to unpack the ramifications of the Christian notion of salvation is to attend to the question: "What is the relationship between salvation and the process of human liberation throughout history?"[111] If salvation is the making of a "new humanity," Christian theologians are to work out how such salvific phenomenon relates to "the struggle against an unjust society."[112] For him, the process of creating a new humanity requires an unwavering commitment to the creation of a just society.[113] Salvation, properly understood, does not only deal with the afterlife but also, and in some significant ways, particularly with *this* life. He writes, "Salvation is not something otherworldly, in regard to which the present life is merely a test. Salvation—the communion of human beings with God and among themselves—is something that embraces all human reality, transforms it, and

---

107. Gutiérrez, *Theology of Liberation*, 84.

108. Rahner, "Christianity and the Non-Christian Religions," 115–34.

109. Vatican II, *Nostra Aetate*, in Flannery, *Vatican Council II*, 738–49; Vatican II, *Guadium et spes*, in Flannery, *Vatican Council II*, 903–11; Vatican II, *Lumen Gentium*, in Flannery, *Vatican Council II*, 350–426.

110. Gutiérrez, *Truth Shall Make You Free*, 106.

111. Gutiérrez, *Theology of Liberation*, 83.

112. Gutiérrez, *Theology of Liberation*, 83.

113. Gutiérrez, *Theology of Liberation*, 121.

leads it to its fullness in Christ."[114] What is required is a robust and a nuanced soteriology that takes seriously the healing aspect of God's salvific work in the world. Salvation is God's ongoing work of healing—directly and indirectly (through human beings)—of the world's ills, which include spiritual, physical, emotional, and social aspects. Poverty—spiritual poverty (spiritual bankruptcy) and material poverty—is one mode of existence of such ills.[115] When understood in light of the sabbatical year (Exod 23:10–12; Lev 25:1–7; Deut 15:1–11) and the Jubilee (Lev 25:8–26; Isa 61:1–2; cf. Luke 4:18–9), salvation is really about a gradual transformation of the world from its social ills to a healthy condition. The sabbatical year, which promotes the idea of *giving a rest to something or someone,* implies creating a society that cares about the environment and cares for the poor (Deut 15:4). The Jubilee is really about the proclamation of freedom and liberty to God's creation. We can also see in Jesus's decision to heal the beggar who asked him for money (Luke 18:35–43) and in Peter's and John's similar response to a beggar (Acts 3:1–10) the overarching theme of transforming the condition that makes someone live in poverty. These examples at the very least suggest that Jesus's disciples are to embody the spirit of healing that he practiced by exposing and tearing down oppressive structures. They ought to press for the establishment of just societies in which people can work toward both creating and enjoying the resources that are necessary for human existence. The poor—those who lack the basic necessities of life—exemplify the shortcomings of unjust societies. They equally accentuate the importance of transforming unjust societies into just societies insofar as many of them are the victims of oppressive political, religious, and socioeconomic structures. In the following section, I examine Gutiérrez's claim that the God of the Bible sides with the poor in their struggles for liberation from oppressive structures.

God's Preferential Love for the Poor

What exactly is the illocutionary act of the utterance "God sides with the poor"? If the point (or purpose) of this theological utterance is to show that God only cares about the poor or that God does not care about the rich, it is theologically misguided. The Christian Scripture does not present God as one who totally dislikes riches, wealth, and the rich. On the contrary, God blesses people and brings about prosperity (Gen 30:29–30; Deut 15:14; 2

114. Gutiérrez, *Theology of Liberation,* 85.

115. Gutiérrez defines "spiritual poverty" only in terms of spiritual humility: it "is an attitude of openness to God and spiritual childhood." Gutiérrez, *Theology of Liberation,* 171.

Chr 32:29; Jer 29:10–14; 1 Tim 6:17–19). How, then, should we understand the expression "God sides with the poor"? It is clear in Scripture that the poor are God's special people. God will take up the case of the poor and fight for them largely because they are oppressed, marginalized, and denied justice. Proverbs 22:22–23 makes this clear: "Do not rob the poor because they are poor, or crush the afflicted at the gate; for the Lord pleads their cause and despoils of life those who despoil them" (NRSV). Isaiah 3:14–15 makes a similar point, albeit more pointedly:

> The LORD enters into judgment with the elders and princes of
> his people: It is you who have devoured the vineyard; the spoil
> of the poor is in your houses. What do you mean by crushing
> my people, by grinding the face of the poor? says the Lord God
> of hosts. (NRSV)

The enemies of the poor, and by implication the enemies of God, are the people that exploit and oppress the poor (Ps 9:16–19; Ezek 18:10, 12). To utter the words "God sides with the poor," therefore, has a directive illocutionary act: it is a directive to Christian communities to take up the case of the poor as God their creator does and will do. This illocutionary act is central to the idea of a preferential option for the poor that has been a prominent feature of the theologies of many Latin American liberation theologians since the late 1960s.

For Gutiérrez, if the poor are the "non-loved," they find a new life in God who has a preferential love for them. This is the genius of the idea of the preferential option for the poor. God is not a neutral observer in the disputes between the oppressors of the poor and the poor. God's preferential love for the poor, in Gutiérrez's view, is demonstrated in the life of the poor Nazarene, Jesus Christ, whose life and work embodied divine liberation of humanity. Here is Gutiérrez's argument for God's preferential love for the poor as manifested in Jesus Christ:

> If we believe that the Kingdom of God is a gift which is received
> in history, and if we believe, as the eschatological promises—so
> charged with human and historical content—indicate to us, that
> the Kingdom of God necessarily implies the reestablishment of
> justice in this world, then we must believe that Christ says that
> the poor are blessed because the Kingdom of God has begun:
> "The time has come; the Kingdom is upon you" (Mark 1:15).
> In other words, the elimination of the exploitation and pov-
> erty that prevent the poor from being fully human has begun;
> a Kingdom of justice which goes even beyond what they could
> have hoped has begun. They are blessed because the coming of

the Kingdom will put an end to their poverty by creating a world of fellowship.[116]

Also, he wrote:

> The taking on of the servile and sinful human condition, as fore-told in Second Isaiah, is presented by Paul as an act of voluntary impoverishment: "For you know how generous our Lord Jesus Christ has been; He was rich, yet for your sake he became poor, so that through his poverty you might become rich" (2 Cor 8:9). This is the humiliation of Christ, his *kenosis* (Phil 2:6–11). But he does not take on the human sinful condition and its consequences to idealize it. It is rather because of love for and solidarity with others who suffer in it. It is to redeem them from their sin and to enrich them with his poverty. It is to struggle against human selfishness and everything that divides persons and allows that there be rich and poor, possessors and dispossessed, oppressors and oppressed.[117]

Gutiérrez cites the christological ode in Paul's epistle to Christians in Philippi to make the case for God's voluntary poverty in the life of God incarnate, Jesus Christ of Nazareth. By incarnating in the life of the poor Nazarene, God (specifically, the divine *Logos*) demonstrates God's determination to partner with humanity in order to expose the manifestations of sin in humans' acts of selfishness, which creates a devastating dualism: poor and rich, possessors and dispossessed, and oppressors and oppressed. Theologically, a particular case of *material poverty* (lack or deprivation of the basic necessities of life) must be the result of oppressive structures and consequently (a manifestation of sin) in order for it to fit into God's *kenotic* act—the self-emptying or self-denying act that constituted the mystery of the Incarnation. To put it differently, if humanity's poverty (excluding voluntary poverty) is inherently linked to sin, it is a part of what God redeems in and through Jesus Christ (God incarnate). By voluntarily becoming poor, God incarnate shows solidarity with the poor, sheds light on their dehumanizing condition, and opposes the structures that cause material poverty.[118]

The project of liberation theology is largely grounded in the belief that "God is a liberating God" who has revealed his liberative work concretely in the "liberation of the poor and oppressed."[119] For Gutiérrez, "voluntary poverty" is a liberative act in which God in and through Christ takes on

116. Gutiérrez, *Theology of Liberation*, 170–71.

117. Gutiérrez, *Theology of Liberation*, 172.

118. Gutiérrez, *Theology of Liberation*, 172.

119. Gutiérrez, "Two Theological Perspectives," 247.

"the sinful human condition to liberate humankind from sin and all its consequences."[120] As followers of Christ, Christians are to imitate him in showing "authentic solidarity with the poor and a real protest against the poverty of our time" through concrete actions.[121] This does not mean that all Christians must become materially poor. Rather, it means that they should follow in the footsteps of Jesus who condemned oppressive structures that created poverty and also demanded that such structures be changed. I will return later in this chapter to explore the idea of preferential option for the poor. It is noteworthy at this point, however, that Gutiérrez does not see commitment to the cause or well-being of the poor as the affairs of the poor people alone. Rather, it should be of concern to all people who desire to create and sustain a just society. The church, for him, should model for the rest of the world such commitment to the poor. I will examine this claim in the section below.

Church's Role in Making God's Kingdom Visible in this World

The salient theological point of the Christian gospel, with reference to humanity, is the triune God's proclamation of liberation to all human beings: the healing and restoring act that expresses God's love, commitment, and care for the well-being of all people. The kind of well-being imagined in this context opposes a dualistic mindset in which the *spiritual* and the *physical* are construed as disparate realms that must be kept apart from each other. On the contrary, well-being in this context is thoroughly holistic: it touches on all aspects of human life. In other words, the Christian gospel is really about God's reign of salvation. The holistic liberation of human beings gives impetus to God's salvific activity in the world. In God's reign (kingdom), therefore, salvation, which is inherently liberative and restorative in nature, is visible as the *good news* (gospel) is proclaimed to the poor, liberty is proclaimed to the captives and the oppressed, and restoration is proclaimed to the blind (Luke 4:18–19; cf. Isa 61:1–2). Given this understanding of the Christian gospel, Gutiérrez argues that material poverty is in direct conflict with God's proclamation of good news to the world. He writes, "In the Bible poverty is a scandalous condition to human dignity and therefore contrary to the will of God."[122]

120. Gutiérrez, *Theology of Liberation*, 172.

121. Gutiérrez, *Theology of Liberation*, 173.

122. Gutiérrez, *Theology of Liberation*, 165.

The theological impetus for Jesus's teaching about the kingdom of God, for Gutiérrez, is the role it plays in the "building up of the world."[123] The church's role is not to ferry people into a future life and to protect them from the realities of this life. Since salvation is a process of creating a new humanity, the church must participate in building a just society.[124] Therefore, Christians are to imagine God's kingdom in the context of eschatology, albeit not merely in a futuristic sense:

> One must be extremely careful not to replace a Christianity of Beyond with a Christianity of Future; if the former tended to forget the world, the latter runs the risk of neglecting a miserable and unjust present and the struggle for liberation . . . To hope does not mean to know the future, but rather to be open, in an attitude of spiritual childhood, to accepting it as a gift. But this gift is accepted in the negation of injustice, in the protest against trampled human rights, and in the struggle for peace and fellowship. Thus hope fulfills a mobilizing and liberating function in history. Its function is not very obvious, but it is real and deep.[125]

For Gutiérrez, liberation offers a better link between Christianity's teaching about God's kingdom and God's salvific work in the world.[126] He challenged Christian theologians to see the historical liberation process not as the "coming Kingdom" but rather as the "historical realization of the Kingdom" and also as what makes God's reign in the world visible, that is, what proclaims its fullness.[127] In what follows, I turn attention to some theological materials that he identified in the Roman Catholic Church tradition, which he used to formulate his liberation theology.

Theological Materials from Church Tradition

I will concentrate on two major theological materials from the Roman Catholic tradition, particularly in the context of Latin American Roman Catholic communities, that figured prominently in Gutiérrez's theology. The first material is the idea of the church as a missional community. The second material is the preferential option for the poor.

123. Gutiérrez, *Theology of Liberation*, 29.
124. Gutiérrez, *Theology of Liberation*, 122.
125. Gutiérrez, *Theology of Liberation*, 124–25.
126. Gutiérrez, *Theology of Liberation*, 104.
127. Gutiérrez, *Theology of Liberation*, 104–5.

Church as a Missional Community

In the mid-twentieth century, Pope John XXIII was determined to bring some fresh air into the Roman Catholic Church by eradicating its previous siege mentality toward some social, economic, and political issues that impacted the world. Rather than legislating on social issues outside of the walls of Roman Catholicism or avoiding a penetrating encounter with the contemporary world by retreating into its safe walls, he aimed to update the Roman Catholic Church's understanding of its relation to the world.[128] In his 1961 encyclical, entitled *Mater et Magistra*, which was largely a commentary on Pope Leo XIII's encyclical entitled *Rerum Novarum*, Pope John XXIII touched on many social, economic, and religious issues, including the dehumanizing condition of the poor.

> As for the problems which face the poorer nations in various parts of the world, we realize, of course, that these are very real. They are caused, more often than not, by a deficient economic and social organization, which does not offer living conditions proportionate to the increase in population. They are caused, also, by the lack of effective solidarity among such peoples. But granting this, we must nevertheless state most emphatically that no statement of the problem and no solution to it is acceptable which does violence to man's essential dignity; those who propose such solutions base them on an utterly materialistic conception of man himself and his life.[129]

One significant result of Pope John XXIII's vision for the world and the Roman Catholic Church in particular was the Second Vatican Council (1962–65, also known as Vatican II). Some of the final documents of the Second Vatican Council have deeply impacted Gutiérrez's theology, especially *Gaudium et spes* and *Lumen Gentium*. However, Gutiérrez frequently returned to the final documents of the Second and Third General Conferences of Latin American Bishops (Medellín 1968; Puebla 1979). For example, in *We Drink from Our Own Wells*, he wrote: "Latin American reality is characterized by a poverty that the Final Puebla Document (PD) describes as 'inhuman' (no. 29) and 'anti-evangelical' (no. 1151). Such poverty represents a situation of 'institutionalized violence,' to use the well-known phrase of Medellín ('Peace,' no. 16)."[130] Both the Medellín and

128. See Twomey, *"Preferential Option for the Poor"*, 37–75.

129. John XXIII, *Mater et Magistra*, nos. 190–191.

130. Gutiérrez, *We Drink from Our Own Wells*, 9. The term "institutionalized violence" also refers to government repression through the use of torture, assassination, and summary arrests to silence the cry of the exploited class in Latin America and also

Puebla conferences emphasized that Latin American Christian communities must reevaluate its understanding of evangelism—the proclamation
of the gospel—in light of its commitment to the liberation of the poor.
Given the pastoral focus of both episcopal conferences, it should not be
surprising that the bishops explored how the church can be in dialogue
with the social and political institutions of the world with the aim to create
a society in which justice, equality, human flourishing, and peace reign.
Accomplishing this task entails that the church of Latin America must be
"free from temporary ties, from intrigues, and from a doubtful reputation;
to be 'free in spirit as regards the chains of wealth,' so that her mission of
service will be stronger and clearer."[131]

Gutiérrez developed his theology in dialogue with three theological
models of church-world (or state) relations. First, he argued that in the
medieval notion of Christendom, the church co-opted the secular realm
for its own benefits but was largely disinterested in participating in it as an
autonomous and distinct entity. The church engaged in the political arena
usually to flex its spiritual muscles as "the exclusive depository of salvation"
and claimed that there is no salvation outside the church.[132] Only for the
purposes of evangelizing mission and safeguarding its interests did the medieval church engage the temporal secular realm.[133]

The French philosopher Jacques Maritain has highlighted five characteristics of Christendom that are useful for understanding the role the
church played in the medieval era.[134] (1) *Maximal organic unity*: the efforts
to unify both temporal and sacred realms, with an emperor attending to
temporal matters, and a pope attending to spiritual matters. (2) *Temporal
realm's ministerial role*: the understanding of the temporal realm as an instrument for achieving the spiritual interests and matters of the church. (3)
Instrumental role of the state: the efforts to use the state's political institution for the spiritual good of people and "for the spiritual unity of the body
itself—for that spiritual unity by reason of which the heretic was not only
a heretic, but indeed a man who attacked the socio-temporal community
at its living sources."[135] (4) *Hierarchical social structure*: the "disparity as of
essence between leader and led," which is grounded in the belief that people

to prevent them from demanding justice and liberation. See Gutiérrez, "Two Theological Perspectives," 239.

131. "Poverty of the Church," III.18, in Second General Conference of Catholic
Bishops, *Church in the Present-Day Transformation*, 219.

132. Gutiérrez, *Theology of Liberation*, 34.

133. Gutiérrez, *Theology of Liberation*, 34–35.

134. Maritain, *Integral Humanism*, 146–53.

135. Maritain, *Integral Humanism*, 150.

in positions of power (e.g., kings, popes, abbots) are inherently superior to their subjects both in terms of authority and sacral relations.[136] (5) *Telos of God's glory*: the establishment of social and juridical structures that are dedicated to the service of God "by the power of baptized [people] and a baptized political life."[137] Maritain proposed a revised understanding of Christendom, which he termed the "New Christendom." For him, "Christendom" is a temporal reign with structures that have the "imprint of Christian conception of life."[138] The "New Christendom" has two main features. Firstly, it is *communal*: it focuses on the common good, which is the right moral and material life of the whole community. Secondly, it is *personalist*: it has an intermediary goal insofar as the temporal common good of the community should "respect and serve the spiritual ends of the human person."[139] The church should provide lay Christians with the impetus and social teaching for engaging actively in the projects and organizations that seek to create a just society.[140] For Maritain, the autonomy of the temporal regime should be preserved and therefore should not be construed as a mere instrument to serve the needs of the church.[141]

Jacques Maritain's *New Christendom* is the second major conception of church-state relations that Gutiérrez engages in his political theology. He rejects Maritain's "New Christendom" on several grounds. He charges Maritain's New Christendom with the crime of "ecclesiastical narcissism" because it gives Christianity a special privilege in the public square insofar as the goal is to build "a society inspired by Christian principles."[142] He also points out that one of the devastating consequences of Maritain's New Christendom is its (perhaps unintended) dualism: its distinction of the

136. Maritain, *Integral Humanism*, 150–151.

137. Maritain, *Integral Humanism*, 153.

138. Maritain, *Integral Humanism*, 132.

139. Maritain, *Integral Humanism*, 133–34.

140. Maritain, *Integral Humanism*, 162. He writes, "The political activity in question, I have often explained, does not need all Christians, nor only Christians: but only those Christians who have a certain philosophy of the world, of society and of modern history; and such non-Christians as recognize more or less completely the cogency of this philosophy. It is normal that on the plane of action these men should constitute autonomous political formations; only in certain exceptional cases would this mean that they would refuse on principle to cooperate with the established regime, or to conclude agreements with other political formations and to collaborate with them. But it is important that they preserve at the same time the germ of a vitally Christian politics against all that which would run the risk of impairing it." See Maritain, *Integral Humanism*, 263–64.

141. Maritain, *Integral Humanism*, 178–80.

142. Gutiérrez, *Theology of Liberation*, 36.

secular (world) and spiritual (church) planes.[143] According to him, although Maritain attempted to distinguish the two spheres without separating them, he paved the way for a "timid" and an "ambiguous" attempt of lay Christians' engagement with the social order. Maritain's position, for Gutiérrez,

> represents an initial effort to evaluate temporal tasks with the eyes of faith as well as to situate the Church in the modern world. This approach led many Christians to commit themselves authentically and generously to the construction of a just society. Those Christians who supported this position often had to endure the enmity of the faithful and Church authorities, both of whom were of a conservative mentality. In fact, nevertheless, this approach amounted only to a timid and basically ambiguous attempt. It gave rise to fundamentally moderate political attitudes—at least in the beginning—which combined a certain nostalgia for the past (reestablishment of guilds, for example) with a modernizing mentality. It is a long way, therefore, from a desire to become oriented towards radically new social forms.[144]

Gutiérrez also argues that Maritain's New Christendom does not quite shake off the traditional mentality; in particular, St. Thomas Aquinas's understanding of grace-nature relations in which grace perfects nature.[145] This theological mindset, for Gutiérrez, is partly responsible for "a more autonomous and disinterested political action" that maintains a distinction between the temporal (secular) plane and sacral (church) plane.[146] The distinction of these planes entails that a priest, as a representative of the church, should not "intervene directly in political action" but must be content with the duty of inspiring and evangelizing the temporal order.[147] In Latin America, however, as Gutiérrez observes, "the greater part of the church remained untouched by this church-world distinction, for it was contradicted by the strong bonds which consciously or unconsciously tied the church to the existing social order."[148] In his view, the church's nonintervention approach is deeply misguided. In the face of social problems, the church ought not restrict its role to "lyrical pronouncements" alone but should also take a clear stand against oppressive structures and also should work actively to

---

143. Gutiérrez, *Theology of Liberation*, 39.
144. Gutiérrez, *Theology of Liberation*, 36.
145. Gutiérrez, *Theology of Liberation*, 35.
146. Gutiérrez, *Theology of Liberation*, 35–36.
147. Gutiérrez, *Theology of Liberation*, 37.
148. Gutiérrez, *Theology of Liberation*, 37–38.

eradicate such structures.[149] He sees the church and the world as a continuum rather than two polar opposites or two separate planes.[150]

The third theological model of church-world relations that Gutiérrez judged to be inadequate could be seen in his critique of "progressivist theology." For him, *progressivist theology* sought to erect theological edifices that showed that Christian theology could pass the test of reason. Such theology aimed to answer the question: "How are we to talk of God in a world come of age?"[151] Departing from this line of thinking, Gutiérrez argues that Latin American liberation theologians ought to ask a different question, namely: "[H]ow are [we] to tell people who are scarcely human that God is love and that God's love makes us one family?"[152] This question, however, should not be relegated to the realm of theory. On the contrary, the point of departure for theological investigation should be the real-life situation of the oppressed.[153] The church can show its commitment to the creation of a just society by siding with the poor in their struggles against oppression. I explore the claim below.

Preferential Option for the Poor

Impelled by the Vatican II, Latin American bishops convened its Second General Conference of Bishops under the theme "The Church in the Present-Day Transformation of Latin America in the Light of the Second Vatican Council."[154] The objectives of the conference, according to the inaugural address of Avelar Vilela, the Archbishop of Teresina, were to "interpret the central problems of the Church and world of today" and to "apply the [second Vatican] Council teachings, the papal directives, the Gospel truths, to the religious and social context of the historical realities in which" Latin American Christian communities find themselves.[155] The

149. Gutiérrez, *Theology of Liberation*, 41–43.

150. He writes, the "affirmation of the single vocation to salvation, beyond all distinctions, gives religious value in a completely new way to human action in history, Christian and non-Christian alike. The building of a just society had worth in terms of the Kingdom, or in more current phraseology, to participate in the process of liberation is already, in a certain sense, a salvific work." Gutiérrez, *Theology of Liberation*, 46.

151. Gutiérrez, "Two Theological Perspectives," 233.

152. Gutiérrez, "Two Theological Perspectives," 241.

153. He writes, "The locus of liberation theology is the common people seeking to be agents of their own history and expressing their faith and hope in the poor Christ through their efforts of liberation." Gutiérrez, "Two Theological Perspectives," 242.

154. Vilela, "Inaugural Address," 69.

155. Vilela, "Inaugural Address," 69.

Second General Conference of Latin American Bishops held in Medellín (Colombia) employed the term "preferential option for the poor" to highlight the condition of the poor in Latin America and also to instruct Latin American churches to participate in the liberation of the poor from their underserved, dehumanizing conditions.[156] The Medellín conference also argued for the need for Christian communities to be in solidarity with the poor and marginalized: "The Lord's commitment to 'evangelize the poor' ought to bring us to a distribution of resources and apostolic personnel that effectively gives preference to the poorest and most needy sectors and to those segregated for any cause whatsoever."[157] The Third General Conference held in Puebla, Mexico, reiterated the points made by the Second General Conference, claiming there was a "need for conversion on the part of the whole church to a preferential option for the poor, an option aimed at their integral liberation."[158]

God-talk, Gutiérrez argues, "presupposes practice: that is, the silence of contemplation and commitment."[159] These two components of God-talk—contemplation and commitment—are a continuum of theologizing. In this section, I focus on one of the concrete ways Gutiérrez imagines "commitment" in Christian theological activity. Perhaps no other theological category captures Gutiérrez's understanding of "commitment" in the context of God-talk vis-à-vis the poor than the idea of *opción preferencial* (preferential option). For him, preferential option for the poor entails

> a commitment that implies leaving the road one is on, as the parable of the Good Samaritan teaches, and entering the world of the other, of the "insignificant" person, of the one excluded from dominant social sectors, communities, viewpoints, and

156. The Medellín conference described three kinds of poverty. *Material poverty* is the "lack of the goods of this world necessary to live worthily as [people]," which the Medellín conference called an "institutionalized violence" and evil." *Spiritual poverty* refers to the "attitude of opening up to God, the ready disposition of one who hopes for everything from the Lord." *Voluntary poverty* is "a personal commitment" that a person "assumes voluntarily and lovingly" because of the "needy of this world in order to bear witness to the evil which it represents and to spiritual liberty in the face of material goods." This act of voluntary poverty is rooted in the "example of Christ who took to Himself all of the consequences of [people's] sinful condition and who 'being rich became poor' in order to redeem us." See "Poverty of the Church," II.4, in Second General Council of Catholic Bishops, *Church in the Present-Day Transformation*, 214–15.

157. "Poverty of the Church," III.9, in Second General Council of Catholic Bishops, *Church in the Present-Day Transformation*, 216–17.

158. "A Missionary Church Serving Evangelization in Latin America," IV.1.1134, in Third General Conference of Latin American Bishops, *Puebla*, 179.

159. Gutiérrez, *God of Life*, 145.

ideas. It is a long and difficult, but necessary, process, and a precondition for authenticity. The priority of the other is a distinguishing mark of a gospel ethic, and nobody embodies this priority more clearly than the poor and the excluded.[160]

Gutiérrez characteristically appeals to the Medellín and Puebla conferences to defend his idea of the preferential option for the poor.[161] Like the Medellín conference, the Puebla conference made the case for the theological value of the concept of the preferential option for the poor. Though the Puebla conference clearly condemned and denounced those who propound "dangerous and erroneous Marxist ideology,"[162] it adopted the preferential option for the poor as a theologically adequate mandate.[163] It equally recognized the need for the church to study the situation of the poor within the historical context of Latin America.[164] The church should also see its service to the poor as one of the concrete ways to assess its commitment to Jesus Christ: "When we draw near to the poor in order to accompany them and serve them, we are doing what Christ taught us to do when he became our poor brother, poor like us. Hence service to the poor is the privileged, though not the exclusive, gauge of our following of Christ."[165] Throughout the *Final Document* of Puebla, one can discern the attempts to recast biblical teaching on the person of Jesus Christ, justice,

160. Gutiérrez, "Option for the Poor Arises from Faith," 148.

161. Gutiérrez, *God of Life*, 165.

162. *Final Document of the Third General Conference of the Latin American Episcopate, Puebla de Los Angeles, Mexico, 27 January—13 February 1979*, no. 1139, in Eagleson and Scharper, *Puebla and Beyond*, 264.

163. "With renewed hope in the vivifying power of the Spirit, we are going to take up once again the position of the Second General Conference of the Latin American episcopate in Medellín, which adopted a clear and prophetic option expressing preference for, and solidarity with, the poor. We do this despite the distortions and interpretations of some, who vitiate the spirit of Medellín, and despite the disregard and even hostility of others. We affirm the need for the conversion on the part of the whole Church to a preferential option for the poor, an option aimed at their integral liberation. . . . Service to them [the poor] calls for constant conversion and purification among all Christians. That must be done if we are to achieve fuller identification each day with the poor Christ and our own poor." See *Final Document of the Third General Conference of the Latin American Episcopate, Puebla de Los Angeles, Mexico, 27 January—13 February 1979*, 1134, 1140, in Eagleson and Scharper, *Puebla and Beyond*, 264.

164. *Final Document of the Third General Conference of the Latin American Episcopate, Puebla de Los Angeles, Mexico, 27 January—13 February 1979*, nos. 1206–1208, in Eagleson and Scharper, *Puebla and Beyond*, 273.

165. *Final Document of the Third General Conference of the Latin American Episcopate, Puebla de Los Angeles, Mexico, 27 January—13 February 1979*, no. 1145, in Eagleson and Scharper, *Puebla and Beyond*, 265.

evangelism, and equality in the peculiar context of Latin America's social-economic and social structures.

Gutiérrez equally drew upon the theological insights of the Puebla conference to make the case against an attitude of indifference toward the poor or the movements that aimed to dismantle the oppressive structures. In the spirit of the Medellín and Puebla documents that called for the church to repent of its indifference toward the situation of the poor, he argued that the church must break its "ties with the present order, ties that it has maintained overtly or covertly, wittingly or unwittingly, up to now."[166] However one imagines the contributions of Gutiérrez to the field of Christian theology, and liberation theology in particular, it is more fruitful to situate his writings in the social, ecclesiastical, and theological contexts of Latin American Christianity in the late nineteenth century. In what follows, I will highlight some criticisms against his liberation theology.

Assessing Criticisms of Gutiérrez's Theology of Liberation

A Christian theology of poverty ought to be grounded in the life of Jesus, the poor Galilean who led a movement against oppressive structures because he was convinced that "the Spirit of the Lord" anointed and commissioned him to proclaim God's good news to the poor (Luke 4:16–21). As Liz Theoharis has noted, "Jesus was a teacher, leader, prophet, and ruler of a budding, revolutionary social movement of the poor that practiced and preached about God's coming reign of abundance, dignity, and prosperity for all."[167] Gutiérrez developed a theology of the poor that drew insights from God's love for the poor. He also drew insights from Jesus's experience as a poor Galilean and also his critique of oppressive structures that cause immense poverty and lead to the horrendous sufferings. Being a disciple of Jesus Christ, for Gutiérrez, requires following in his footsteps in proclaiming freedom and liberation to the poor by opposing (in words and deeds) the forces that create poverty or perpetuate it.

Gutiérrez wrote his theological works both in the spirit of constructive theology and in the spirit of apologia. As I showed throughout this chapter, he used different sources to construct his theology. As a constructive theologian, he was interdisciplinary in his efforts to develop fresh theological ideas in dialogue with other disciplines, particularly social sciences. In the spirit of apologia, he was constantly haunted by the criticism of other Roman Catholic theologians who scorned Latin American liberation

166. Gutiérrez, *Power of the Poor in History*, 29.
167. Theoharis, *Always with Us?*, 144.

theology movements. He was constantly defending his theological orthodoxy against detractors and critics.[168] Like many Latin American liberation
theologians who drew inspiration from the discourse on Christian-Marx-
ism relations, he has been criticized for being Marxist in his theological
thinking. Interestingly, some of the strenuous critics of liberation theology
were key members of CELAM. For example, Bishop Alfonso Lopez Trujillo
criticized some liberation theologians for promoting the image of a Zealot
Christ who condones the use of violence as a viable option to bring about
a social change. Though Trujillo did not say that all liberation theologians
were implicated in violent revolutions, he saw Marxist thought, class
struggle, and revolutions as the major characteristics of the Latin American liberation movements and most Latin American liberation theologies.
In *Liberation or Revolution?*, Trujillo argued that Jesus Christ is neither "a
guerrilla [fighter] nor a pacifist."[169] Presenting Jesus as one who was unwavering in his commitment to exposing injustices without resorting to
the use of violence, Trujillo claimed that it is disingenuous for liberation
theologians who support social revolutions, especially the violent forms, to
appeal to Jesus as an ally. Accordingly, Jesus Christ

> asks for the betterment and purification of tradition. He exposes
> injustices, but he is not oriented towards the destruction of "or-
> der" or towards a reform of institutions or structures; neither
> is he caught in immobility. He preaches on a fundamental con-
> version from love according to the present Kingdom. For that
> particular reason, he does not accept political messianisms.[170]

Though the project of liberation theology is not *de facto* dangerous to the
Christian faith, for Trujillo, its proclivity towards a socialist revolution and
Marxist thought demands distinguishing it from the biblical teaching of
liberation.[171] He named Gustavo Gutiérrez an example of a liberation theologian who cautiously favors socialism over capitalism.[172] Ironically Trujillo,
like Gutiérrez, blames capitalism for many of the social, economic, and political ills of Latin America. He describes capitalism as "a human failure."[173]
However, unlike Gutiérrez, he is unapologetically critical of socialism. In
his general criticism of socialism, Trujillo asserts that many liberation theologians do not have a complete understanding of socialism as a system, fail

168. See Gutiérrez, *Truth Shall Make You Free*, 62–81.

169. Trujillo, *Liberation or Revolution?*, 17.

170. Trujillo, *Liberation or Revolution?*, 17–18.

171. Trujillo, *Liberation or Revolution?*, 38, 50.

172. Trujillo, *Liberation or Revolution?*, 97.

173. Trujillo, *Liberation or Revolution?*, 101.

to acknowledge and deal with the failures of Marxist socialism, and do not ground their arguments for socialism in scientific and systematic research on its actual form of existence, particularly in Europe.[174]

Cardinal Joseph Ratzinger was also an ardent critic of Gutiérrez's use of Marxist thought. In his general criticism of the project of Latin American liberation theology, Ratzinger scolded liberation theologians for using Marxian thought in their theological construction, warning them that such a theological move was detrimental to the Roman Catholic faith. In his 1986 "Instruction on Some Aspects of Theology of Liberation," Ratzinger wrote,

> The present instruction has a much more limited and precise purpose: to draw the attention of pastors, theologians, and all the faithful to the deviations, and risks of deviation, damaging to the faith and to Christian living, that are brought about by certain forms of liberation theology which use, in an insufficiently critical manner, concepts borrowed from various currents of Marxist thought.[175]

Is it possible to create a just social order—a society that is just—without accepting socialism? My goal here is not to explore in detail the complex phenomenon of socialism and the reasons for its acceptance or rejection in several parts of the world. I have a more modest goal: to highlight the role the concept of "socialism" played in the imagination of some Latin American liberation theologians. In the early 1970s, some priests from several Latin American countries convened to explore the proposal that socialism was a "necessary precondition for the construction of a just and humane society."[176] Such theological exploration was driven in part by the Christians for Socialism movement, which emerged in Chile during the presidency of Salvador Allende. In several of its documents, Christians for Socialism argued for the use of scientific analysis in understanding the social conditions, particularly poverty, in Latin America. At the heart of its objectives is the option for revolution and the role of Christians in the revolution:

> Through the characteristic feature of the convention itself, we want to give public expression to the scope and variety and concrete effectiveness of the option for revolution among Christians on our continent. Through this public manifestation we want

---

174. Trujillo, *Liberation or Revolution?*, 98–102.

175. Benedict XVI, *Instruction on Certain Aspects of the "Theology of Liberation."*

176. "Draft Agenda," in Eagleson, *Christians and Socialism*, 17–15.

to bear clear witness to the fact that the scope of this effort is as broad as Latin America itself.[177]

In 1973, the Chilean episcopate issued its own document, distancing itself from Christians for Socialism, condemning it for employing a "Marxist-Leninist method of interpreting history in economic terms."[178] Commenting on this method, the documents says:

> This method reduces the religious life of humanity to an ideology reflecting the economic infrastructure and the class struggle. In every instance where religion claims to be a-political, to be above and beyond conflicting dialectics in the social struggle (e.g., that of the bourgeoisie and that of the proletariat), this method sees alienation on the one hand and complicity with the dominant social groups on the other hand. It is not for us here to spell out to what extent this method can contribute valid elements to the social and historical sciences, and hence to people's social and political action. But we certainly can state that many of its elements and its essential postulates—e.g., materialism, dialectics, and atheism—are not scientific at all; nor can they claim the label of science in order to disqualify the spiritual and supernatural import of the Church's life. We can also say that these presuppositions and conclusions, which are formally philosophical and ideological in character but not scientific, are contrary to the Catholic faith. As the magisterium of the Church has repeatedly pointed out, they do not dovetail with the existence of God, human liberty, the autonomy of moral and spiritual values, and so forth.[179]

The episcopal document scolds the members of Christians for Socialism for bad science and for endangering the doctrines of the Roman Catholic Church. The criticism advanced in the document will set the tone for subsequent criticisms against liberation theology. Alfonso Trujillo also condemned the priests who endorsed the project of Christians for Socialism, accusing them of ignoring the magisterium of the Church.[180] However, it is not entirely clear how appealing to an ecclesiastical magisterium would be a viable argument against liberation theologians that construed capitalism

177. "Christians For Socialism: Draft Agenda of Proposed Convention," in Eagleson, *Christians and Socialism*, 21.

178. "Christian Faith and Political Activity: Declaration of the Chilean Bishops," 22, in Eagleson, *Christians and Socialism*, 191.

179. "Christian Faith and Political Activity: Declaration of the Chilean Bishops," 22, in Eagleson, *Christians and Socialism*, 191.

180. Trujillo, *Liberation or Revolution?*, 103.

as a prime culprit in the exploitation of many people in Latin America. The church's endorsement of capitalism or rejection of socialism is irrelevant insofar as the issue is discerning the socioeconomic structures and systems responsible for the massive scale of poverty that instigated the liberation theology movements in Latin America. One of the major arguments of Latin American liberation theologians was that the church should not take for granted how it was implicated in the social structures that created or sustained poverty. They encouraged Christian communities, as we saw in the writings of Gutiérrez, to engage in self-reflection and to rethink their relationship with the structures of the society that impede them from becoming a strong moral voice against social problems.

Another issue that is noteworthy is how to bring theological ideas that are grounded in the Christian faith into the pluralistic context of Latin America without making the public square a Christian colony. Though Christianity has a strong presence in Latin America, it is one among many religious traditions, therefore Christians are to constantly negotiate their theological reflections and beliefs in relation to other religious communities and also *a*religious communities. Gutiérrez at different junctures in his writings approached this issue by appealing to the idea of human freedom from oppression as a *human* problem and not merely a religious or Christian problem. He equally acknowledges the difficulty of presenting a *Christian* solution to poverty in the public square:

> The mission of the church, as the community of Jesus' disciples, is to communicate and bear witness to this total liberation of the human being. The liberation has, indeed, aspects that have a degree of autonomy (social liberation, liberation of the human person) but these are not watertight compartments into which the saving grace of Christ does not reach. The church must respect the inner coherence proper to each of these several areas; it does not have a right to give directives in fields that are the proper objects of human efforts. On the other hand, it does have a duty to show the connection of these areas with the kingdom of God and its ethical demands.[181]

Working out how Christians are to bring their theological beliefs and practices into the public square is a complex endeavor that has haunted Christians from their earliest beginnings. In many contexts, Christians are unable to (and should not) impose the Christian faith on non-Christian religious communities. The tasks of Christian theologians who venture into the treacherous path of engaging a social issue in the public square from

181. Gutiérrez, *Truth Shall Make You Free*, 141.

their own religious traditions, it seems to me, are (1) to show the utility of their proposal for addressing the problem in ways that will benefit the society and (2) to show why people who are non-Christians should be interested in such a proposal.[182] In the next chapter, I will return to these two issues, albeit focusing on contemporary Nigerian Christianity.

182. For discussions on different models for Christian public engagement tailored for the Western world, see Williams, *Faith in the Public Square*; Volf, *Public Faith*; Kaveny, *Prophecy Without Contempt*; Dulles, *Church and Society*.

6

Christian Abandonment and the Pursuit of Spiritual Solutions in Nigerian Christianity

A major goal that can be ferreted out of Jesus's public ministry is *discipleship*: his invitation to people to commit to him by submitting to his teaching and guidance in their exploration of God-world relations. Though Jesus did not write a manual on discipleship, a close look at the four canonical Gospels shows certain qualities that may be understood as disciple-making properties in his mode of discipleship. I will explore these disciple-making properties and also use them to assess the practice of discipleship in Nigerian Christianity. The primary context of this exploration will be the phenomenon of intermittent abandonment of Jesus by some Nigerian Christians in their pursuit of spiritual solutions to existential needs. I undertake a theological interpretation of this phenomenon, focusing on what it might tell us about the ways some Nigerian Christians appropriate their understandings of Jesus in the contexts of existential needs, spiritual solutions to such needs, and Christian discipleship. Like in the preceding four chapters, I will begin first with a terse summary and historical background of the main theological issues of this chapter.

Theological Case: Intermittent Desertion of Jesus in Pursuit of Spiritual Solutions to Existential Needs

Summary of the Issues

- The proclivity of some Nigerian Christians to desert Jesus, albeit intermittently, for spiritual solutions to existential needs and the theological problems it poses to Christian discipleship.

- The freedom of disciples to explore alternative spiritual solutions to their existential needs, particularly when Jesus appears to be disinterested in providing such solutions.

Historical Background

For several years now, I have studied Nigerian Christianity, focusing on some Christians' penchant for forswearing Jesus if he appeared to delay solutions to their daily needs.[1] What is particularly revealing about this phenomenon is that some Christians sometimes consult oracles of the deities of traditional Nigerian religion in their search for and pursuit of spiritual solutions to their existential needs.[2] I will call this proclivity of deserting Jesus for spiritual solutions to existential needs "Christian abandonment." Some exogenous factors—for example, failing healthcare systems, largely ineffective security against threats to life and property, and the growing scale of extreme poverty—are partly the reasons Christian abandonment is taken for granted.[3] These exogenous factors exert a considerable pressure on many Nigerian Christians, pulling their faith allegiance in two different directions—towards Jesus and towards deities of traditional Nigerian religion.[4] I will explore later in this chapter some examples of these exogenous factors. It is important to note here that echoes of what Emile Durkheim described as *anomie*—a disordered division of labor—can be discerned in some of the factors that cause Christian abandonment in Nigerian Christianity.[5] Existential problems in Nigeria reflect the pervasive social anomie, a situation where old and established ways of doing things, such as the rules guiding expectations or aspirations and the means for realizing them, have been undermined and new effective ones have not been established.[6]

1. A theological analysis of some of my findings was published in Ezigbo, *Re-imagining African Christologies*.

2. I will return to define how the terms *spiritual solutions* and *existential needs* are used in this chapter.

3. For data on poverty in Nigeria, see Canagarajah and Thomas, "Poverty in a Wealthy Economy."

4. The phrase *traditional Nigerian religion* refers to one of the religious traditions that have been subsumed under the terms *African Religions* or *African Traditional Religions*. For more discussions on these religions, see Mbiti, *Introduction to African Religion*; Olupona, *African Traditional Religions in Contemporary Society*; Olupona, *African Religions*; Imasogie, *African Traditional Religion*.

5. For Durkheim's discussion on anomie, see Durkheim, *Division of Labor in Society*.

6. I am indebted to Dr. Samuel Zalanga for Durkheim's discussion on anomie and its implications for understanding social problems in contemporary Nigeria.

The term *existential needs* is used here to describe what many Nigerian Christians believe to be essential to their existence and well-being. Good health, safety, fertility, food, and shelter are examples of such needs. These needs typically cause immense suffering and pain. Therefore, seeking solutions to these needs, either from Jesus or oracles of a local deity, should be understood as an exercise in practical judgment: an attempt to alleviate real suffering and pain. *Spiritual solutions* are divinely induced miraculous acts that appear in different forms, such as an unexpected deliverance from threats to one's life and provision of funds to cater for pressing needs. Some recipients of spiritual solutions in Igbo Christian communities call Jesus *ọtụmụọkpo ndị kwere ekwe* (literally the "amulet of believers") as a way of describing their belief that Jesus is a source of spiritual solution.

Interestingly, in the traditional worldviews of many Nigerian communities, it is common belief that local deities also give spiritual solutions to their worshippers and seekers. Many Nigerian Christians believe that some members of their communities who desire quicker solutions to their existential needs consult priests and oracles of the traditional religion.[7] In the words of Moses Attah, an Evangelical Christian from northern Nigeria:

> In the North, you may have problems with somebody and if you call on Jesus the problems may not be solved immediately. Some people will do as we normally say, "Let me put off the shirt of Jesus Christ and put on the cultural shirt." Then they will go to [a] shrine [of a local deity] or any other place to look for help, forgetting that Jesus will help them. And sometimes during either tribal war or religious war between Christians and Muslims, some Christians . . . collect charms [from native doctors or oracles of local deities] in order to protect themselves, forgetting that Jesus is there to protect them.[8]

I do not aim to prove or disprove the spiritual solutions that Christians claim to get either from Jesus or other religious sources.[9] I have a more

7. Strikingly, in matters of existential needs, Jesus may not be the preferred option. The agencies of traditional Nigerian religion, such as priests and oracles of local deities, are usually the preferred options.

8. Moses Attah, interview by Victor I. Ezigbo, tape recording, Aba, February 29, 2006.

9. Such ambitious tasks are beyond the scope of this chapter. Also, since claims about spiritual solutions from Jesus and other religious sources belong to the realm of religious experiences, which are notoriously slippery and unpredictable, they are largely closed to independent verifications. For helpful discussions on the history and complexity of the concept of religious experience, see Proudfoot, *Religious Experience*; James, *Varieties of Religious Experience*.

modest task, to explore the question: What christological problem does Christian abandonment raise about the nature and *raison d'être* of Christian discipleship? At the core of this question are the issues of how best to imagine Jesus's discipleship and also its place and cogency in appraising Christian abandonment in Nigerian Christianity, particularly in the present climate of religious violence. In order to address these issues, I will attend to the phenomenon of religious violence in Nigeria, the christological issues that underlie Christian abandonment, Jesus's mode of discipleship, and some lessons from Jesus's teaching for confronting religious violence.

Religious Violence in Nigeria: Its Context and Outcomes

The term "religious violence" is notoriously difficult to define. Given that scholars have not reached a consensus on a particular way of understanding it, I will describe how I intend to use it in this chapter. I use the term "religious" for the diverse and recognizable ways a community expresses and responds to its awareness of divine-world relations.[10] The term "violence" refers to a lethal or nonlethal act that is intended to destroy human lives or properties. Violence can take different forms, including physical (the use of force to cause bodily harm or destroy properties) and rhetorical (the use of words to injure people emotionally, psychologically, and spiritually). "Religious violence" is used here to describe extrajudicial violent acts carried out by some adherents of Nigeria's religions in defense of

10. For discussions on the complexity and the diverse usage of the term "religion," see Smith, *Meaning and End of Religion*, especially chs. 2 and 3. As a contextual theologian, I am drawn to William Cavanaugh's claim that there is no such thing as a "religion—a genus of which Christianity, Islam, Hinduism, and so on are species, which is necessarily more inclined toward violence than are ideologies and institutions that are identified as secular." Cavanaugh's point is that the "category of religion," as it is imagined in the post-Enlightenment Western world, is an arbitrary construction that emerged as a strategy to create "a dichotomy between the religious and the secular" with the intent to denigrate the religious as "an irrational and dangerous impulse that must give way in public to rational, secular forms of power." Cavanaugh also notes that one of the underlying agendas of construing religion and the religious in this way is to justify "the killing and dying in the name of the nation-state" and to demonize the "killing and dying in the name of one's religion." Without attempting to excuse either of these forms of killing and dying, Cavanaugh argues that "there is no transhistorical and transcultural essence of religion and that essentialist attempts to separate religious violence from secular violence are incoherent." In other words, the causes of and motivations for the so-called religious violence and secular violence are "not immune to historical circumstances" but rather are conditioned by "the empirically observable actions" of specific communities that carry out such violence. Cavanaugh, *Myth of Religious Violence*, 3–5.

their religious community's interests.[11] A community's act of defense may be a preemptive attack done to ward off a potential threat to its interest. It could also be in the form of a counterattack in response to the harm done to its members. The community's interests need not, as they are often the case, be purely religious.

The phenomenon of religious violence in Nigeria has a complex history. Therefore, it is useful to attend to the broader climate in which it has taken its different forms of existence in response to different factors, which include political, economic, social, and ethnic cleavages.[12]

Socio-political Context of Religious Violence in Contemporary Nigeria

With a quizzical look, she asked: "Is he a Christian? Isn't Bethel a Christian university?" A Nigerian (Igbo) woman who was studying at Bethel University asked me those questions when I said to her that another Nigerian scholar, from northern Nigeria, teaches sociology at the university. As one familiar with some of the ethnic and religious stereotypes that are prevalent in Nigeria, I understood the woman's assumption: my colleague (let's call him Dr. Z) must be a Muslim because he is from northern Nigeria. (In fact, he was born into a Christian evangelist's home and grew up a Christian.) In 2017, I visited the hometown of Dr. Z, which is predominantly Muslim in terms of cultures and demographics. I still remember the sardonic tone of some of my extended family members living in Nigeria when I told them I was going to spend some time in Bauchi State. They thought I couldn't possibly be saying what they were hearing. One of my outspoken cousins said: "Well, come back to us alive." He clearly assumed that my life would be in grave danger. He feared that some northerners might hurt me either because I am an Igbo or because I am a Christian. While in Zalanga (a village in Bauchi state), I learned that Christians and Muslims have lived peacefully together for decades and sometimes have intermarried. I share these personal stories in order to highlight some ethnic and religious assumptions that largely condition social relations in contemporary Nigeria. My cousin's assumption and fears were not atypical.

11. An "extrajudicial violence" is any lethal or non-lethal act intended to destroy human lives and property that is not authorized by a nation's constituted government or judicial authority.

12. Some Nigerians with ethnic and political agendas have sometimes used religion to inspire camaraderie among those they hope to recruit or have already recruited to join their cause.

I chose to study Nigerian Christianity in this chapter for two main reasons. Firstly, in the wake of the rapid expansion of Christianity in the global south, Nigeria has emerged as a major center of Christianity. Allan Anderson has rightly observed that some of "the largest gatherings of Christians in the world occur in the compounds of . . . Nigerian churches, where hundreds of thousands of people attend all-night Friday prayer meetings in places with names like Redemption Ground and Canaan Land."[13] One possible factor for the expansion of Christianity in Nigeria is that most Nigerians are deeply religious. Many of them would see the separation of religious and secular into two polemical spheres like in several parts of the Western world as an anomaly, arbitrary, and unrealistic.[14] Religious and secular are rather understood as a dyad that ought to shape Nigeria's public square. However, how best to imagine the relationship of the religious and secular has continued to be a source of intense debates and disagreements in Nigeria. For example, though Nigerian constitution prohibits a state religion, Christians and Muslims harbor fears of Islamization or Christianization of Nigeria. Depending on the religious identity of principal political officers such as presidents, governors, and local government chairpersons, many Christians and Muslims fear marginalization, which may come in the form of unfavorable policies.[15] Some of these political officers freely meddle in religious affairs for political gains or ethnic agendas.

13. Anderson, *Introduction to Pentecostalism*, 112.

14. Writing from the Western context, Rowan Williams has noted two forms of secularism, one of which poses a serious threat to religious freedom. "Procedural secularism," for example, guarantees equal protection to all religious institutions under the law. A government that adopts a procedural secular policy "declines to give advantage or preference to any religious body over others." Unlike procedural secularism, a government that adopts "programmatic secularism" seeks to relegate religious convictions to the private realm in order to ensure an undivided loyalty to the state. Though procedural secularism does not pose any serious threat to Christianity, programmatic secularism poses a serious problem to Christianity and to other religious communities. Programmatic secularism operates with a parochial understanding of loyalty, which wrongly assumes that "only one sort of loyalty is really possible." Contrary to this assumption, Williams contends that people can simultaneously show loyalty to their faith and to their state. Also, he rejects the assumption of the programmatic secularists that a "neutral public order of rational persons" requires relegating religious values to the private sphere. Williams, *Faith in the Public Square*, 1–3.

15. The section on "Fundamental Rights" in the Nigerian Constitution makes provision for religious freedom, freedom of religious education within certain parameters, and freedom of religious association: (1) "Every person shall be entitled to freedom of thought, conscience and religion, including freedom to change his religion or belief, and freedom (either alone or in community with others, and in public or in private) to manifest and propagate his religion or belief in worship, teaching, practice and observance." (2) "No person attending any place of education shall be required to receive

Secondly, Nigeria has continued to witness bloody violence between religious communities, especially between Christian and Muslim communities in many parts of northern Nigeria. It is noteworthy at this point that some Christians are increasingly becoming open to the idea of preemptive strikes or counterattacks against adherents of traditional Nigerian religion and Muslim communities. Yet, in spite of the destructive and violent conflicts between Nigerian religious communities, the roles that these communities can play in promoting and preserving the sacredness of human life, human dignity, and peace in Nigeria should not be ignored. As Olufemi Vaughan has noted, "Christian, Muslim, and indigenous religious structures are integral to the formation of the modern Nigerian state and society. . . . [The] intersections of these competing religious traditions—Islam, Christianity, and indigenous religions—are decisive in the making of the modern Nigeria."[16] Adherents of these three major religious traditions negotiate their religious identities and viabilities within the matrix of the ethnic, economic, and political milieu of contemporary Nigeria. As the adherents of each of these religions enter into such negotiation, they confront what they consider serious threats to the existence of their own religious beliefs and communities. In what follows, I will survey the historical context of interreligious conflicts in Nigeria. The survey will illuminate several complex factors that condition and amplify violent interactions between religious communities.

Nigerians are now witnessing the dawning of a new and terrifying epoch. This new and emerging epoch is, however, intersecting with the receding old epoch. In the receding epoch, the utility of religious communities as an essential factor in building a peaceful, flourishing, and prosperous nation was a default position. In the new and emerging epoch, the usefulness of religious communities in making Nigeria a peaceful, flourishing, and prosperous nation is no longer a default position. In the receding epoch, interreligious conflicts were an anomaly and a state of interreligious harmony was the normal experience. In the emerging epoch, the state of affairs is reversed: interreligious conflicts have increasingly become the normal experience and

religious instruction or to take part in or attend any religious ceremony or observance if such instruction ceremony or observance relates to a religion other than his own, or religion not approved by his parent or guardian." (3) "No religious community or denomination shall be prevented from providing religious instruction for pupils of that community or denomination in any place of education maintained wholly by that community or denomination." (4) "Nothing in this section shall entitle any person to form, take part in the activity or be a member of a secret society." *Constitution of the Federal Republic of Nigeria*, Act No. 24, May 5, 1999, ch. IV, 38.1–4, available at: https://publicofficialsfinancialdisclosure.worldbank.org/sites/fdl/files/assets/law-library-files/Nigeria_Constitution_1999_en.pdf.

16. Vaughan, *Religion and the Making of Nigeria*, 1.

a peaceful coexistence of religious communities is becoming an anomaly or an aberration. In the receding epoch, there were limited attempts to engage in interreligious conversations with the intent to promote mutual understanding of faiths in a less adversarial circumstance. In this new and emerging epoch, several concerted efforts are being made to promote interfaith dialogues, albeit in more adversarial circumstances.

Painting with a broad brush, the receding epoch, whose beginnings could be traced back to 1914, witnessed the optimism of religion's usefulness as an important factor in nation-building. Some inheritors of the Sokoto reformist jihad (1804–8) and the Niger Mission (1841–91) in Abeokuta and other parts of the southwest region were prepared to use their religious ideas to shape the political and social life of the communities that eventually became part of Nigeria in 1914.[17] Many people, both locals and foreigners, had high hopes of witnessing the flourishing of foreign religions, particularly Islam and Christianity, as bridges connecting the southern and northern protectorates, which were amalgamated, and also the numerous ethnic groups that constituted the protectorates. Interestingly, such high hopes coincided with a period of Nigerian history when there were fewer churches, fewer mosques, and more shrines dedicated to local gods and deities. Although the signs of its receding were felt in a few areas of the nation, sometime around the early 1990s, the decline of the old epoch was brought into the nation's consciousness in ways that surprised many dreamers. Many Nigerians began to say with frustrations: "We thought that religion was the factor that would unite many of our warring communities and diverse ethnic groups!" As the old epoch is receding to the periphery of national consciousness, it is becoming glaringly clear that the utility of religion as a unifying factor and an essential element for building a successful, peaceful, and prosperous Nigeria can no longer be taken for granted.

The early beginnings of the new and emerging epoch could be traced back to the 1990s at a time when interreligious conflicts and violence were arising in some parts of northern Nigeria. In this epoch, religion's role as an essential player in Nigeria's nation-building project no longer has the wider public confidence and unquestioned support it previously enjoyed in the receding epoch. In fact, since religion's seat at the table may no longer be a default position, the adherents of Nigeria's religions would need to demonstrate why religion is an essential factor in the project of building a strong, secure, flourishing, and prosperous Nigeria. Merely appealing to the pervasiveness of religion in all areas of Nigerians' personal as well as public

17. For further discussions on how Christianity and Islam shaped Nigeria in the early twentieth century, see Vaughan, *Religion and the Making of Nigeria*, especially chs. 1–4.

life does not quite get Nigeria's religious communities off the hook in the judicial court of nation-building. As each religious community engages in self-reflection and also rethinks how it can contribute to Nigeria's prosperity, safety, and flourishing, it will be confronted with what may be described as Nigeria's "crisis of being"—the feeling of brokenness that is displayed in the ubiquitous anxiety of Nigerians about the viability of Nigeria's existence as a unified entity amidst the conflictual relations of its communities (religious, ethnic, social, and political). Religious violence is one of the noticeable and devastating ways Nigeria's crisis of being is manifested in the public square. I will now briefly describe the nature and scope of this crisis.

Crisis of Being and National Identity

Nigeria's crisis of being is eroding away the idea of *national identity*: the commitment to the well-being of Nigeria in terms of its sovereignty, security, prosperity, goals, and inhabitants. Many Nigerians now believe that religiously, ethnically, and politically motivated conflicts are like a ticking bomb that could explode at any time and plunge Nigeria back into silos of warring groups and sub-groups. Some salient turning points of Nigeria's crisis of being are noteworthy. The origins of the crisis can be traced back to Great Britain's arbitrary lumping together of disparate ethnic communities into protectorates and the subsequent amalgamation of the northern and southern protectorates in 1914.[18] British colonialists and imperialists were more interested in their geographical acquisitions than preserving the different vernaculars, dialects, cultures, forms of governance, and religions of the ethnic communities they forced into a unified nation or colony. Like the Koine Greek in the era of Hellenization, English became more than a *lingua franca,* for it was also a tool that Great Britain used to control its subjects. The process of *indirect rule*—the use of local forms of governance (native authority) as British proxies—did not quite smooth out the rough

---

18. The amalgamation officially took place on January 1, 1914. In 1906, the colony and protectorate of Lagos and the southern protectorate were merged together under the name "Protectorate of Southern Nigeria." See Akinola, *Party Coalitions in Nigeria,* 2. Nigeria was indeed the economic and political project (*experiment* may be a better term) of the British imperialists and colonialists. Dissatisfied with the cumbersomeness of names such as "The Hausa Territories," "Central Sudan," and "The Royal Niger Company Territories," which were used for different regions that would eventually become part of modern-day Nigeria, Flora Shaw (1852–1929), who later became the wife of Sir Frederick Lugard (the first Governor-General of the amalgamated southern and northern protectorates in 1914), first suggested "Nigeria" as a simpler and novel name for the territories in her January 8, 1897, article published in *The Times* (a British daily newspaper). See Crowder, *Short History of Nigeria,* 21–23, 231–34.

edges of an arbitrary amalgam of disparate identities.[19] It should, of course, be noted that the British colonialists and imperialists did not institute an indirect rule purely as an act of political altruism; it was also a strategy to make the "subject people in the image of their alien masters."[20] Dividing the southern protectorate into two provinces—eastern (with Enugu as its headquarter) and western (with Ibadan as its headquarter)—in 1939 and preserving the northern province (with Kaduna as its headquarter), in Anthony Akinola's assessment, "marked the birth of three geographically distinct and politically hostile cultures."[21] At the national level, political affiliations and agendas of Nigerians have roughly followed the three main regional ethnic bloc—Hausa, Igbo, and Yoruba.[22]

In the early years following Nigeria's independence on October 1, 1960, from British colonial rule, Nigeria's crisis of being resurfaced in the events that led to the civil war (1967–70). The government of Nigeria resisted with deadly force against the Igbos for wanting to secede from Nigeria and to create the state of Biafra under the leadership of Chukwuemeka Odumegwu Ojukwu (1933–2011). Among several economic and political factors that led to the civil war, one main factor was a breakdown in negotiations as the political elites from the three major ethnic regions (north, southwest, and southeast) struggled to harness different political, ethnic, cultural, and religious currents that had gone into the nationalist movements' efforts to secure Nigeria's independence from Great Britain. The movements exemplified Nigerians' commitment to national identity. As Michael Crowder has noted, the nationalist movements were led by a class of people who "began to think of themselves as Nigerians rather than Ibo, Hausa and Yoruba."[23] Inspired by pan-Africanist intellectuals such as the West Indian Edward Blyden (1832–1912) and the Liberian John Payne Jackson (1848–1915), who were committed to the liberation of Africans from European colonial rule and cultural colonialism, Olayinka Herbert Macaulay (1864–1946), Nnamdi Azikiwe (1904–96) and others fought for Nigeria's independence. Azikiwe, an Igbo, became the first Nigerian president, serving from 1963–1966.[24] Obviously, the nascent Nigeria's democracy was cut short by the civil war. The Nigerian Civil War sowed a lasting seed of mistrust between Igbos and the

19. Osaghae, "Managing Multiple Minority Problems," 4–5.

20. Whitaker, Politics of Tradition, 27.

21. Akinola, Party Coalitions in Nigeria, 5.

22. Vinson, Religion, Violence, and Local Power-Sharing in Nigeria, 9–10.

23. Crowder, Short History of Nigeria, 253.

24. The Nigerian Independence Act (1960) preserved Queen Elizabeth II as the monarch of Nigeria from 1960 to 1963.

rest of the country, especially people from the northern region. Many derogatory stereotypes in Nigeria are symptomatic of how people belonging to the traditional three main regional blocs—Igbo, Hausa, and Yoruba—relate to each other. For example, when an Igbo calls another Igbo person *onye awusa* (a Hausa person), it could mean, depending on the context of the conversation, a fool, an illiterate, or a beggar. People from the northern region (including the middle belt) generally refer to the Igbos as *nyamiri,* sometimes to remind them that they are the defeated foe because they lost in the civil war (1967–70) or that they are foreigners when referring to the Igbos residing in northern Nigeria. These kinds of derogatory stereotypes are symptomatic of a prevalent way of seeing and naming among Nigerians that is rooted in degrading perceptions of one ethnic group by other groups.

The event of June 12, 1993, was another turning point in Nigeria's crisis of being. On this day, for some bizarre reasons, General Ibrahim Babangida, the military head of state, annulled the result of a democratic presidential election won by the Yoruba Bashorun M. K. O. Abiola (1937–98). Many feared that people of the southwest region of Nigeria would attempt secession that could lead to another civil war. In 2009, Babangida for the first time made public his reasons for annulling the election. In his view, Nigeria was not quite ready for a democratic government. He feared that Abiola would have been ousted out of office by a military coup d'état.[25] The recent decision of President Muhammadu Buhari to move Nigeria's Democracy Day from May 31 to June 12 in recognition of the successful, albeit annulled, democratic election of 1993, could be a double-edged sword.[26] On one hand, it could pacify the southwestern Nigerians and other Nigerians who were infuriated by the 1993 annulment. On the other hand, it could, in the future, reopen an old political wound that could cause some to seek compensations. If such compensations are not granted, Nigeria may find itself in another political crisis or a civil war.

The reintroduction of Sharia has amplified Nigeria's crisis of being. Some Nigerians viewed the introduction of Sharia in Zamfara State in 1999 as an insidious effort that would erode away the unity of Nigerians and also undermine the nascent transition from a military to a democratic rule.[27] Many non-Muslim Nigerians have remained suspicious of some Muslims who are holding national political offices, fearing that they might

25. Nwachukwu, "'Why I Annulled June 12 1993 Presidential Election'—Babangida."

26. President Buhari made the announcement in his speech on May 29, 2018. For the full speech, see "President Muhammadu Buhari's 2018 Democracy Day speech."

27. For extensive discussions on the resistance (both violent and nonviolent) to the 1999 pro-Sharia movements in some parts of northern Nigeria, see Vaughan, *Religion and the Making of Nigeria,* 181–222.

allow structures that would lead to the Islamization of Nigeria. Such fears are usually heightened during presidential elections. For example, in the 2015 presidential election, some Muslims from northern Nigeria geared up for conflicts when it was rumored that President Goodluck Jonathan, a Christian, might rig the election if the retired General Muhammadu Buhari won the election. Though some people from the southwest region reminded other Nigerians that they would not be excluded from the national *cake* (political influence), many people from the southeast region threatened to secede from Nigeria if President Jonathan was ousted from the office. The political decision of the then-candidate Muhammadu Buhari to choose a Yoruba Christian (who is also a pastor) as his vice-presidential running mate highlighted the roles that ethnicity and religion play in Nigeria's national politics.

The crisis of being I have outlined above paints a gloomy picture about Nigeria's future. But what if Nigeria's crisis of being is approached, not from the perspective of doom, but rather by exploring the opportunities that it could provide for rethinking the oneness of Nigeria, to use the words of the Nigerian national anthem, as "one nation bound in freedom, peace, and unity"? This question is not intended to undermine the seriousness of the conflictual relations that characterize many communities in Nigeria. The question is also not intended as an insidious strategy to circumvent the past and present events that have caused conflicts in Nigeria, especially along ethnic, political, and religious lines. It is rather intended to explore a counter-narrative to the language of doom about Nigeria's disintegration into silos and sub-silos of warring groups. That many Nigerian religious communities—Muslims, Christians, and adherents of traditional religions, in particular—continue to coexist peacefully in several villages, towns, and cities show that the narrative of doom need not be the final word on the matter. Rather than succumbing to fears of disintegration, Nigerians can explore the opportunities that Nigeria's crisis of being can create for them to reimagine the idea of oneness in a national context.

Nigeria's oneness should be reimagined in ways that go beyond *federalism*—a political arrangement in which regional and sub-regional political blocs agree to form a unified government.[28] Laura Vinson has proposed that

28. Emilian Kavalski and Magdalena Zolkos have described two forms of federalism that capture the different practice of federalism in Nigeria: "We distinguish between two dominant interactive processes of federalism: territorial federalism and multinational federalism—sometimes referred to as 'plural federalism.' The former provides a means by which 'a single national community' can divide and diffuse power, while the latter indicates a conscious intention to accommodate the desire of national minorities for self-government." Kavalski and Zolkos, "Approaching the Phenomenon of Federal Failure," 2.

"power-sharing," particularly at the level of the Local Government Areas (LGAs), will reduce or prevent inter-communal violence in Nigeria:

> Ultimately, the findings hold out—not only that religious violence is not an inevitable feature of strongly religious communities in weak states—but that there is no one path to power-sharing and no one historical experience that can definitively eliminate the possibility of religious peace. Despite the saliency and acrid nature of religion in Nigerian national and local politics, the data and comparative case studies . . . show that local elites in power-sharing LGAs are less likely to exploit religious cleavages, and they are more conciliatory in their actions and rhetoric. Similarly, the local population is less likely to perceive local issues of inequality and political competitions through the lens of religion or to see religion as a basis for violent mobilization.[29]

Vinson's argument would explain politically charged issues, especially at a local level but not at the regional and national levels. Of course, power-sharing at the local government level does not eliminate political corruption or embezzlement of public funds that partly explain the debilitating state of basic amenities such as roads, electricity, water supply, and security, all of which make some people vulnerable or prone to violence. Vinson fails to account for the complexity of several cases of inter-communal violence in Nigeria that are the result of an international issue (like the Danish representation of Prophet Muhammad in cartoons).[30] Also, it is not clear how power-sharing at the level of LGAs would deal with fears of Islamization or Christianization that haunt many Nigerians today. The practice of power-sharing at the local government level does not really address ethnically motivated violence.[31] For example, in 2015, the Oba of

---

29. Vinson, *Religion, Violence, and Local Power-Sharing in Nigeria*, 30.

30. The report on the violence that occurred in Nigeria as a result of the publication of the cartoons can be accessed: "16 die in cartoon protests in Nigeria," *CNN*, February 19, 2006, http://www.cnn.com/2006/WORLD/africa/02/18/cartoon.roundup/index.html.

31. In his response to the question, "Does democratic transition help to resolve or aggravate violent political conflicts in general, and ethnic and religious conflicts in particular?" Muhammad Umar argues: "Democracy does not resolve preexisting violent political conflicts, particularly those with religious and ethnic dimensions. In fact, democracy could aggravate such conflicts by transforming them into contests that are characteristic of democracy: contests of elections, ideas, policies, privileges, and positions of power." Umar, "Weak States and Democratization," 259.

Lagos threatened to drown Igbos if they voted against his preferred candidate in the gubernatorial election.[32]

I propose that a reimagination of Nigeria's oneness in the context of nationhood ought to be grounded in the notion of well-being that upholds the human worth and dignity of all Nigerians. By "well-being," I mean a state of wellness that springs from the worthiness of human life, extending to various aspects of human existence. The term "worthiness" should be understood broadly to include value, dignity, freedom, and respect. I propose that one of the ways to redress religiously motivated violence in Nigeria is for Nigerians to rediscover their oneness as a people belonging to one community. The word "redress" refers to the process of exposing the complex casual factors of religiously motivated violence, prosecuting perpetrators, rehabilitating perpetrators, compensating victims, and preventing future extrajudicial violence through a judicial system. Oneness in this context should go beyond political power-sharing and Nigeria's *lingua franca* (i.e., the English language—the residue of British colonialism—in all of its metastasized forms). Oneness, as it is used here, is to be pursued with the intent to promote the well-being of all Nigerians. Promoting Nigerians' well-being will require seeing their oneness in a tripartite way: (1) *oneness of substance*, people who possess the essential quality of humans; (2) *oneness of relationship*, people who share a common national identity; and (3) *oneness of purpose*, people who share a common task of promoting the well-being of all Nigerians. These three interrelated ways of imagining Nigerians' oneness can serve as guardrails in the discussion on the complex issues of religious violence in contemporary Nigeria and effective ways to combat it. In what follows, I describe the current state of affairs of religious violence in Nigeria.

Current State of Affairs of Religious Violence

Religious violence has reached epidemic proportions in Nigeria. Countless lives and properties have been lost to religious violence. Three factors are of particular importance for understanding religious violence in contemporary Nigeria. These factors provide helpful backgrounds to the conflictual relationships between many Nigerian religious communities. The first factor is the common belief in the effectiveness of violence as a deterrent to real and perceived threats to a community's life, practices, and interests. Some religious communities adopt banditry and jungle justice as the last resort to redress harms done to them by people of other faiths. Increasingly, many communities use violence (both rhetorical and

32. To view Oba's speech, see SaharaTV, "RAW VIDEO."

physical) as the most viable option to protect themselves against threats to properties and ways of life. For instance, in January 2010, some Christians in Dogo Nahawa preemptively attacked Muslim communities as a way of preventing them from building a mosque in a predominantly Christian quarter of the village.[33] Several months later, some Muslims retaliated, killing between three hundred and five hundred Christians in the village of Dogo Nahawa.[34] In 2011, Christians and Muslims clashed in the city of Jos when some Muslims trekked into "a predominantly Christian neighborhood to pray at an abandoned mosque—destroyed in previous inter-religious violence—against the warning of security personnel."[35] While at Jos ECWA Theological Seminary (JETS) as a visiting scholar in the summer of 2017, I learned that some Berom Christians who, for unclear reasons, chose to roast and eat the body parts of some fallen Muslim militants, was the worst-kept secret among Christian communities in Jos.[36] Some Christians sometimes engage in preemptive attacks against other religious communities. To cite an example, Pastor Wale Fagbere destroyed a shrine dedicated to a deity from a traditional Yoruba religion in Ketu, Ogun State, as a public display of the powerlessness of non-Christian gods when confronted with the almighty power of Jesus.[37]

The second factor is the propensity to uphold religious identity and ethnic identity above national identity. Bishop David Oyedepo of the Living Faith Church Worldwide International preached an infamous sermon in 2015 that was replete with echoes of religious and ethnic interests or agendas.[38] For example, he said: "Must the north continue to rule? What devils! God has anointed me to lead a revolution against the Islamic jihadist and as the Lord liveth and . . . we declare them extinct in the name of Jesus!" The word "north" refers to the political elite from the northern part of Nigeria, which is predominantly Muslim. Some echoes of religious agenda can be found in the expression "Islamic Jihadist." It is also evident in the words "name of Jesus," which represent the Bishop's source of power for the revolution he claims to lead. Loyalty to religious and ethnic interests, when pursued at the expense

33. Handley, "Violence in Nigeria."

34. Nossiter, "Toll from Religious and Ethnic Violence in Nigeria Rises to 500."

35. Vinson, *Religion, Violence, and Local Power-Sharing in Nigeria*, 1.

36. On this cannibalistic act, Laura Vinson wrote, "At least 24 people were killed, and gruesome reports emerged that Christian youth had not only beheaded some Muslims, but also roasted and eaten their flesh." Vinson, *Religion, Violence, and Local Power-Sharing in Nigeria*, 1.

37. Awoyinfa, "Pastor who Destroyed Shrine in Ogun Denies Being Stricken by 'Gods.'"

38. Onyeji, "Living Faith Church Reacts to Video."

of national interests (such as promoting the welfare of all Nigerians) may cause nonviolent religious people to protect the members of their communities that engage in violent acts rather than aid government authorities to capture and prosecute them as the culprits of extrajudicial violence. Some people who have such blind allegiance to their religious community may see the government's crackdowns on religiously motivated crimes within their communities as persecutions.

The third factor is public mistrust of the Nigerian government as a neutral and reliable arbiter of religious freedom. Oyedepo's sermon also highlights this mistrust of the Nigerian government: "Every agent of destruction in [Nigerian] Government today, call fire down on their head, call fire down on their head. Everyone sponsoring evil against the nation [Nigeria]; let your fire fall on him!" One can also hear the Bishop's mistrust of Nigerian government in the words "There is no reporting to anybody."[39] Rather than defer to government authorities, Bishop Oyedepo seems to encourage his members to be both the judge and executioner in cases relating to an "Islamic Jihadist" who might attack his congregation. In 2016, Kamal-deen Olawale Sulaiman argued that strengthening the Nigerian constitution and also enforcing the rule of law are needed to combat religious violence. He wrote,

> The Constitution must be strengthened and respected. This includes the respect for the rule of law, respect for the fundamental human rights, independence of the judiciary and respect to all democratic norms and values. This is the running of government affairs in a positive and progressive manner that will be beneficial to the governed by following due process and the rule of law.[40]

Apart from the fact that Sulaiman did not say precisely the area of the Nigerian constitution that needed strengthening, it is not entirely clear if what is needed is a constitutional amendment. What is needed the most is how to restore Nigerians' faith in the Nigerian government as an effective and neutral institution that protects religious freedom. Sulaiman rightly notes that the "Nigerian Government should, at the Federal, State and Local Levels, adopt an open and uncompromising neutral attitude towards religious groups in the country."[41] In order to attain this state of affairs, "anyone in the position of power in a multi-religious country should not allow his religious inclination to override common interests. Nigerians should be treated equally and be given equal rights and privileges irrespective of their

39. Onyeji, "Living Faith Church Reacts to Video."

40. Sulaiman, "Religious Violence in Contemporary Nigeria," 96.

41. Sulaiman, "Religious Violence in Contemporary Nigeria," 96.

religious background."[42] But how can this be enforced? Relying solely on individuals' morality might not quite eradicate the abuses of people who are holding political, military, and judicial offices who consider their religious and ethnic allegiances as more important than the national interest. The complexity of interreligious relations and religious violence in Nigeria requires collaborative efforts of Nigerians who uphold the national interest of Nigeria and at the same time duly attend to the diverse ethnic and religious interests of religious communities. Each religious community, for example, should iron out how it can contribute to the efforts being made to promote Nigeria's well-being and also to bring about the peaceful coexistence of religious communities in the country. A religious community should examine itself by attending to the ways in which some of its members have misused its sacred texts and religious beliefs to justify their violent actions in pursuit of either religious or nonreligious agendas. It should equally be proactive in expounding its religious teachings that can motivate its members to become good citizens of Nigeria: those who promote the common good of Nigeria and attend duly to the needs (social, economic, political, ethnic, and religious) of all Nigerians.

Underlying these three factors are several socioeconomic and political conditions that have relegated some Nigerian communities to the periphery of the nation in which they are subjected to vulnerabilities. Sometimes, scarcity of resources, which has led to poverty and economic hardships, conditions how these three factors are expressed and embodied.[43] It is sometimes difficult to differentiate the violence perpetrated by some religious people for the sake of safeguarding a purely religious interest from the violence perpetrated by religious people for the sake of safeguarding ethnic, economic, and political interests. In other words, some of the violent acts that are usually lumped together under the category of religious violence may have nothing really to do with a religious tradition in itself but rather with religious people who are conditioned by nonreligious currents in their own communities. In *The Myth of Religious Violence*, William Cavanaugh challenged the notion of "a transhistorical and transcultural concept of religion that is essentially prone to violence."[44] Against this juxtaposition of religion and violence, which is prevalent in Western societies, Cavanaugh argues that the so-called religious violence shares more in common with secular violence than most

42. Sulaiman, "Religious Violence in Contemporary Nigeria," 96.

43. For more discussions on how socioeconomic factors contribute to religious violence in Nigeria, see Falola and Heaton, *History of Nigeria*, 238–41; Falola and Oyebade, *Hot Spot*, 82–84; Vinson, *Religion, Violence, and Local Power-Sharing in Nigeria*.

44. Cavanaugh, *Myth of Religious Violence*, 4.

Western thinkers are willing to admit.[45] It is also very difficult to discern if religious beliefs in themselves or a misrepresentation of such beliefs by some adherents of the religious tradition incite people to violence against people of other faiths. Religious people can manipulate the beliefs of their faiths for the purposes of recruiting sympathizers and comrades who might otherwise not participate in nefarious and violent acts.

What sort of issues do some Nigerian Christians' act of seeking spiritual protection from oracles or the priests of local deities during religious conflicts and violence raise for the Christian theologian? I suggest that Christian abandonment—some Nigerian Christians' intermittent act of deserting Jesus in pursuit of spiritual solutions from local deities—constitutes a christological problem when examined in light of Christian discipleship. In the next section, I examine the nature and content of the christological problem.

Christian Abandonment as a Christological Problem

The proclivity of some Nigerian Christians to seek spiritual solutions to their existential needs from other sources such as the oracles of local deities is an act of abandonment. Such Christians have given up, albeit temporarily, an exclusive relationship with Jesus as the source of the spiritual solutions to their needs. How are we to interpret this act of intermittent abandonment of Jesus? If we understand it as a cultural-gap issue, we may focus attention on developing christological models or categories that will clarify the conceptual confusions or ambiguities that inhibit some Nigerian Christians from being discipled in a manner that is consistent with Jesus's mode of discipleship. By "cultural-gap issue," I mean two related things. First, the issue of how twenty-first-century Nigerian Christians can interpret and concretely appropriate the teaching of a first-century Jew they believe in, devote themselves to, and follow. Obviously, the two centuries do not share the same social, religious, linguistic, and economic matrix. The second issue is the freedom of Nigerian Christians to contextualize their faith by drawing upon the traditional religious values, beliefs, and practices of Nigeria to explain and appropriate the teaching of Jesus. Some African Indigenous Churches (AICs) and Pentecostal churches exemplify this freedom of contextualization in their liturgy, sermons, and doctrines.[46] The Nigerian theologian Enyi Ben Udoh in his 1983 doctoral dissertation, entitled "Guest Christology: An Interpretative View

45. Cavanaugh, *Myth of Religious Violence*, 16.

46. See Anderson, *Introduction to Pentecostalism*; Oduro et al., *Mission in an African Way*.

of the Christological Problem in Africa," argued that many African Christians suffered from "faith schizophrenia": the act of devoting themselves to
the Christian faith and traditional African religions simultaneously.[47] Udoh
blamed such faith schizophrenia on some Western missionaries' presenta-
tions of Jesus as a stranger who largely detested African cultures. For Udoh,
the phenomenon of faith schizophrenia, which includes occasional desertions
of Jesus to seek help from agents of traditional religions of Africa, is a cultural-
gap issue. Udoh argued that presenting Jesus as a "guest" is a possible solution to the problem of faith schizophrenia. As a guest, Jesus will be protected
and respected as long as he abides by the traditions and values of African
communities.[48] Udoh might have succeeded in offering an image of Jesus
who respects and learns about African cultures but who lacks the insights
to critique and redirect them. Like Udoh, the Ghanaian theologian Kwame
Bediako proposed an ancestor Christology as the most viable option to deal
with the problem of dual religious allegiances of many African Christians. For
Bediako, seeing Jesus as an ancestor, although he is ontologically different and
superior to African ancestors, allowed a theologian to successfully relate Jesus
to Africa's ancestral mediation—a major religious belief of traditional African
religions.[49] Bediako's ancestor Christology might have successfully interpreted
the person and work of Jesus with a recognizable religious category (ancestor
mediation) of Africa traditional religions but at the expense of some essential
beliefs about ancestors. It remains to be seen if Jesus would have met the cri-
teria for becoming an ancestor in Africa if he was found guilty of violating the
traditions of the community as many of his Jewish contemporaries believed.[50]
However, what both Udoh and Bediako have shown is that the phenomenon
of Christian abandonment permeates African Christianity.

If we understand the intermittent desertion of Jesus as a pragmatic
issue, we may focus our attention on the moral rectitude of Nigerian
Christians who consult with oracles of local deities for solutions to their
existential needs, while retaining their commitment to Jesus. A "pragmatic
problem" refers to the moral and practical decisions of Christians to seek

47. Udoh, "Guest Christology."

48. A guest in many traditional African communities was somewhat sacred and,
therefore, is protected from harm. The guest is, however, expected to respect the cultures and traditions of the society.

49. See Bediako, *Jesus as the Gospel in Africa*, 3–33; Bediako, "Doctrine of Christ,"
110–11; Bediako, *Christianity in Africa*, 212–27; Bediako, "Biblical Christologies in the
Context of African Traditional Religions."

50. For an extensive assessment of Bediako's ancestor Christology, see Ezigbo, *Re-
imagining African Christologies*, 71–80; Ezigbo, "Jesus as God's Communicative and
Hermeneutical Act," 49–52.

effective and efficient solutions to their existential needs. If going to Jesus will delay solutions to one's existential needs, why stick with him when there are quicker and more effective paths to solving those needs? The pragmatic reasons for deserting Jesus could be fueled by other motives such as defiance (a bold disobedience designed to get Jesus's attention), protest (resisting Jesus's seemingly disinterested attitude towards their needs and requests), and exasperation (displaying anger towards Jesus who appears to abandon them in the time of need). Christians who are driven by these motives might well have retained the belief that Jesus is the savior of the world but doubted his commitment to their well-being in this present world.

Though Christian abandonment is a complex phenomenon that requires a multi-angled response, many Nigerian Christians see it primarily as a pragmatic issue.[51] Christians who intermittently desert Jesus in pursuit of spiritual solutions are believed to be lacking patience or genuine *conversion*: changing one's previous loyalties for an exclusive relationship with Jesus. Chetachukwu Ibe represents such Christians:

> Some do [seek solutions to existential needs from agents of local deities] but those committed ones don't. A real child of God, born-again, will seek the face of Jesus and will every time learn to wait for the Lord's plans [for her] to come through in [her life]. True Christians will wait for God's deliverance and not seek help from here and there [oracles of a local deity]. They will wait for Jesus to solve their problems no matter the time [i.e., no matter how long it takes]. The Bible says, "Is there anything I [God] cannot do, is there any problem that is bigger than me, is there anything so difficult for me to solve?" [Jer 32:27]. If Christians understand this they will wait on the Lord and will not go here and there. And I know, with time, Jesus will solve their problems. I know of a woman that for 18 years did not have a child and after so many [pieces] of advice from people—"Go to this native doctor and go to that oracle"—she tried them and it did not work. She stopped going there [oracles of local deities] and decided to wait on the Lord [Jesus]. After she stopped going there and focused her hope on Jesus, the next year she conceived and gave birth to a child. She now has three children. So, that's an example of those who wait on the Lord.[52]

51. I use the term "grassroots Christologies" here to describe the imaginations and appropriations of the person, work, and significance of Jesus Christ by Nigerian Christians with no formal theological education. Such Christologies can be discerned in their prayers, songs, liturgy, and other practices.

52. Chetuchukwu Ibe (pseudonym), interview by Victor I. Ezigbo, tape recording, Aba, May 28, 2006.

Ibe's words provide a glimpse of some theological currents that shape discussions on conversion, Christian identity, and Christian discipleship in Nigerian Christianity. Expressions such as "real child of God," "born-again," and "true Christians" in his thinking serve as the markers of true conversion. However, unless sinlessness or perfection is viewed as the outward sign of true conversion it would be misleading to assume that all Christians who occasionally deserted Jesus to seek solution from local deities were not genuine converts or believers in Jesus. A more plausible explanation is a misguided understanding of Christian discipleship, especially how Jesus mediates the connection between what Christians *should do* and what they *actually do* in the face of existential needs. This means that the intermittent desertion of Jesus is not only cultural-gap and pragmatic issues but also a christological issue. A "christological issue" in this context refers to an underlying belief that Jesus is merely a solution—the answer to human existential needs—and that he is obligated to solve the needs of his followers.

I propose that the phenomenon of Christian abandonment invites a Christian theologian to make a theological, or to be more precise, a christological judgment. For example, one may ask: How is Christian abandonment in Nigerian Christianity to be understood in relation to Jesus's mode of discipleship? To answer this question, I will use James Arum, a Nigerian Christian musician, as an interlocutor. I begin with a quotation from Arum's melodic refrains in one of his well-known songs: "Jesus settle me so that I will stop disturbing you. Jesus settle me so that I will rejoice like others."[53] Arum cites Jesus's parable of a persistent widow in Luke 18:1–8 and Jesus's invitation to his followers to ask, seek, knock (Matt 7:7) to justify his plea for a settlement.[54] This is a form of plea that arises from the belief about what a person rightly deserves. As one who is fascinated by grassroots Christologies of Nigerian Christianity, Arum's song nudges me to ask: Why does he imagine the benefits that Jesus offers his followers in terms of settlement? Answering this question will require attending to the notions of "settlement" in Igbo cultures and communities. Apprenticeship (*igbaboyi*), which is grounded in a relationship between a master (*oga*) and a servant (*nwaboyi*), is one contextual factor that might help us to understand the force of the language of settlement to an Igbo audience.[55] Many parents send their male children (typically teens and young adults) to wealthy businessmen to learn the ropes. Such businessmen are called

53. In Igbo language, "Jisọs setụlụọ nụ mụ ka mụ kwụsị inye gị nsogbu. Jisọs setụlụọ nụ mụ ka mụ soro ibe mụ ñụria." James Arum is a Nigerian musician.

54. Settlement in this context refers to a positive answer from Jesus to one's prayer request or a divine blessing mediated by Jesus.

55. The Igbos constitute one of the major ethnic groups in Nigeria.

ndịọga (masters) and their apprentices are called *umuboyị* (servants). In some cases, an apprentice is expected also to serve his master by completing domestic tasks such as household chores.

Two salient features of *settlement* in the context of apprenticeship that are pertinent to Christian discipleship are noteworthy. First, settlement is not an option: an apprentice who has successfully completed the terms of the agreements between him and his master has earned the rights to demand a settlement, which could be in monetary form or in the form of goods with monetary value.[56] The christological content of Arum's plea for a deserved settlement from Jesus is particularly revealing. The assumption is that by being a follower of Jesus, one has earned the right to demand the benefits he offers.[57] For instance, a disciple suffering a debilitating illness has the rights to ask Jesus for the blessing of healing. The second feature is that settlement invokes freedom: a settled apprentice is free to pursue any line of business or way of life without recourse to the guidance and precept of his former master. In the event that a new partnership is developed between an ex-apprentice and a former master, it will not be based on the master-apprentice relationship. These two features of settlement have conditioned the ways in which some Nigerian Christians relate to Jesus and also seek him for answers to their existential needs. The ubiquitous presence of faith-healing and prosperity-gospel sermons, especially by some Pentecostal preachers, has amplified some Christians' urge to follow Jesus for reasons of gaining answers to their needs and requests. Though it could well be unintended, faith-healing and prosperity-gospel sermons have reduced Jesus to a person who is at the service of his followers.[58] Consequently, when some Nigerian Christians that have internalized such

56. This social-economic arrangement, which interestingly is not codified in any existing state laws in southeast Nigeria, is culturally binding. An aggrieved party could report the matter to *alusi*—a local deity. Typically, a priest of a local deity will summon both parties to appear before the deity. Many believe that the local deities, unlike Jesus Christ or the Christian God, do not defer judgment to the end of times. The judgments and punishments of the local deities are believed to be swift and immediate.

57. Arums also cites Matt 11:28 to make the case for his plea for a settlement from Jesus. In a rhetorical fashion, he posed the following question to Jesus: "Would you want me to return home with my burdens?"

58. Paul Gifford has noted that "Faith Gospel," which characterizes many charismatic churches in Africa, presents God as having "met all the needs of human beings in the suffering and death of Christ, and every Christian should now share the victory of Christ over sin, sickness, and poverty. A believer has a right to the blessings of health and wealth won by Christ, and he or she can obtain these blessings merely by a positive confession of faith." See Gifford, *African Christianity*, 39. Similar beliefs are also present in other contexts in which prosperity gospel and faith healings are emphasized. See Bowler, *Blessed*.

sermons assume Jesus is no longer at their beck and call—solving their problems how and when they want it—they are tempted to desert him for other religious sources of spiritual solutions.[59] Christian abandonment, therefore, is corrosive of Jesus's mode of discipleship. I will show later that imagining the benefits in becoming Jesus's disciple in terms of settlement erodes the substratum of Jesus's mode of discipleship, namely, following in his footsteps and yielding to his work of redirection.

The journey between what Christians should do and what they actually do as disciples of Jesus in the face of existential needs may be likened to a treacherous terrain that sometimes result in unpredictable decisions and choices. Some observations are in order when exploring how Jesus mediates the relationship between what Christians should do and what they actually do if they are confronted with an existential need such as a terminal illness. I will highlight four assumptions. First, Christian identity—its content and parameter—cannot be successfully mapped out in isolation from the life, experience, and teaching of Jesus. Christians are by definition followers of Jesus, the Christ. In some ways, Christian identity is really about how Christians can learn from Jesus to "present their bodies as a living sacrifice, holy and acceptable to God" (Rom 12:1 ESV). Second, Christian identity involves discipleship: following in the footsteps of Jesus and also submitting to his redirection. Christians ought not to follow Jesus as a morality star like someone follows an esteemed and beloved movie star. On the contrary, following Jesus in this context, to borrow the Apostle Paul's line, is to say: "I have been crucified with Christ. It is no longer I who live, but Christ who lives in me. And the life I now live in the flesh I live by faith in the Son of God, who loved me and gave himself for me" (Gal 2:20 ESV). Third, Christian identity is not an esoteric project but rather a *this*-world affair. Jesus in his famous Sermon on the Mount taught his followers to serve as the "salt of the earth" and "the light of the world" (Matt 5:13–16). Christians ought to embody the way of Jesus in this world. Fourth, Jesus has a considerable advantage over his followers. It is his way of life that Christians strive to learn, adopt, and practice.

Jesus attends to the existential needs of his disciples by guiding them, on the one hand, to rethink their needs and requests for solutions in light of his teaching, and on the other hand, to come to him in faith for the grace and wisdom to address their needs. I have argued elsewhere that the term "revealer" is a robust and befitting christological category that can bridge the dichotomy separating Jesus as a "question" and as a "solution" in the

---

59. One example of such sermons is Ogbonnaya, *I Am Too Big to Be Poor*. See also the sermon of Bishop David Oyedepo entitled, "You Will Become What You Believe." You can find it at Ajao, "You Will Become What You Believe."

context of Christian identity formation.[60] As a "question," Jesus—his life and teaching—should shape the content of Christians' existential requests. As a "solution," he should shape and inform the content of the solutions that Christians anticipate. The master-servant relationship, which the idea of settlement accentuates, nudges us to imagine Christian discipleship as requiring a dutiful life of following Jesus in obedience to his precepts and demands.[61] Though this is commendable, it raises a serious christological problem that might betray the genius of Christian discipleship. As I imagine it, the genius of Christian discipleship is following Jesus not primarily as a means to an end but rather as an end in itself. This way of imagining Christian discipleship rules out the idea of demanding of Jesus what one believes to be what is rightly earned by choosing to pursue a relationship with him. A lurking temptation beneath the belief of following Jesus for the reasons of what a person can earn, gain, or deserve is deserting him when he appears not to hold up his end of a bargain. One possible way to equip Nigerian Christians to face such temptation is by recovering Jesus's role in the formation of Christian discipleship. If we see Jesus only as a *solution,* it is most likely that we will follow him for what we can gain from him or only when it is convenient for us. Conversely, seeing Jesus as simultaneously constituting a *question* and a *solution* will prompt as well as safeguard two mutually reinforcing disciple-making properties, namely: *following* and *redirecting.* I will explain this claim later. In the meantime, it will be useful to explore the connection between the phenomenon of intermittent desertion of Jesus and the moral strangeness of Jesus's mode of discipleship.

Jesus's Mode of Discipleship: Its Moral Strangeness and Disciple-Making Properties

One way to define Christian discipleship is to see it as an embodied *yes* or a lived-out response to the New Testament's summons of human beings to a relationship that is modeled by Jesus of Nazareth. To many New Testament writers, Jesus models for his followers how they are to live obediently as creatures of God.[62] If my reading of the New Testament is correct,

60. Ezigbo, *Re-imagining African Christologies,* 143–74; Ezigbo, "Jesus as God's Communicative and Hermeneutical Act," 37–58.

61. In some cultures, construing Jesus as a master in the context of Christian discipleship may be a useful category. Williams, *Being Disciples,* 1–19.

62. To "follow Jesus is to become his disciple. To become a disciple of Jesus is to pursue a way of living that is shaped by his teaching and life." See Ezigbo, "Violent Christians," 236–59.

Christian abandonment, as previously described, betrays the genius of Christian discipleship. Yet, exactly what constitutes a *desertion* of Jesus is not easily identifiable. For instance, does Christian discipleship permit or reject multiple religious allegiances? Is a Nigerian Christian seeking spiritual solutions from the priests of a local deity guilty of desertion? Does rendering to "Caesar the things that are Caesar's and to God the things that are God's" (Mark 12:17 ESV) translate into multiple religious (not just civic) allegiances?[63] Does Jesus's commitment to his disciples' welfare warrant their freedom to seek solutions to threats to their well-being from every available source? Or should Jesus's disciples seek spiritual solutions to their needs from him alone? These are important questions that are help-ful for exploring the phenomenon of Christian abandonment in Nigerian Christianity. Given that most Christians who seek spiritual solutions from resources and agents of local deities still regard themselves as disciples of Jesus and sometimes appear unfettered by the difference between the Christian faith and the traditional religion, it should be assumed that the act of desertion need not be permanent. The main issue is not whether deities of the traditional religion are reliable and trustworthy, but rather Christians' mistrust of Jesus who has called them into a particular way of living. To put it differently, forswearing Jesus to pursue spiritual solutions from the deities of traditional Nigerian religions is a sign of what may be called a *failed Christian discipleship*: wanting to become a disciple of Jesus in ways that either negate or disregard his mode of discipleship.

The phenomenon of Christian abandonment brings into sharp focus the moral strangeness of Jesus's mode of discipleship. The term "strangeness" implies a state of difference. The depth of the difference will vary depending on how one understands the roots of the difference and also the nature of the objects or people being assessed and compared. If by *moral strangeness* we mean the difficulty—"impossibility" might be a better term—of embodying Jesus's vision for what it is to live in the world as moral beings who are sum-moned by their Creator, then, it is a state of affairs that has a long history. To

---

63. Many Christian communities throughout history, as H. Richard Niebuhr has observed, have "sometimes found the counsel of the Cross quite as inexpedient as have national and economic groups. In dealing with such major social evils as war, slavery, and social inequality," many of the communities have "discovered convenient ambi-guities in the letter of the Gospel which enabled [them] to violate their spirit and to ally [themselves] with the prestige and power those evils had gained in their corporate organization. In adapting [themselves] to the conditions of a civilization which [their] founder had bidden [them] to permeate with the spirit of divine love, [they] found that it was easier to give to Caesar the things belonging to Caesar if the examination of what might belong to God were not too closely pressed." Niebuhr, *Social Sources of Denominationalism*, 3.

cite an example, a would-be disciple of Jesus asked him: "What must I do to inherit eternal life?" (Mark 10:17 ESV). Mark notes that he departed with sadness after hearing Jesus's response: "Go, sell all that you have and give to the poor, and you will have treasure in heaven; and come, follow me" (Mark 10:21–22 ESV). Mark comments that the would-be disciple was saddened because he was unwilling to relinquish the wealth he had accumulated. The disciples, clearly bewildered by Jesus's response, asked him: "Then who can be saved?" (Mark 10:26 ESV). This story shows that embodying Jesus's vision for entering into the kingdom of God is an extremely difficult and a humanly impossible task for both disciples and would-be disciples. Mark quotes Jesus as saying, "With man it is impossible, but not with God. For all things are possible with God" (Mark 10:27 ESV). Why, one might ask, is it humanly impossible to embody the *way of Jesus*—being Jesus's disciple—in the face of existential needs?[64] Is it because he is demanding what is logically possible but practically impossible? In other words, is the problem with the moral task itself? If, for example, deserting Jesus, albeit intermittently, to pursue spiritual solutions to existential needs from deities of traditional Nigerian religion is a witness to the practical impossibility of embodying his way of life, is the problem with the task itself? However one approaches these questions, they are indicative of the moral strangeness of Jesus, particularly when they are explored in light of the kind of discipleship and relations that Jesus demands of his disciples.

Changes in the cultures of a country—for example, being more or less religious in its public sphere—do not quite explain the roots of Jesus's moral strangeness.[65] Though national cultural changes can inform both the reception and rejection of Jesus's message, they only provide a partial explanation for his moral strangeness. In this section, I explore the question: Is being a moral stranger essential to Jesus's mode of discipleship? I suggest that it is more fitting to answer it in the affirmative. By "mode of discipleship," I mean the particular ways Jesus summons people to learn from and be informed by his teachings. In his famous prayer recorded in John, Jesus noted that though his disciples "are in the world" but "not of the world" (John 17). Part of John's agenda, it seems, is to show that Jesus has created a moral

64. By "way of Jesus," I mean the teachings and precepts of Jesus that are described in the New Testament, particularly those relating to how his disciples are to live as a people striving to love God and also love their neighbors (Mark 12:30–33).

65. I find Charles Taylor's description of a "public sphere" useful and will adopt it in this chapter. For Taylor, the public sphere is "a common space in which the members of society are deemed to meet through a variety of media: print, electronic, and also face-to-face encounters; to discuss matters of common interest; and thus to be able to form a common mind about these." Taylor, *Secular Age*, 185.

space within which his disciples and followers can work out how to be his disciples in relation to both his mode of discipleship and their own context. As I have written elsewhere,

> The clause "they are not of the world" (John 17:14) . . . should be understood in light of "I do not ask you to take them out of the world" (John 17:15). To say that Christians are "not of the world" does not mean they are immune to the ways of the world. Christians are "not of the world" precisely because Jesus has called them into a life of discipleship and it is through that way of seeing that they are to relate to God and other people.[66]

It is his form of discipling, which demands what are sometimes uncommon to people's way of living, that originates his moral strangeness.

If Jesus's moral strangeness is intrinsic to his mode of discipleship, as I am suggesting, it follows that a Christian theologian's task is not to erase or minimize the strangeness. On the contrary, the theologian should examine the opportunities and dilemmas it creates for reimagining his identity and also his significance for Christian theological reflection and praxis. There are real theological pitfalls in erasing or diminishing Jesus's strangeness as a moral authority who calls people into a particular way of life. One such pitfall is a form of domestication in which he is stripped of the powers to critique and redirect his followers. He becomes too passive to engage people who encounter him because he has been reduced to an unschooled figure in the art of discipleship, lacking in the abilities to effectively contest the attempts to reduce him into what a community wants him to be. He also lacks the sensibilities to raise sobering questions about some of his disciples and followers who attempt to bring his teaching into their society only when it conveniently suits their own selfish agendas.[67] He equally loses the ability to marshal out a formidable corrective to discipline the confidence of his disciples that intermittently abandon him to seek alternative sources of solutions to existential needs without recourse to his teachings. These kinds of distortive domestications of Jesus perhaps prevent some Christians in Nigeria from seeing the contradiction in preaching Jesus as good news while remaining silent in the face of dehumanizing actions that are grounded in ethnic and religious bias.[68] To mitigate against the pitfalls of

66. Ezigbo, "Violent Christians," 248.

67. See Bonhoeffer, *Cost of Discipleship*, 46–78.

68. This is, of course, not peculiar to Christians in Nigeria. Christians in other countries face similar issues. For example, many white American Christians fail to see the contradiction in preaching Jesus as good news while remaining silent in the face of racism. To borrow the words of James Cone, they fail to make a symbolic connection

domesticating Jesus in the sense outlined above, I have suggested in several of my writings that Jesus is to be imagined as a "revealer": one who embodies, for his disciples in particular, what it is to live in relation to God, who interprets such embodied life for them, and who redirects them from their misconceptions of God-human relations.

As I noted earlier, Jesus disciples people by instructing them, on the one hand, to rethink their identity, their needs, and to anticipate solutions to those needs in the light of his teachings, and on the other hand, to come to him in faith for grace and wisdom in order to grow in their relationship with him.[69] Seeing Jesus as a "revealer" of God-human relations is theologically useful for bridging the dichotomy separating him as a "question" and as a "solution" in the context of discipleship.[70] Seeing Jesus as simultaneously constituting a question and a solution will prompt as well as safeguard two mutually reinforcing disciple-making properties, namely, *following* and *redirecting*. In this context, following properly belongs to the disciples and redirecting belongs to Jesus. What prompts the act of following—selfish or selfless reasons—in the end matters less in light of the redirecting act of Jesus. To unpack my claim, I will discuss the nature of following and redirecting.

---

between the cross of Jesus and the lynching tree. See Cone, *Cross and the Lynching Tree*. Perhaps it is equally because of the failure of many white American Christians to make a clear theological connection between the cross of Christ and the "cross" of African Americans who suffered under the weight of slavery and racial segregation that compelled Jacquelyn Grant to make a distinction between "White women's Christ" and "Black women's Jesus." In Grant's assessment, in spite of feminist theology's achievements, for example, its impressive discussions on the damaging impact of patriarchy on Christian theology and practices, it has remained blind to the peculiar experience of black women. Grant contends that feminist theology, as practiced in the West and by white women, has been successful in dealing with the issue of gender in theological discourse but has failed to grapple with the issues of race and class. See Grant, *White Women's Christ and Black Women's Jesus*.

69. See his discussions and sayings in John 15–17.

70. Jesus performs three related functions as the "revealer" of God-human relations, particularly in the context of Christian understanding of the relationship between true divinity and true humanity. First, as "revealer," he is an embodiment of the knowledge of true divinity and humanity and also the embodiment of a form of relationship that ought to exist between the Christian God and human beings. Second, as "revealer," he is the interpreter for the Christian communities on how to imagine and appropriate God-world relations. Disciples of Jesus, therefore, ought to see him as a hermeneutical lens through which to assess their interpretations of Scripture and also their understanding of God-world relations. Thirdly, as "revealer," he is the boundary-maker of Christianity's language of God and also its knowledge of God-world relations. For extensive discussions on revealer Christology, see Ezigbo, *Re-imagining African Christologies*, 143–74; Ezigbo, "Jesus as God's Communicative and Hermeneutical Act," 37–58.

Following Jesus in discipleship involves several features. Four such features are decision-making, commitment, learning, and purposefulness. Several factors condition a person's decision-making process, including freedom of choice and constraining factors. In discipleship, *decision-making* should be grounded in freedom of choice.[71] Christians are not (and should not) be docile followers who are at the mercy of Jesus's discipleship. On the contrary, they ought to be active followers who freely respond to his discipleship. Decision-making should arise from people's freedom to act upon the range of religious and nonreligious options available to them. To put it bluntly, people are to become disciples of Jesus without compulsion. Jesus clearly instructs his disciples to make other disciples through a peaceful means that guarantees freedom of choice:

> Whenever you enter a town and they receive you, eat what is set before you. Heal the sick in it and say to them, "The kingdom of God has come near to you." But whenever you enter a town and they do not receive you, go into its streets and say, "Even the dust of your town that clings to your feet we wipe off against you. Nevertheless know this, that the kingdom of God has come near to you." (Luke 10:9–11 NIV)

The disciples are to announce that the "kingdom of God has come near" both to those who welcome them and those who do not. The act of shaking off the dust clinging to the disciples' feet as they peacefully leave the place where they are rejected serves two related purposes. On the one hand, it is a witness that they have obediently carried out the instructions of Jesus, and on the other hand, it is a witness that judgment is God's prerogative.

Discipleship involves commitment: a disciple's steadfast dedication to the guidance and character-molding teaching of Jesus. Faith is the beginning point of commitment in discipleship. Without faith it is impossible to commit to Jesus or heed his summon to "take up" one's "cross" and follow him (Matt 10:38; see also 16:24; Mark 8:34; Luke 9:23). Faith is sometimes expressed in a creedal formula, "I believe." Whatever else the creedal formula might mean, it implies saying yes to Jesus's faithfulness. In *Tokens of Trust*, Rowan Williams argues that the creedal formula "I believe" is "the beginning of a series of statements about where I find the anchorage of my life, where I find solid ground, home."[72] Disciples of Jesus are to actively commit to him, showing allegiance and loyalty to him, and also relying

---

71. We need not be detained by abstract discussions on whether a person is truly free to act given human finitude. Human beings are constrained by limited lifespan, power, knowledge, and so on.

72. Williams, *Tokens of Trust*, 6.

on him to successfully follow in his footsteps. Writing about the nature of Christian discipleship in the context of public engagement, Miroslav Volf and Ryan McAnnally-Linz state:

> [I]f we are committed to following Jesus in the power of the Holy Spirit, we are committed to letting him determine the character of our whole lives—no exceptions. We are his disciples in our judgements, words, and deeds that affect the common good, just as we are his disciples in every other aspect of our lives.[73]

Discipleship also requires learning from Jesus as the moral authority for *his* community. Learning in this context does not merely mean an acquisition of knowledge. It also means heeding Jesus's voice as a moral authority (John 10:27 ESV). Traditionally, many Christian theologians ground Jesus's moral authority in his ontology. Jesus is believed to be a different class of being from other human beings because he is God incarnate.[74] This implies that he did not become the moral authority of his followers merely because of his moral perfections but primarily because he is the revealer—embodiment and interpreter—of divinity and humanity for Christian communities.[75] Learning, in the context of discipleship, is a process of developing a deeper relationship with God (the Father) by heeding the voice (teaching) of Jesus, and relying on the help of the Holy Spirit in all matters regarding being a disciple.

Finally, discipleship requires purposeful living. "But he who lives without an aim," writes Pope Shenouda III, "feels that life is monotonous and too heavy to bear. His life is meaningless and tasteless, wavering without direction."[76] In his discussion on the Christian life, which he couched in the language of sports, Paul wrote: "I do not run aimlessly; I do not box as one beating the air. But I discipline my body and keep it under control, lest after preaching to others I myself should be disqualified" (1 Cor 9:26–27 ESV). Engaging in a spiritual exercise—for instance, studying Scripture—is no guarantee of purposeful living. Jesus is rather the one who guarantees the purposeful living of his disciples. To live a purposeful life is to discover and

73. Volf and McAnnally-Linz, *Public Faith in Action*, 7.

74. Generally, discussions on the Christian doctrine of Incarnation have followed two broad pathways. While some describe the belief that God's *Logos* became a human being in the person of Jesus of Nazareth as a myth, others see it as a mystery—an event that has not been fully revealed by God. For introductory discussions, see Hick, *Myth of God Incarnate*; Goulder, *Incarnation and Myth*.

75. Presenting Jesus as a moral authority in a pluralistic context raises serious questions about totalitarianism and fanaticism. For discussions on morality and moral authority in the public square, see Engelhardt, *Foundations of Bioethics*, 32–101.

76. Shenouda, *Characteristics of the Spiritual Path*, 13.

also internalize the belief that the disciples of Jesus have been "crucified with him" and that he now lives through them (Gal 2:20). To be crucified with Jesus among other things means to submit oneself to him for the process of transformation that requires his redirecting work, which are embedded in his teachings and animated by the Holy Spirit.[77]

Jesus does not enter into a relationship with his disciples simply to solve their problems in ways *they* choose. Rather, he engages their previously held views about God-human relations and human-human relations, redirecting their beliefs, expectations, and actions. For instance, his disciples are gravely mistaken if they expect him to support their views on oaths sworn to "the Lord" as a way of establishing one's truthfulness. He instructs them to be truthful at all times—"let your yes be yes, and your no, no"—with or without the provision of oaths sworn in the name of God (Matt 5:33–37). The redirecting work of Jesus implies that he will dominate the lives of his disciples without being domineering, he will nudge them to conform to his ways without suffocating them, he will sanctify them without erasing their individual personalities, and he will mold them into his way of life with his teaching without paralyzing them. Disciples of Jesus should surrender to his correction. Jesus's juxtaposition of "food that spoils" and "food that endures to eternal life" (John 6:22–29) is relevant in the exploration of the nature of the acts of following and redirecting in his form of discipleship. Though his disciples are within their rights to frame the kind of "food" or benefits they expect to get by following him, as their shepherd (John 10), Jesus is well within his rights to define the parameters of the benefits he offers to them. Such parameters may likely appear quite strange to his disciples (and followers). What does this way of imagining Jesus's way of discipling entail in terms of engaging and confronting religious violence? I will attend to this question in the remainder of this chapter, using Nigeria and Nigerian Christianity as the primary context of my exploration.

Confronting Religious Violence in Nigeria: Lessons from Jesus's Teaching

Many Nigerians are increasingly recognizing religious communities' insights in the attempts to bring about a more peaceful Nigeria. Though some religious communities stoke violence, the role of religious communities,

77. The cross of Jesus, theologically speaking, brings together God's act of justifying sinners and making them righteous. Separating these two divine acts is at best misleading. A helpful book that explores these issues in the context of the dialogue between Protestant and Roman Catholic thinkers is Stumme, *Gospel of Justification in Christ*.

particularly traditional religious, Muslim, and Christian communities, in promoting the sacredness of human life, human dignity, and peace, should not be ignored.[78] It would seem appropriate to ask religious communities in Nigeria to show from the wells of their faiths how to prevent or provide curbs on religious violence. It is in the spirit of such faith-based responses that I explore the question: How should Christians in Nigeria act, as disciples of Jesus, in the climate of religious violence? This question is intended to bring into focus some principles from Jesus's life and teaching that ought to inform how Christians practice their faith in the context of conflictual relationship with people of other faiths. Jesus clearly does not have, as far as we can see in the Gospels, a well-developed theology of religions.[79] However, the story about Jesus's conversation with a certain woman of Samaria in John 4 is perhaps the closest we come to what could be described as his interfaith theological activity. In chapter 2, I discussed the historical milieu of this story. My goal here is to extract some principles from the story that can aid Christians in Nigeria in their attempts to confront religious violence. This story is appropriate for several reasons. It highlights the tensed relationship between some adherents of Judaism and religions of Samaria. The tensed relationship is analogous to the conflictual relationship between many adherents of Christianity, Islam, and traditional religion in contemporary Nigeria. Also, we can discern ethnic tensions between Jews and Samaritans in the story that are equally analogous to the ethnic tensions, to use a traditional broad category, between the Igbos, Yorubas, and Hausas.[80]

I have discerned four principles in Jesus's conversation with the Samaritan woman that can guide Nigerian Christians who desire interfaith or intercultural conversations with the goal of de-escalating religious violence in contemporary Nigeria. The first is the principle of a *pre-emptive interfaith initiative*. Jesus initiated the conversation knowing full well he would be crossing ethnic, cultural, and religious boundaries.[81] In other

78. Vaughan, *Religion and the Masking of Nigeria*, 1.

79. See ch. 2 for more discussions.

80. See ch. 2 for an extensive discussion on the relationship between Jews and Samaritans.

81. On realizing that Jesus was a Jew, the Samaritan woman reminded him of their ethnic and religious differences and disagreements, which, for her, should permeate all forms of relationship between Jews and Samaritans, even in a basic act or gesture such as getting a cup of water. Responding to Jesus's request for a drink, the Samaritan woman posed a question to him, perhaps with a sardonic tone: "How is it that you, a Jew, ask a drink of me, a woman of Samaria?" (John 4:9 NRSV). For a helpful discussion on how identity-makers of a human society can acquire a militant edge, see Martin, *Does Christianity Cause War?*

words, Jesus had ethnic, cultural, and religious reasons to avoid any contact with the Samaritan woman. As Judith M. Gundry-Volf has noted, "Jesus' request for a drink of water, therefore, is deceptively simple. To make it, he had to cross great gulfs—geographical, ethnic, religious, and gender in nature."[82] It is not quite clear why Jesus did not use the Perean route for his journey to Galilee.[83] It is also surprising that he started an unwarranted conversation with a Samaritan woman (John 4:4–8).[84] As I noted in chapter 2, John does not tell us why exactly it was necessary (*edei*, "had to") for Jesus to travel through Samaria. It was as if Jesus had concluded that the benefits of going through Samaria outweighed the risks of going through Perea. That Jesus struck an unwarranted conversation with a woman of Samarian would suggest that it was possible his reason was missional: he wanted to teach his disciples (and the people of Samaria) to reimagine their understandings of God-human relations (in the context of true worship) and human-human relations (in the context of ethnic and religious biases). Whatever the actual reasons that occasioned his action, Jesus was willing to critique and engage both the Jewish and Samarian religious traditions in light of his theological reading of Scripture.

Jesus refused to take the woman's bait: the woman wanted the conversation to be settled within the spheres of ethnic and religious hostility. He, however, moved the conversation to the sphere of God-human relationship. Without discarding the seriousness of their religious, social, political, and ethnic differences, Jesus nudged her towards the sacredness of human beings and the worth of human life in relation to God's gift of salvation. In response to the woman's hesitation to give him a drink because he was a Jew, Jesus said to her: "If you knew the gift of God, and who it is that is saying to you, 'Give me a drink,' you would have asked him, and he would have given you living water" (John 4:10 NRSV). In her commentary on this verse, Teresa Okure, wrote:

> Jesus does not debate the issue of mutual national antagonism
> between Jews and Samarians. Rather, he transfers the discussion

82. Gundry-Volf, "Spirit, Mercy, and the Other," 509–10.

83. For extensive discussions on both the Judaist and Samaritan versions of the origins of the religious and ethnic conflicts, see Macdonald, *Theology of the Samaritans*.

84. Ben Sira cautions men against spending time alone with women who are not their wives: "Do not be jealous of the wife of your bosom, or you will teach her an evil lesson to your own hurt. Do not give yourself to a woman and let her trample down your strength. Do not go near a loose woman, or you will fall into her snares. Do not dally with a singing girl, or you will be caught by her tricks. Do not look intently at a virgin, or you may stumble and incur penalties for her. Do not give yourself to prostitutes, or you may lose your inheritance" (Sir 9:3–6 NRSV).

from this socioreligious context of reciprocal contempt and separatism [John 4:9] to the sphere of God's relationship and dealings with human beings, where the governing principle is his generous bounty or "free gift."[85]

The second is an *irenic principle*. The violent spirit of some of the earliest disciples of Jesus was displayed in their attempt to destroy the Samaritans (Luke 9:51–54). The irenic spirit of Jesus was evident in his stern rebuke (Luke 9:55). Also, a nonviolent, albeit unhelpful, attitude of Jesus's disciples towards Samaritans was equally on display in John's account of Jesus's encounter with the Samaritan woman (John 4:27). According to John, Jesus chose to engage the Samaritan woman in a peaceful conversation. Throughout the conversation, which could have easily denigrated into insults given the historical enmity between Jews and Samaritans, one can discern recurring attempts to bridge the schism between Jews and Samaritans. Of course, both Jesus and the woman went out of their way to keep the conversation peaceful even though they had numerous opportunities to steer the conversation in a non-peaceful direction. For example, on discovering that Jesus was a Jew, the woman could have hurled abusive words and slurs at him (4:9). She kept the conversation civil and peaceful (4:11). The woman most likely thought that Jesus was boasting of offering her *fresh water* (living water) that is better than the *still water* of cisterns. She also had another opportunity to move the conversation in a non-peaceful direction but chose not to do so when Jesus was clearly prying into her personal life (4:16–18).

Nigerian Christians, of course, should not assume that people of other faiths would take the peaceful route the Samaritan woman followed. Therefore, they need to return to Jesus's choice of an irenic conversation with a woman of a different faith or a distinct variant of the Jewish faith. It could be possible that Jesus chose an irenic approach for personal reasons: he was thirsty and needed some water that the woman could provide. However, given that Jesus could have sought an alternative solution to his thirst (for example, joining his disciples in the city to find food and water; see John 4:8), it was probably because he wanted to bridge the divide between Jews and Samaritans. Pursuing an irenic goal in interfaith conversations ought to govern Christians' engagement with people of other faiths.[86]

The third principle is a *concession of religious difference*. Jesus acknowledged and upheld the difference in the theological beliefs of Jews and Samaritans. He told the woman, "You worship what you do not know;

85. Okure, *Johannine Approach to Mission*, 96.
86. See Volf, "Social Meaning of Reconciliation," 158–72.

we worship what we know, for salvation is from the Jews" (4:22). Like a typical Jew, Jesus reminded the woman of a long history of religious conflicts and competitions between Jews and Samaritans that have driven a wedge between the two ethnic groups. In order for us to have sustainable and substantive interfaith dialogues and conversations, we must discard, as Lamin Sanneh rightly notes, "complacent pluralism." This is a form of pluralism that displaces "any serious thinking about particular and rival claims to truth and to encourage complacency among . . . people."[87] Sanneh notes that this form of "complacent pluralism . . . can blind us to the real opportunities of interfaith encounter, with platitudes replacing commitment and accountability."[88]

The fourth principle is a *concession of God's prerogatives on true worship*. Jesus reminded the woman that neither the religion of Jews nor the religion of Samaritans could effectively function as the arbiter of true worship of God. On the contrary, God alone is one who rules on humans' acts of worship. Jesus seems to suggest there is a divine surplus in the context of God-human relationship that rules out any possibility of worshippers colonizing God and limiting God's presence in their own religious spheres.[89] He said:

> Woman, believe me, the hour is coming when you will worship the Father neither on this mountain nor in Jerusalem . . . But the hour is coming, and is now here, when the true worshipers will worship the Father in spirit and truth, for the Father seeks such as these to worship him. God is spirit, and those who worship him must worship in spirit and truth. (4:21, 23–24 NRSV)

Without diminishing the differences in the theological convictions of Jews and Samaritans, Jesus invited the woman to explore a new way of approaching the religious differences and tensions between Jewish and Samaritan communities. The role that Jesus plays in guiding worshipers (his disciples) to the true knowledge of God and to true worship of God fits John's theological aim to show that Jesus was superior to Israel's ancestors such as Jacob (John 4:12), Moses (John 6:32–59), and Abraham (John 8:53).[90]

One of the controversial theological insights of Jesus was his claim to dispense God's "living water" or salvific blessing. The Samaritan woman's question highlights the difficulty of understanding Jesus's claim. Obviously, Jesus couldn't possibly be speaking literally when he said to the woman

87. Sanneh, *Piety and Power*, 113.

88. Sanneh, *Piety and Power*, 113.

89. Ezigbo, "Religion and Divine Presence," 178–203.

90. Neyrey, "Jacob Traditions," 420–421.

that he could give her the "living water." It is unsurprising that the woman sardonically remarked: "Sir, you have no bucket, and the well is deep. Where do you get that living water? Are you greater than our ancestor Jacob, who gave us the well, and with his sons and his flocks drank from it?" (John 4:11-12 NRSV). Also, she said: "Sir, give me this water, so that I may never be thirsty or have to keep coming here to draw water" (John 4:15 NRSV). The woman clearly misunderstood Jesus's point: the "living water," a metaphor for God's salvific blessing, is more important than the natural water that has temporal value. Jesus told the woman, "Everyone who drinks of this water will be thirsty again, but those who drink of the water that I will give them will never be thirsty. The water that I will give will become in them a spring of water gushing up to eternal life" (John 4:13-14 NRSV). As I argued in chapter 2, Jesus most probably was echoing the figural usages of "living water" in the Hebrew Bible. In this context, "Water" and "living water" signified God's salvific blessing.

True worship, for Jesus, consists in worshiping God—approaching and calling upon God—"in spirit and truth" (4:24). For Jesus, true worship is not really about a location of worship (either Jerusalem or Mt. Gerizim) but rather the content of our worship. True worship requires living obediently to God that naturally arises from having right beliefs about God-human relationship. We need to look elsewhere in the teaching of Jesus for the content of his understanding of believing and living rightly in the context of true worship. Mark 7:5-9 and Luke 4 provide a helpful starting point. In Mark, Jesus told "the Pharisees and teachers of the law" that obeying the "commands of God" requires worshiping God with one's heart and not merely "holding on to the traditions of men" (Mark 7:5-8 NIV). For Jesus, practicing hand washing ritualistically does not amount to worshiping God truthfully. In Luke 4, true worship of God entails participating in the drama of God's salvation in which those who are suffering from illness (spiritual and physical) receive healing.

Any attempts to bring Jesus into the public sphere either as a neutral or an uncomplicated moral authority is doomed to failure for at least two reasons. First, as I have shown, cultural currents of societies condition the reception or rejection of his teachings. Given that almost all modern societies are pluralistic (they house and protect, albeit in different ways, diverse religious beliefs and communities), the best Christians can do is to show either *indirectly* (through discursive acts) or *directly* (through concrete acts) how Jesus might contribute to the betterment of humans as moral beings. Second, Jesus's moral strangeness is an inherent attribute of his mode of discipleship. He offers a particular way of imagining God-human relations and human-human relations that is quite strange to common human experience. Accepting his offer of discipleship, for example, requires countering some aspects of common human experience such as serving God and money (Matt 6:24), disregarding the poor and the oppressed (Luke 4:16–21), and hating one's enemies (Matt 5:43–48). Therefore, when Jesus appears no longer to be a moral stranger, it could be indicative of the presence of the distortional strain of domestication that I highlighted.

In *Politics of Jesus*, John Howard Yoder argued that Jesus demanded a peaceful revisionary movement as *the* means to confront social and political evils in the world.[91] It is, of course, debated whether Jesus's choice to lead a peaceful revisionary movement should be understood as a contrast to the Zealots, who might not have existed during his time.[92] What is clear, however, is that Jesus was not an idle spectator in political and religious realms: he engaged actively with the intent to overcome domination. One need not accept Yoder's version of pacifism in order to take seriously Jesus's teaching on a peaceful engagement that aimed to promote the love of oneself in ways that are thoroughly judged by and also grounded in one's love of God and love of one's neighbor (Matt 22: 34–40). It seems that the ends of Jesus's peaceful engagement is *shalom*: the enacting of the well-being of human beings that should be grounded in God's reign in which, to paraphrase Isaiah and Luke, the gospel is preached to the poor, people in captivity are set free, the blind receive sight, the oppressed are set free, and the year of the Lord is proclaimed to all people (Isa 61:1–2; Luke 4:18–19).

Jesus's mode of discipleship has a transformative effect: the remaking of this world, transforming it from its unhealthy condition to a healthy condition. Christian abandonment undermines this transformative effect. Participation in the long and zigzag process of bringing the world from an unhealthy condition to a healthy condition will obviously require that Nigerian Christians engage in self-discipline, which can impede the gravitational force of Christian abandonment.[93] Though Nigerian Christians are to engage in self-discipline, they may not generate it without the kind of discipleship that I have described in this chapter. When internalized, Jesus's teaching on discipleship would orient Nigerian Christians to act in a manner that conforms to his way of life. On the contrary, when Nigerian Christians reject Jesus's mode of discipleship, which, as I have shown, involves following in his footsteps and submitting to his redirection, they

91. Yoder, *Politics of Jesus*. See also Yoder, *Nevertheless*.

92. See Horsley and Hanson, *Bandits, Prophets, and Messiahs*, xii–xvi.

93. The Apostle Paul's words in 1 Cor 9:27 remind us that self-discipline, in the context of discipleship, entails a denial of certain gratification or a form of mortification of some desires: "But I discipline my body and keep it under control, lest after preaching to others I myself should be disqualified" (ESV).

will deprive themselves of the insights Jesus provides on how his followers are to act during conflicts. For example, Nigerian Christians who get an amulet from an oracle of a deity of traditional Nigerian religion to protect themselves during interfaith conflicts will most likely lose sight of how they are to act in such situations as disciples of Jesus, which requires preemptive interfaith initiatives, an irenic spirit, a concession of religious difference, and a concession to God's prerogatives on true worship.

Conclusion

C hristian theology ought to be useful to the Christian life and the spiritual development of Christian communities. What does this conception of the relationship between theology, the Christian life, and Christian
communities demand in terms of how to theologize? The main issue here is
the implementation of the belief that theology has a significant role to play
in clarifying for Christian communities how they are to imagine and construct their Christian identities. The field of contextual theology explores this
issue with the aim of advancing the theological processes for imagining and
constructing Christian identity. A helpful way to understand how contextual
theology advances these theological processes is to attend to its telos.

It may seem at first that the telos of contextual theology is to offer a
jeremiad: a form of theological rhetoric or a way of doing theology that
uses the sharpest possible voice to call attention to the dangers besetting
the Christian theologies that fail what might be described as the "test of
contextuality." Any Christian theology that is not formulated with the theological materials that are generated from within a context of a Christian
community will likely fail the test of contextuality. I have argued in this
book, from the reflections on the echoes of contextual theologizing in some
sayings of Jesus to the exploration of Dalit theology, African theology, and
Latin American liberation theology, that the context of each Christian community can (and ought to) contribute substantively to the content, form,
and identity of Christin theology. A community's context can yield unique
theological materials, which have the potential for opening new vistas for a
Christian theologian to develop insightful theological responses to specific
issues. But how can a theologian discern the theological materials without
studying (or learning about) the community? And how can the theologian
develop an adequate theology for the community without attending to the
context that conditions or influences the actions of the members of the

community? For instance, how are theologians able to give insightful theological responses to questions of the ontological value, dignity, and worth of the lives of African Americans and other black folks residing in the United States of America, which George Floyd's death highlights, without attending to the historical context of police brutality in the nation? In a 2018 essay, I wrote that theologians should tackle the social problem of police brutality and excessive use of deadly force, which the Black Lives Matter movements have brought to the fore.[1] However, theologians who are interested in providing insightful theological responses to this perennial social problem in the United States of America, "should exegete the contemporary questions embedded in (1) America's responses to police brutality and use of deadly force, (2) the history of the victims of police brutality, and (3) the victims' experience—their ongoing encounter with the police."[2] When I penned these words, I did not foresee that the death of another African American (George Floyd) in police custody on May 25, 2020, would generate global outcries over racial injustices that black people suffer, particularly in the United States of America. Formulating a theology, which is grounded in the deity of Jesus Christ, *for* an American Christianity community "whose faith in Jesus Christ is being tested by the church's silence on police brutality and killings may be praised for being faithful to scripture" and church traditions.[3] If such theology lacks the knowledge of the historical manifestations of systemic racism and injustices in the United States of America or does not engage them, it will be discarded on the grounds that "it has nothing important to say about exposing police brutality, preventing [unnecessary] killings or empowering the American people to create a more just society, which does not allow such inhumane actions to flourish."[4]

As I pointed out in chapter 1, Christian theology is inherently contextual insofar as it is formulated by human beings who are conditioned by their contexts. Even those who do not see the context of a Christian community as an essential source of Christian theology are not completely immune to the effects of the contextual demands of theology. Theologians do not create theologies *ex nihilo*. They create and formulate theologies with the resources that are either partly or completely informed by particular contexts. The jeremiads of contextual theologians against the theologies that fail the test of contextuality, therefore, is not grounded in the question of whether every theology is in principle conditioned by a context. Rather,

1. Ezigbo, "Contextual Theology Response," 178–79.
2. Ezigbo, "Contextual Theology Response," 179.
3. Ezigbo, "Contextual Theology Response," 181.
4. Ezigbo, "Contextual Theology Response," 181.

their jeremiads are grounded in the failure of some theologians to generate and utilize theological materials from the context of a Christian community to construct their theologies. Theological materials vary from context to context. Therefore, theologians ought to attend to the peculiarities of theological materials that are embedded in the context of a Christian community for which they develop their theologies.

A jeremiad is, of course, one of the features of contextual theology insofar as it calls attention to the problems of grounding Christian theology in bare abstraction and in isolation from the life situations of Christian communities. As I showed in chapters 3–6, some European and North American theologies that were brought into Africa, Asia, and Latin America by missionaries, explorers, and merchants, gave rise to jeremiads and theological responses from African, Asian, and Latin American contextual theologians. They bemoaned the stifling influence of colonialism and the Enlightenment on European and North American Christianity. The main issue here is not how successfully or unsuccessfully European and North American Christianity adjusted to the phenomena of colonialism and the Enlightenment. It is rather the attempts of some European and North American missionaries and theologians to superimpose their contextualized theologies on Christian communities in Africa, Asia, and Latin America. The repudiation of such European and North American contextualized theologies on the grounds that they lacked adequate knowledge of the cultures and peculiar needs of Africa, Asia, and Latin America is evident in the rise of ecclesial communities that developed as a result of the concerted efforts of local agencies. Examples of such ecclesial communities are African Indigenous Churches (AICs) and Basic EcclesiaL Communities (BECs). Contextual theological movements that gave rise to African theology, Dalit theology, and Latin American liberation theologies, which are discussed in this book, equally display the difficulties and dangers of foisting foreign theologies on a Christian community.

The telos or ultimate aim of contextual theology is to advance the theological processes that are required to successfully imagine and formulate Christian identity by situating such processes within the *context* (history, culture, and contemporary state affairs) of each Christian community. It seeks to accomplish this task without subordinating other forms of theology such as philosophical theology, practical theology, missional theology, systematic theology, and biblical theology. Unlike many of these forms of theology, contextual theology explores a fresh pathway to overcome the difficulties that repel the attempts to construct a theology that meets the unique theological needs of a Christin community, without doing so either in isolation from (or overreliance on) the theological

212 The Art of Contextual Theology

resolutions achieved by Christian communities of different contexts and eras. Granted, each form of theology faces these difficulties. What contextual theology contributes to the discussions on how to overcome the difficulties is the recognition of *context* as one of the essential or indispensable sources of Christian theology. Where a context is not pressed for essential theological materials that are useful for constructing Christian theology, contextual theology does not exist. Dalit theology, African theology, and Latin American liberation theology that are discussed in this book are contextual theologies precisely because their authors pressed their different contexts for theological materials and utilized them to formulate Christian theologies for their own communities.

A theology seeking the status of Christian identity must successfully pass important tests. Theological materials extracted from Christian Scripture and church traditions supply the necessary Christian *vernacular*—the language, thoughts, concepts, and conventions—that can aid theologians to pass the tests. Theological materials extracted from the context of a Christian community also can aid theologians to construct theologies that qualify for and merit the status of Christian identity.[5] Attending to the contexts of Christian communities is required to pass the test of contextuality. To pass the test of contextuality, a theology must show convincingly that it correctly identified and insightfully responded to the peculiar theological needs and questions of its Christian audience—the Christian community for which the theology is formulated. This is one of the important lessons of the rulings of the Council of Jerusalem (Acts 15), which showcases how the earliest Jewish Christian communities rethought the viability and problems of proselytism for imagining Christian identity in response to the burden it created for non-Jewish Christians residing in Antioch. The council's rejection of proselytism as the only means by which non-Jewish Christians can benefit from Jesus's gospel paved the way for Gentile Christians in Antioch and also for future communities that would become a part of the church to explore the incarnational nature of the Christian faith. As Andrew Walls wrote in his commentary on the incarnational nature of the Christian faith,

> Christ is to be formed among those who receive him in faith; the Word is to take flesh again. And the Word does not take flesh in a generalized humanity, for there is no such thing. Humanity is always culture specific, reflecting the conditions of a particular time and place, and with an identity formed by a particular past.[6]

5. For descriptions of these tests and their unique contributions to Christian theology, see ch. 1.

6. Walls, *Crossing Cultural Frontiers*, 263.

Each Christian community, defined by its contextual accents, can rightly participate in and contribute to the furtherance of the inherent global, multicultural, and diverse outlooks of the Christian faith. Contextual theology nudges Christians to concede that the different theological representations and expressions of the Christian faith are partial and fragmentary. Only together can the contextualized expressions of the Christian faith with their particular theologies, to borrow the words of Walls, "realize the full stature of Christ."[7]

7. Walls, *Crossing Cultural Frontiers*, 263.

Bibliography

Adebayo, Bukola. "Nigeria Overtakes India in Extreme Poverty Ranking." *CNN*, June 26, 2018. https://www.cnn.com/2018/06/26/africa/nigeria-overtakes-india-extreme-poverty-intl/index.html.

Ajao, Ibukun. "You Will Become What You Believe with Bishop David Oyedepo." YouTube video, 35:59. August 23, 2017. https://www.youtube.com/watch?v=EEkKqCGd2c4.

Ajayi, J. F. A. *Christian Missions in Nigeria 1841–1891: The Making of a New Elite.* Evanston: Northwestern University Press, 1965.

Akinola, Anthony A. *Party Coalitions in Nigeria: History, Trends and Prospects.* Ibadan: Safari, 2014.

Amoah, Elizabeth, and Mercy Amba Oduyoye, "The Christ for Africa Women." In *With Passion and Compassion: Third World Women Doing Theology*, edited by Virginia Fabella, 35–46. Maryknoll, NY: Orbis, 1988.

Anderson, Allan Heaton. *An Introduction to Pentecostalism.* 2nd ed. Cambridge: Cambridge University Press, 2014.

Anderson-Rajkumar, Evangeline. "Turning Bodies Inside Out: Contour of Womanist Theology." In *Dalit Theology in the Twenty-First Century: Discordant Voices, Discerning Pathways*, edited by Sathianathan Clarke, Deenabandhu Manchala, and Philip Vinod Peacock, 199–214. New Delhi: Oxford University Press, 2010.

Appiah-Kubi, Kofi. "Indigenous African Christian Churches: Signs of Authenticity." In *African Theology en Route: Papers from the Pan-African Conference of Third World Theologians, December 17–23, Accra, Ghana*, edited by Kofi Appiah-Kubi and Sergio Torres, 117–25. Maryknoll, NY: Orbis, 1979.

———. "Preface." In *African Theology en Route: Papers from the Pan-African Conference of Third World Theologians, December 17–23, Accra, Ghana*, edited by Kofi Appiah-Kubi and Sergio Torres, viii–x. Maryknoll, NY: Orbis, 1979.

Atherton, John. *Public Theology for Changing Times.* London: SPCK, 2000.

Awoyinfa, Samuel. "Pastor Who Destroyed Shrine in Ogun Denies Being Stricken by 'Gods.'" *Punch*, September 25, 2016. http://punchng.com/pastor-stuck-shrine-trying-destroy-idols/.

Ayandele, E. A. *Holy Johnson, Pioneer of African Nationalism, 1836–1917.* London: Frank Cass, 1970.

Banerjea, Krishna Mohan. *The Arian Witness, or, The Testimony of Arian Scripture in Corroboration of Biblical History and the Rudiments of Christian Doctrine Including Dissertation on the Original Home and Easy Adventure of Indo-Arians*. Calcutta: Asiatic Society of Bengal, 1875.

―――. "The Relation between Christianity and Hinduism." In *Krishna Mohan Banerjea: Christian Apologist*, by T. V. Philip, 181–201. Madras: Christian Literature Society, 1982.

Barbu, Liviu. "The Poor in Spirit and Our Life in Christ: An Eastern Orthodox Perspective on Christian Discipleship." *Studies in Christian Ethics* 22 (2009) 261–74.

Barnett, Paul. *Jesus and the Rise of Christianity: A History of New Testament Times*. Downers Grove: InterVarsity, 1999.

Barr, James. *The Scope and Authority of the Bible*. London: Xpress Reprints, 1993.

Barrett, C. K. *The Gospel according to St. John: An Introduction with Commentary and Notes on the Greek Text*. London: SPCK, 1962.

Barth, Karl. *Church Dogmatics 1.1: The Doctrine of the Word of God*. Translated by G. W. Bromiley. 2nd ed. 1975. Reprint, Peabody: Hendrickson, 2010.

―――. *The Word of God and the Word of Man*. Translated by Douglas Horton. New York: Harper & Row, 1956.

Bauckham, Richard. *Gospel of Glory: Major Themes in Johannine Theology*. Grand Rapids: Baker Academic, 2015.

―――. *Jesus and the Eyewitnesses: The Gospels as Eyewitness Testimony*. Grand Rapids: Eerdmans, 2006.

Bediako, Gillian Mary. "Christianity in Interaction with the Primal Religions of the World: A Historical and Global Perspective." In *Christianity and Religious Plurality: Historical and Global Perspectives*, edited by Wilbert R. Shenk and Richard J. Plantinga, 181–207. Eugene, OR: Cascade, 2016.

Bediako, Kwame. "Biblical Christologies in the Context of African Traditional Religions." In *Sharing Jesus in the Two-Thirds World: Evangelical Christologies from the Contexts of Poverty, Powerlessness, and Religious Pluralism*, edited by Vinay Samuel and Chris Sugden, 81–121. Grand Rapids: Eerdmans, 1983.

―――. *Christianity in Africa: The Renewal of a Non-Western Religion*. Edinburgh: Edinburgh University Press, 1995.

―――. "The Doctrine of Christ and the Significance of Vernacular Terminology." *International Bulletin of Missionary Research* 22 (1998) 110–11.

―――. "Epilogue." In *On Their Way Rejoicing: The History and Role of the Bible in Africa*, by Ype Schaaf, 243–54. Carlisle: Paternoster, 1994.

―――. "Five Theses on the Significance of Modern African Christianity: A Manifesto." *Transformation* 13 (1996) 20–29.

―――. *Jesus and the Gospel in Africa: History and Experience*. Maryknoll, NY: Orbis, 2004.

―――. "The Roots of African Theology." *International Bulletin of Missionary Research* 13 (1989) 58–65.

―――. *Theology and Identity: The Impact of Culture upon Christian Thought in the Second Century and Modern Africa*. Oxford: Regnum, 1992.

Benedict XVI. *Instruction on Certain Aspects of the "Theology of Liberation."* Vatican website. August 6, 1984. http://www.vatican.va/roman_curia/congregations/cfaith/documents/rc_con_cfaith_doc_19840806_theology-liberation_ en.html"Instruction on Certain Aspects of the 'Theology of Liberation,'" accessed from http://www.vatican.va/roman_curia/congregations/cfaith/documents/rc_con_cfaith_doc_19840806_theology-liberation_en.html.

Berger, Mark T. "After the Third World? History, Destiny and the Fate of Third Worldism." *Third World Quarterly* 25 (2004) 9–39.

Bergsma, John S. *The Jubilee from Leviticus to Qumran: A History of Interpretation.* Supplements to Vetus Testamentum 115. Leiden: Brill, 2007.

Bevans, Stephen B. *Models of Contextual Theology.* Rev. and exp. ed. Maryknoll, NY: Orbis, 2002.

Bird, Adrian. *M. M. Thomas and Dalit Theology.* Bangalore: BTESSC, 2008.

Bishops' Conference of England and Wales. *The Common Good and the Catholic Church's Social Teaching.* London: Catholic Bishops' Conference of England and Wales, 1996.

Bloomberg, Craig L. *Matthew.* The New American Commentary. Nashville: Broadmans, 1992.

Boff, Leonardo. *Ecclesiogenesis: The Base Communities Reinvent the Church.* Maryknoll, NY: Orbis, 1986.

———. "The Originality of the Theology of Liberation." In *The Future of Liberation Theology: Essays in Honor of Gustavo Gutierrez,* edited by Marc H. Ellis and Otto Maduro, 38–48. Maryknoll, NY: Orbis, 1989.

Bonhoeffer, Dietrich. *The Cost of Discipleship.* Translated by R. H. Fuller. New York: Touchstone, 1995.

Bonino, Jose Miguez. *Christians and Marxists: The Challenge to Revolution.* Grand Rapids: Eerdmans, 1976.

Booth, Roger P. *Jesus and the Laws of Purity: Tradition History and Legal History in Mark 7.* Sheffield: JSOT, 1986.

Bourgel, Jonathan. "The Destruction of the Samaritan Temple by John Hyrcanus: A Reconsideration." *Journal of Biblical Literature* 135 (2016) 505–23.

Bowler, Kate. *Blessed: A History of the American Prosperity Gospel.* New York: Oxford University Press, 2013.

Braedley, Susan, and Meg Luxton. "Competing Philosophies: Neoliberalism and Challenges of Everyday Life." In *Neoliberalism and Everyday Life,* edited by Susan Braedley and Meg Luxton, 3–21 Montreal: McGill-Queen's University Press, 2010.

Brown, Robert McAffee. *Gustavo Gutiérrez.* Makers of Contemporary Theology. Atlanta: John Knox, 1980.

Bujo, Benezet. *African Theology in Its Social Context.* Translated by John O'Donohue. Maryknoll, NY: Orbis, 1992.

Bultmann, Rudolf. *Theology of the New Testament.* Translated by Kendrick Grobel. New York: Charles Scribner's Sons, 1951.

Busia, K. A. "The African Worldview." In *Christianity and African Culture: The Proceedings of a Conference Held at Accra Gold Coast, May 2–6, 1955, under the Auspices of the Christian Council,* 1–6. Accra: Christian Council of the Gold Coast, 1955.

———. "Ancestor Worship, Libation, Stools, Festival." In *Christianity and African Culture: The Proceedings of a Conference Held at Accra Gold Coast, May 2–6, 1955, under the Auspices of the Christian Council,* 17–23. Accra: Christian Council of the Gold Coast, 1955.

Caird, G. B. *New Testament Theology*. Completed and edited by L. D. Hurst. Oxford: Clarendon, 1995.

Canagarajah, Sudharshan, and Saji Thomas. "Poverty in a Wealthy Economy: The Case of Nigeria." *IMF Working Paper* 02.114 (July 1, 2002). https://www.imf.org/en/Publications/WP/Issues/2016/12/30/Poverty-in-a-Wealthy-Economy-The-Case-of-Nigeria-15789.

Carter, J. Kameron. *Race: A Theological Account*. New York: Oxford University Press, 2008.

Cavanaugh, William T. *The Myth of Religious Violence: Secular Ideology and the Roots of Modern Conflict*. New York: Oxford University Press, 2009.

The Christian Council of the Gold Coast. *Christianity and African Culture: The Proceedings of a Conference Held at Accra Gold Coast, May 2–6, 1955, under the Auspices of the Christian Council*. Accra: Christian Council of the Gold Cost, 1955.

Collins, Nina L. *Jesus, the Sabbath and the Jewish Debate: Healing on the Sabbath in the 1st and 2nd Centuries CE*. New York: T&T Clark, 2014.

"Communiqué: Ecumenical Dialogue of Third World Theologians, Dar es Salaam, August 12, 1976." In *The Emergent Gospel: Theology from the Underside of History*, edited by Sergio Torres and Virginia Fabella, 272–74. Maryknoll, NY: Orbis, 1978.

Cone, James H. *Black Theology of Liberation*. Maryknoll, NY: Orbis, 1986.

———. *The Cross and the Lynching Tree*. Maryknoll, NY: Orbis, 2011.

Clarke, Sathianathan, Deenabandhu Manchala, and Philip Vinod Peacok. "Introduction." In *Dalit Theology in the Twenty-First Century: Discordant Voices, Discerning Pathways*, edited by Sathianathan Clarke, Deenabandhu Manchala, and Philip Vinod Peacok, 1–16. New Delhi: Oxford University Press, 2010.

Clarke, Steve. *The Justification of Religious Violence*. Chichester: Wiley-Blackwell, 2014.

Clooney, Francis X. *Comparative Theology: Deep Learning across Religious Borders*. Chichester: Wiley-Blackwell, 2010.

Cranfield, C. E. B. *The Gospel according to St. Mark*. Cambridge: Cambridge University Press, 1963.

Crossan, John Dominic. *The Historical Jesus: The Life of a Mediterranean Jewish Peasant*. New York: HarperOne, 1991.

———. *Who Killed Jesus? Exposing the Roots of Anti-Semitism in the Gospel Story of the Death of Jesus*. New York: HarperCollins, 1996.

Crowder, Michael. *A Short History of Nigeria*. Rev. and enl. ed. New York: Frederic A. Praeger, 1966.

Danaher, William J. "Music That Will Bring Back the Dead? Resurrection, Reconciliation, and Restorative Justice in Post-apartheid South Africa." *Journal of Religious Ethics* 38 (2010) 115–41.

Dawkins, Richard. *The God Delusion*. Boston: Houghton Mifflin, 2006.

Dawson, Andrew. *The Birth and Impact of the Base Ecclesial Community and Liberative Theological Discourse in Brazil*. San Francisco: Catholic Scholars, 1999.

Deliege, Robert. "Replication and Consensus: Untouchability, Caste and Ideology in India." *Man* 27.1 (1992) 155–73.

Dickson, Kwesi A. "The African Theological Task." In *The Emergent Gospel: Theology from the Underside of History*, edited by Sergio Torres and Virginia Fabella, 46–49. Maryknoll, NY: Orbis, 1978.

———. *Theology in Africa*. London: Darton, Longman and Todd, 1994.

Dulles, Avery. *Church and Society: The Laurence J. McGinley Lectures, 1988–2007.* New York: Fordham University Press, 2008.

Dumont, Louis. *Homo Hierarchicus: The Caste System and Its Implications.* Translated by Mark Sainsbury, Louis Dumont, and Basia Gulati. Complete rev. english ed. Chicago: University of Chicago Press, 1970.

Durkheim, Emile. *The Division of Labor in Society.* Translated by George Simpson. New York: Free Press, 1964.

———. *Suicide: A Study in Sociology.* Translated by John A. Spaulding and George Simpson. New York: Free Press, 1966.

Dzalto, Davor. "'The Logos as Reason and Love: A Response to 'Tradition as Reason and Practice' by A. Papanikolou." *St. Vladimir's Theological Quarterly* 59 (2015) 113–19.

Eagleson, John, ed. *Christians and Socialism: The Christians for Socialism Movement in Latin America.* Translated by John Drury. Maryknoll, NY: Orbis, 1975.

Eagleson, John, and Philip Scharper, eds. *Puebla and Beyond: Documentation and Commentary.* Maryknoll, NY: Orbis, 1979.

Engelhardt, H. Tristram. *The Foundations of Bioethics.* 2nd ed. New York: Oxford University Press, 1996.

Evans, C. Stephen, ed. *Exploring Kenotic Christology: The Self-Emptying of God.* New York: Oxford University Press, 2006.

Ezeh, Uchenna A. *Jesus Christ the Ancestor: African Contextual Christology in the Light of the Major Dogmatic Christological Definitions of the Church from the Council of Nicaea (325) to Chalcedon (451).* Bern: Lang, 2003.

Ezigbo, Victor I. "African Christian or Christian African? Identity Relations in African Christianity." In *Sources of Christian Self: A Cultural History of Christian Identity,* edited by James M. Houston and Jens Zimmermann, 664–82. Grand Rapids: Eerdmans, 2018.

———. "Contextual Theology: God in Human Context." In *Evangelical Theological Method: Five Views,* edited by Stanley E. Porter and Steven M. Studebaker, 93–115. Downers Grove: InterVarsity, 2018.

———. "A Contextual Theology Response." In *Evangelical Theological Method: Five Views,* edited by Stanley E. Porter and Steven M. Studebaker, 177–87. Downers Grove: InterVarsity Academic, 2018.

———. "Imagining Mutual Christian Theological Identity: From Apologia to Dialogic Theologizing." *Journal of Ecumenical Studies* 50 (2015) 452–72.

———. *Introducing Christian Theologies: Voices from Global Christian Communities.* Vol. 1. Eugene, OR: Cascade, 2013.

———. "Jesus as God's Communicative and Hermeneutical Act: African Christians on the Person and Significance of Jesus Christ." In *Jesus without Borders: Christology in the Majority World,* edited by Gene L. Green, Stephen T. Pardue, and K. K. Yeo, 37–58. Grand Rapids: Eerdmans, 2014.

———. *Re-imagining African Christologies: Conversing with the Interpreting and Appropriations of Jesus in Contemporary Africa.* Eugene, OR: Pickwick, 2010.

———. "Religion and Divine Presence: Appropriating Christianity from within African Indigenous Religions' Perspective." In *African Traditions in the Study of Religion in Africa,* edited by Afe Adogame, Ezra Chitando, and Bolahi Bateye, 178–203. Surrey: Ashgate, 2012.

———. "Violent Christians, the Nigerian Public Square, and the Utility of Jesus' Forgiveness Sayings for Tackling Religious Violence." *International Journal of Public Theology* 12 (2018) 236–59.

Falola, Toyin, and Matthew M. Heaton. *A History of Nigeria*. New York: Cambridge University Press, 2008.

Falola, Toyin, and Adebayo O. Oyebade. *Hot Spot: Sub-Saharan Africa*. Denver: Greenwood, 2010.

Farmer, Paul. "Health, Healing, and Social Justice: Insights from Liberation Theology." In *The Preferential Option for the Poor beyond Theology*, edited by Daniel G. Groody and Gustavo Gutierrez, 199–228. Notre Dame: University of Notre Dame Press, 2014.

Fee, Gordon D. "The New Testament and Kenosis Christology." In *Exploring Kenotic Christology: The Self-Emptying of God*, edited by C. Stephen Evans, 25–36. New York: Oxford University Press, 2006.

Fergusson, David. *Faith and Its Critics: A Conversation*. New York: Oxford University Press, 2009.

"Final Statement: Ecumenical Dialogue of Third World Theologians, Dar es Salaam, August 5–12, 1976." In *The Emergent Gospel: Theology from the Underside of History*, edited by Sergio Torres and Virginia Fabella, 259–71. Maryknoll, NY: Orbis, 1978.

Fine, Steven, ed. *Jews, Christians, and Polytheists in the Ancient Synagogue: Cultural Interaction during the Greco-Roman Period*. New York: Routledge, 1999.

Flannery, Austin, ed. *Vatican Council II: The Conciliar and Post-Conciliar Documents*. Collegeville, MN: Liturgical, 1975.

Forrester, Duncan B. *Caste and Christianity: Attitudes and Policies on Caste of Anglo-Saxon Protestant Missionaries in India*. London: Curzon, 1979.

Freire, Paulo. *Pedagogy of the Oppressed*. Translated by Myra Bergman Ramos. New York: Continuum, 2000.

Frykenberg, Robert Eric. *Christianity in India: From Beginnings to the Present*. Oxford: Oxford University Press, 2008.

Funk, Robert W., Roy W. Hoover, and the Jesus Seminar. *The Five Gospels: The Search for the Authentic Words of Jesus*. New York: Polebridge, 1993.

Gaussen, L. *Divine Inspiration of the Bible*. Translated by David D. Scott. Grand Rapids: Kregel, 1971.

Gifford, Paul. *African Christianity: Its Public Role*. Bloomington: Indiana University Press, 1998.

Gordon, D. H. *The Prehistoric Background of Indian Culture*. Bombay: Bhulabhai Memorial Institute, 1958.

Gorringe, T. J. *The Common Good and the Global Emergency: God and the Built Environment*. Cambridge: Cambridge University Press, 2011.

Gott, Richard. "Introduction." In *The Rebel Church in Latin America*, edited by Alain Gheerbrant, 9–13. Baltimore: Penguin, 1974.

Goulder, Michael, ed. *Incarnation and Myth: The Debate Continued*. Grand Rapids: Eerdmans, 1979.

Graham, Elaine. "Rethinking the Common Good: Theology and the Future of Welfare." *Colloquium* 40 (2008) 133–56.

Grant, Jacquelyn. *White Women's Christ and Black Women's Jesus: Feminist Christology and Womanist Response*. Atlanta: Scholars, 1989.

Griffin, James. *Well-Being: Its Meaning, Measurement, and Moral Importance.* New York: Oxford University Press, 1986.

Grillmeier, Aloys. *Christ in Christian Tradition.* Vol. 1, *From the Apostolic Age to Chalcedon.* 2nd ed. Atlanta: John Knox, 1975.

Grudem, Wayne, and Barry Asmus. *The Poverty of Nations: A Sustainable Solution.* Wheaton: Crossway, 2013.

Gundry-Volf, Judith M. "Spirit, Mercy, and the Other." *Theology Today* 51 (1995) 508–23.

Gunton, Colin. "Historical and Systematic Theology." In *The Cambridge Companion to Christian Doctrine,* edited by Colin E. Gunton, 3–20. Cambridge: Cambridge University Press, 1997.

Gutiérrez, Gustavo. "Expanding the View." In *Expanding the View: Gustavo Gutierrez and the Future of Liberation Theology,* edited by Marc H. Ellis and Otto Maduro, 3–36. Maryknoll, NY: Orbis, 1988.

———. "Faith as Freedom: Solidarity with the Alienated and Confidence in the Future." *Horizons* 2 (1975) 25–60.

———. *The God of Life.* Translated by Matthew J. O'Connell. Maryknoll, NY: Orbis, 1991.

———. "The Indian: Person and Poor—the Theological Perspective of Bartolomé de Las Casas." In *Witness: Writings of Bartolomé de Las Casas,* edited by George Sanderlin, xi–xxii. Maryknoll, NY: Orbis, 1992.

———. *On Job: God-Talk and the Suffering of the Innocent.* Translated by Matthew J. O'Connell. Maryknoll, NY: Orbis, 1985.

———. *The Power of the Poor in History.* Translated by Robert R. Barr. Maryknoll, NY: Orbis, 1983.

———. "Response." In *Liberation and Change,* edited by Ronald H. Stone, 181–84. Atlanta: John Knox, 1977.

———. "Saying and Showing to the Poor: 'God Loves You.'" In *In the Company of the Poor: Conversations with Dr. Paul Farmer and Fr. Gustavo Gutierrez,* edited by Michael Griffin and Jennie Weiss Block, 27–34. Maryknoll, NY: Orbis, 2013.

———. *A Theology of Liberation.* Translated and edited by Caridad Inda and John Eagleson. Maryknoll, NY: Orbis, 1988.

———. *The Truth Shall Make You Free: Confrontations.* Translated by Matthew J. O'Connell. Maryknoll, NY: Orbis, 1990.

———. "Two Theological Perspectives: Liberation Theology and Progressivist Theology." In *The Emergent Gospel: Theology from the Underside of History,* edited by Sergio Torres and Virginia Fabella, 227–55. Maryknoll, NY: Orbis, 1978.

———. *We Drink from Our Own Wells: The Spiritual Journey of a People.* Translated by Matthew J. O'Connell. Maryknoll, NY: Orbis, 2003.

Hachlili, Rachel. "Synagogues: Before and After the Roman Destruction of the Temple." *Biblical Archaeology Review* 41 (2015) 30–38, 65.

Hanciles, Jehu. "Anatomy of an Experiment: The Sierra Leone Native Pastorate." *Missiology* 29.1 (January 2001) 63–82.

Handley, Meg. "The Violence in Nigeria: What's behind the Conflict?" *Time,* March 10, 2010. http://content.time.com/time/world/article/0,8599,1971010,00.html.

Hanson, Paul D. "The Identity and Purpose of the Church." *Theology Today* 42 (1985) 342–52.

Harvey, David. *A Brief History of Neoliberalism*. New York: Oxford University Press, 2005.

Hays, Richard B. *Echoes of Scripture in the Gospels*. Waco: Baylor University Press, 2016.

Hellwig, Monika. "Liberation Theology: An Emerging School." *Scottish Journal of Theology* 30 (1977) 137–51.

Hick, John, ed. *The Myth of God Incarnate*. Philadelphia: Westminster, 1977.

Horsley, Richard A. *Archeology, History, and Society in Galilee: The Social Context of Jesus and the Rabbis*. Valley Forge: Trinity International, 1996.

Horsley, Richard A., and John S. Hanson. *Bandits, Prophets, and Messiahs: Popular Movements at the Time of Jesus*. New York: Harper & Row, 1985.

Hough, James. *A Reply to the Letters of the Abbe Dubois on the State of Christianity in India*. London: Watts, 1824.

Hurtado, Larry W. *How on Earth Did Jesus Become a God? Historical Questions about Earliest Devotion to Jesus*. Grand Rapids: Eerdmans, 2005.

Idowu, E. Bolaji. "Introduction." In *Biblical Revelation and African Beliefs*, edited by Kwesi A. Dickson and Paul Ellingworth, 9–16. London: Longmans, 1969.

———. *Towards an Indigenous Church*. London: Oxford University Press, 1965.

Imasogie, Osadolor. *African Traditional Religion*. Ibadan: University Press, 1985.

International Theological Commission. "The Hope of Salvation for Infants Who Die without Being Baptized." Vatican website. January 19, 2007. http://www.vatican.va/roman_curia/congregations/cfaith/cti_documents/rc_con_cfaith_doc_20070419_un-baptised-infants_en.html.

Irvin, Dale T. "World Christianity: An Introduction." *Journal of World Christianity* 1 (2008) 1–26.

Isasi-Diaz, Ada Maria. *La Lucha Continues: Mujerista Theology*. Maryknoll, NY: Orbis, 2004.

James, William. *The Varieties of Religious Experience*. New York: Vintage, 1990.

Jenkins, Philip. *The New Faces of Christianity: Believing the Bible in the Global South*. New York: Oxford University Press, 2006.

Jeremiah, Anderson H. M. "Exploring New Facets of Dalit Christology: Critical Interaction with J. D. Crossan's Portrayal of the Historical Jesus." In *Dalit Theology in the Twenty-First Century: Discordant Voices, Discerning Pathways*, edited by Sathianathan Clarke, Deenabandhu Manchala, and Philip Vinod Peacock, 150–67. New Delhi: Oxford University Press, 2010.

Jodhka, Surinder S. *Caste in Contemporary India*. New Delhi: Routledge, 2015.

John Paul XXIII. *Mater et Magistra*. Encyclical Letter. Vatican website. May 14, 1961. http://w2.vatican.va/content/john-xxiii/en/encyclicals/documents/hf_j-xxiii_enc_15051961_mater.html.

Johnson, Luke Timothy. *The Real Jesus: The Misguided Quest for the Historical Jesus and the Truth of the Traditional Gospels*. New York: HarperCollins, 1996.

Josephus. "Antiquities." In *The Works of Josephus*, translated by William Whiston, 23–426. Peabody, MA: Hendrickson, 1987.

Judge, Paramjit S. "Between Exclusion and Exclusivity: Dalits in Contemporary India." *Polish Sociological Review* 178 (2012) 265–79.

Justin. "Apologia I." In *The Early Christian Fathers: A Selection from the Writings of the Fathers from St. Clement of Rome to Athanasius*, edited by Henry Bettenson, 58–64. New York: Oxford University Press, 1956.

Kärkkäinen, Veli-Matti. *Introduction to the Theology of Religions: Biblical, Historical, and Contemporary Perspectives*. Downers Grove: InterVarsity, 2003.

Kato, Byang H. "Evaluation of Black Theology." *Bibliotheca Sacra* 133 (1976) 243–52.

———. "Theological Issues in Africa." *Bibliotheca Sacra* 133 (1976) 143–53.

———. *Theological Pitfalls in Africa*. Kisumu: Evangel, 1975.

Kavalski, Emilian, and Magdalena Zolkos. "Approaching the Phenomenon of Federal Failure." In *Defunct Federalisms: Critical Perspectives on Federal Failure*, edited by Emilian Kavalski and Magdalena Zolkos, 1–16. Burlington, VT: Ashgate, 2008.

Kaveny, Cathleen. *Prophecy Without Contempt: Religious Discourse in the Public Square*. Cambridge: Harvard University Press, 2016.

Keener, Craig S. *A Commentary on the Gospel of Matthew*. Grand Rapids: Eerdmans, 1999.

Keith, Chris. *Jesus against the Scribal Elite: The Origins of the Conflict*. Grand Rapids: Eerdmans, 2014.

Kelly, J. N. D. *Early Christian Doctrines*. London: Adam & Charles Black, 1958.

Kelsey, David H. *The Uses of Scripture in Recent Theology*. Philadelphia: Fortress, 1975.

Kimball, Charles. *When Religion Becomes Evil: Five Warning Signs*. New York: HaperOne, 2008.

Kinkupu, Léonard Santedi, Gérard Bissainthe, and Meinrad Hebga. *Des prêtres noirs s'interrogent: Cinquante ans après . . .* Paris: Karthala/Présence Africaine, 2006.

Klancher, Nancy. *The Taming of the Canaanite Woman: Constructions of Christian Identity in the Afterlife of Mathew 15:21–28*. Berlin: De Gruyter, 2013.

Küng, Hans. *Does God Exist? An Answer for Today*. Translated by Edward Quinn. New York: Doubleday, 1978.

Levin, Andrew. "Marxism and Poverty." In *Poverty and Morality: Religious and Secular Perspectives*, edited by William A. Galston and Peter H. Hoffenberg, 242–64. New York: Cambridge University Press, 2010.

Levine, Lee I. *The Ancient Synagogue: The First Thousand Years*. New Haven: Yale University Press, 2000.

Lowery, Stephanie A. *Identity and Ecclesiology: Their Relationship among Select African Theologians*. Eugene, OR: Pickwick, 2017.

Luka, Reuben Turbi. *Jesus Christ as Ancestor: A Theological Study of Major African Ancestor Christologies in Conversation with the Patristic Christologies of Tertullian and Athanasius*. Carlisle: Langham, 2019.

Macchia, Frank D. *Baptized in the Spirit: A Global Pentecostal Theology*. Grand Rapids: Zondervan, 2006.

Macdonald, John. *The Theology of the Samaritans*. London: SCM, 1964.

Macquarrie, John. *Principles of Christian Theology*. 2nd ed. New York: Charles Scribner's Sons, 1977.

Marcus, Joel. "Rivers of Living Water from Jesus' Belly (John 7:38)." *Journal of Biblical Literature* 117 (1998) 328–30.

Maritain, Jacques. *Integral Humanism: Temporal and Spiritual Problems of a New Christendom*. Translated by Joseph W. Evans. New York: Charles Scribner's Sons, 1968.

Martin, David. *Does Christianity Cause War?* Oxford: Clarendon, 1997.

Massey, James. "Christianity to Be Renewed? Rethink Theology." In *Rethinking Theology in India: Christianity in the Twenty-First Century*, edited by James Massey and T. K. John, 25–82. New Delhi: Manohar, 2013.

———. *Dalit Theology: History, Context, Text and Whole Salvation.* New Delhi: Manohar, 2014.

———. "Dalits in India: Key Problems/Issues and Role of Religion." In *Another World Is Possible: Spiritualties and Religions of Global Darker People,* edited by Dwight N. Hopkins and Marjorie Lewis, 20–30. London: Equinox, 2009.

———. *Dalits in India: Religion as a Source of Bondage or Liberation with Special Reference to Christians.* New Delhi: Manohar, 1995.

———. *Downtrodden: The Struggle of India's Dalits for Identity, Solidarity and Liberation.* Geneva: WCC, 1997.

———. *Dr. B. R. Ambedkar: A Study in Just Society.* New Delhi: Manohar, 2003.

———. "Ingredients for a Dalit Theology." In *Towards a Dalit Theology,* edited by M. E. Prabhakar, 57–63. New Delhi: ISPCK, 1988.

———. "Need of a Dalit Theological Expression." In *Confronting Life: Theology out of the Context,* edited by M. P. Joseph, 194–201. New Delhi: ISPCK, 1995.

———. *Roots of Dalit History, Christianity, Theology and Spirituality.* Delhi: ISPCK, 1996.

———. *Towards Dalit Hermeneutics: Rereading the Text, the History, and the Literature.* Delhi: ISPCK, 1994.

Matheny, Paul Duane. *Contextual Theology: The Drama of Our Times.* Eugene, OR: Pickwick, 2011.

Mbefo, Luke. *Christian Theology and African Heritage.* Onitsha: Spiritan, 1996.

Mbiti, John. "Christianity and Traditional Religions in Africa." In *Crucial Issues in Missions Tomorrow,* edited by Donald A. McGavran, 144–58. Chicago: Moody, 1972.

———. *Introduction to African Religion.* 2nd ed. Oxford: Heinemann, 1991.

———. "The Ways and Means of Communicating the Gospel." In *Christianity in Tropical Africa: Studies Presented and Discussed at the Seventh International African Seminar, University of Ghana, April 1965,* edited by C. G. Baëta, 329–50. Oxford: Oxford University Press, 1968.

McGovern, Arthur F. *Liberation Theology and Its Critics: Toward an Assessment.* Maryknoll, NY: Orbis, 1989.

Meier, John P. "On the Veiling of Hermeneutics (1 Cor 11:2–16)." *The Catholic Biblical Quarterly* 40 (1978) 212–26.

Moe-Lobeda, Cynthia D. *Healing a Broken World: Globalization and God.* Minneapolis: Fortress, 2002.

Moffatt, M. *An Untouchable Community in South India: Structure and Consensus.* Princeton: Princeton University Press, 1979.

Morris, Thomas V. *Our Idea of God: An Introduction to Philosophical Theology.* Vancouver: Regent College Publishing, 2002.

Mosse, David. *The Saint in the Banyan Tree: Christianity and Caste Society in India.* Berkeley: University of California Press, 2012.

Mulackal, Shalini. "Women: Theology and Feminist Movements in India." In *Rethinking Theology in India: Christianity in the Twenty-First Century,* edited by James Massey and T. K. John, 151–77. New Delhi: Manohar, 2013.

Mulago, V. "Christianisme et culture africaine: Apport africain à la theeologie." In *Christianity in Tropical Africa: Studies Presented and Discussed at the Seventh International African Seminar at the University of Ghana, April 1965,* edited by C. G. Baëta, 308–28. Oxford: Oxford University Press, 1968.

Neyrey, Jerome H. "Jacob Traditions and the Interpretation of John 4:10–26." *The Catholic Biblical Quarterly* 41 (1979) 419–37.

Nickoloff, James B. "Introduction." In *Gustavo Gutiérrez: Essential Writings*, edited by James B. Nickoloff, 1–22. Minneapolis: Fortress, 1996.

Niebuhr, H. Richard. *The Social Sources of Denominationalism*. New York: Meridian, 1929.

Nirmal, Arvin P. "A Dialogue with Dalit Literature." In *Towards a Dalit Theology*, edited by M. E. Prabhakar, 64–82. New Delhi: ISPCK, 1988.

———. "Toward a Christian Dalit Theology." In *Frontiers in Asian Christian Theology: Emerging Trends*, edited by R. S. Sugirtharajah, 27–40. Maryknoll, NY: Orbis, 1994.

Nossiter, Adam. "Toll from Religious and Ethnic Violence in Nigeria Rises to 500." *The New York Times*, March 8, 2010. https://www.nytimes.com/2010/03/09/world/africa/09nigeria.html.

Nwachukwu, John Owen "'Why I Annulled June 12 1993 Presidential Election'–Babangida." *Daily Post*, June 12, 2017. http://dailypost.ng/2017/06/12/annulled-june-12-1993-presidential-election-babangida/.

Oduro, Thomas, et al. *Mission in an African Way: A Practical Introduction to African Instituted Churches and Their Sense of Mission*. Wellington: Christian Literature Fund, 2008.

Oduyoye, Mercy Amba. "Doing Theology from Beyond the Sahara." In *Confronting Life: Theology out of the Context*, edited by M. P. Joseph, 159–71. Delhi: ISPCK, 1995.

———. "Feminist Theology in an African Perspective." In *Paths of African Theology*, edited by Rosino Gibellini, 166–81. Maryknoll, NY: Orbis, 1994.

———. "The Value of African Religious Beliefs and Practices for Christian Theology." In *African Theology en Route: Papers from the Pan-African Conference of Third World Theologians, December 17–23, 1977, Accra, Ghana*, edited by Kofi Appiah-Kubi and Sergio Torres, 109–16. Maryknoll, NY: Orbis, 1979.

O'Donovan, Oliver. *The Just War Revisited*. Cambridge: Cambridge University Press, 2003.

Ogbonnaya, Clement A. *I Am Too Big to Be Poor: How You Can Unlock the Powers of Psalm 84:11*. Aba: Footprints Communications, 2004.

Okure, Teresa. *The Johannine Approach to Mission: A Contextual Study of John 4:1–42*. Tubingen: J. C. B. Mohr, 1988.

Olanisebe, Samson Olusina. "Sabbatical and Jubilee Regulations as a Means of Economic Recovery." *Jewish Bible Quarterly* 46 (2018) 196–202.

Olsson, Birger, and Magnus Zetterholm, eds. *The Ancient Synagogue from Its Origins until 200 C.E.: Papers Presented at an International Conference at Lund University, October 14–17, 2001*. Stockholm: Almqvist & Wiksell, 2003.

Olupona, Jacob K., ed. *African Religions: A Very Short Introduction*. New York: Oxford University Press, 2014.

———. *African Traditional Religions in Contemporary Society*. St. Paul: Paragon, 1991.

Onyeji, Ebuka. "Living Faith Church Reacts to Video Showing Founder, Oyedepo, Urging Members to 'Kill.'" *Premium Times*, January 14, 2017. http://www.premiumtimesng.com/news/top-news/220482-living-faith-church-reacts-video-showing-founder-oyedepo-urging-members-kill.html.

Osaghae, Eghosa E. "Managing Multiple Minority Problems in a Divided Society: The Nigerian Experience." *The Journal of Modern African Studies* 36 (1998) 1–24.

Ott, Craig, and Harold A. Netland, eds. *Globalizing Theology: Belief and Practice in an Era of World Christianity.* Grand Rapids: Baker Academic, 2006.

Papanikolaou, Aristotle. "Tradition as Reason and Practice: Amplifying Contemporary Orthodoxy Theology in Conversation with Alasdair MacIntyre." *St. Vladimir's Theological Quarterly* 59 (2015) 91–104.

Parratt, John. *Reinventing Christianity: African Theology Today.* Grand Rapids: Eerdmans, 1995.

Philip, T. V. *Krishna Mohan Banerjea: Christian Apologist.* Madras: Christian Literature Society, 1982.

Piggott, Stuart. *Prehistoric India.* Baltimore: Penguin, 1950.

Placher, William C. *Mark.* Louisville: Westminster John Knox, 2010.

Plantinga, Alvin. *Warranted Christian Belief.* New York: Oxford University Press, 2000.

Powell, Mark Allan. "Matthew's Beatitudes: Reversals and Rewards of the Kingdom." *Catholic Biblical Quarterly* 58 (1996) 460–469.

Prabhakar, M. E. "The Search for a Dalit Theology." In *Towards a Dalit Theology*, edited by M. E. Prabhakar, 35–47. New Delhi: ISPCK, 1988.

Prasad, D. Manohar Chandra. "Dalit Theology: Methodological Issues in a Contextual Theology of Liberation." *The Asian Journal of Theology* 23 (2009) 166–75.

Premawardhana, Devaka. "Between Logocentrism and Lococentrism: Alambrista Challenges to Traditional Theology." *The Harvard Theological Review* 101 (2008) 399–416.

"President Muhammadu Buhari's 2018 Democracy Day speech." *Vanguard*, May 29, 2018. https://www.vanguardngr.com/2018/05/president-muhammadu-buharis-2018-democracy-day-speech/.

Proudfoot, Wayne. *Religious Experience.* Berkeley: University of California Press, 1985.

Rahner, Karl. "Christianity and the Non-Christian Religions." In vol. 4 of *Theological Investigations*, edited by Karl H. Kruger, 115–34. Baltimore: Helicon, 1966.

Rajkumar, Peniel. *Dalit Theology and Dalit Liberation: Problems, Paradigms, and Possibilities.* Surrey: Ashgate, 2010.

———. "The Diversity and Dialectics of Dalit Dissent and Implications for a Dalit Theology of Liberation." In *Dalit Theology in the Twenty-First Century: Discordant Voices, Discerning Pathways*, edited by Sathianathan Clarke, Deenabandhu Manchala, and Philip Vinod Peacock, 55–73. New Delhi: Oxford University Press, 2010.

Rapaka, Yabbeju. *Dalit Pentecostalism: A Study of the Indian Pentecostal Chrch of God, 1932–2010.* Lexington: Emeth, 2013.

Ryan, Jordan J. "Jesus and Synagogue Disputes: Recovering the Institutional Context of Luke 13:10–17." *The Catholic Biblical Quarterly* 79 (2017) 41–59.

SaharaTV. "RAW VIDEO: Oba of Lagos Threatens Igbos over Governorship Election." YouTube video, 10:42. April 6, 2015. https://www.youtube.com/watch?v=eCLK m8UZCcU.

Sankalia, H. D. *Prehistory and Protohistory in India and Pakistan.* Bombay: University of Bombay, 1963.

Sanneh, Lamin. *Disciples of All Nations: Pillars of World Christianity.* New York: Oxford University Press, 2008.

————. *Piety and Power: Muslims and Christians in West Africa.* Maryknoll, NY: Orbis, 1996.

————. "The Significance of the Translation Principle." In *Global Theology in Evangelical Perspective: Exploring the Contextual Nature of Theology and Mission,* edited by Jeffrey P. Greenman and Gene L. Green, 35–49. Downers Grove: InterVarsity Academic, 2012.

————. *Translating the Message: The Missionary Impact on Culture.* Maryknoll, NY: Orbis, 1989.

Satyavrata, Ivan M. *God Has Not Left Himself without Witness.* Eugene, OR: Wipf and Stock, 2011.

Scanlon, T. M. *The Difficulty of Tolerance: Essays in Political Philosophy.* New York: Cambridge University Press, 2003.

————. *What We Owe to Each Other.* Cambridge: Harvard University Press, 1998.

Schneiders, Sandra M. "A Case Study: A Feminist Interpretation of John 4:1–42." In *The Interpretation of John,* edited by Jon Ashton, 235–59. 2nd ed. Edinburgh: T&T Clark, 1997.

Schreiter, Robert J. *Constructing Local Theologies.* Maryknoll, NY: Orbis, 1985.

————. *The New Catholicity: Theology between the Global and the Local.* Maryknoll, NY: Orbis, 1997.

Schweitzer, Albert. *The Quest of the Historical Jesus.* Edited by John Bowden. Minneapolis: Fortress, 2001.

Second General Conference of Latin American Bishops. *The Church in the Present-Day Transformation of Latin America in the Light of the Council.* Bogotá: General Secretariat of CELAM, 1970.

Shenouda, H. H. *Characteristics of the Spiritual Path.* Translated by Mary Bassill and Amani Bassill. 2nd ed. Cairo: St. Shenouda, 2015.

Siddiqui, Mona. *Christians, Muslims, and Jesus.* New Haven: Yale University Press, 2013.

Sievers, Joseph. *The Hasmoneans and Their Supporters: From Mattathias to the Death of John Hyrcanus I.* Atlanta: Scholars, 1990.

Simonetti, Manlio, ed. *Matthew 1–13.* Ancient Christian Commentary on Scripture. Downers Grove: InterVarsity, 2001.

Smith, Robert H. "'Blessed Are the Poor in (Holy) Spirit'? (Matthew 5:3)." *Word & World* 18 (1998) 389–96.

Smith, Wilfred Cantwell. *The Meaning and End of Religion: A New Approach to the Religious Traditions of Mankind.* New York: Mentor, 1964.

Srinivas, M. N. "A Note on Sanskritization and Westernization." *The Far Eastern Quarterly* 15 (1956) 481–96.

————. *Religion and Society among the Coorgs of South India.* New York: Oxford University Press, 1952.

Stein, Robert H. *A Basic Guide to Interpreting the Bible: Playing by the Rules.* Grand Rapids: Baker, 1994.

Stumme, Wayne C., ed. *The Gospel of Justification in Christ: Where Does the Church Stand Today?* Grand Rapids: Eerdmans, 2006.

Sugirtharajah, R. S. *The Bible and the Third World: Precolonial, Colonial, and Postcolonial Encounters.* Cambridge: Cambridge University Press, 2001.

Sulaiman, Kamal-deen Olawale. "Religious Violence in Contemporary Nigeria: Implications and Options for Peace and Stability." *Journal for the Study of Religion* 29 (2016) 85–103.

Sullivan, Francis Aloysius. "The Development of Doctrine about Infants Who Die Unbaptized." *Theological Studies* 72 (2011) 3–14.

Tanner, Kathryn. *Christianity and the New Spirit of Capitalism.* New Haven: Yale University Press, 2019.

Tappa, Louise. "The Christ-Event from the Viewpoint of African Women: A Protestant Perspective." In *With Passion and Compassion: Third World Women Doing Theology*, edited by Virginia Fabella and Mercy Amba Oduyoye, 30–34. Maryknoll, NY: Orbis, 1988.

Taylor, Edward. *Primitive Culture.* New York: Harper, 1958.

Taylor, John V. *The Primal Vision: Christian Presence amid African Religion.* London: SCM, 1963.

Temple, William. *Christianity and Social Order.* London: SCM, 1942.

Tertullian. *Against Praxeas.* Translated by A. Souter. New York: Macmillan, 1919.

Theoharis, Liz. *Always with Us? What Jesus Really Said about the Poor.* Grand Rapids: Eerdmans, 2017.

Thiessen, Matthew. "Abolishers of the Law in Early Judaism and Matthew 5,17–20." *Biblica* 93 (2012) 543–56.

Third General Conference of Latin American Bishops. *Puebla: Evangelization at Present and in the Future of Latin America; Conclusions.* Washington, DC: National Conference of Catholic Bishops, 1979.

Thomas, M. M. *The Acknowledged Christ of the Indian Renaissance.* Madras: CLS, 1970.

Thomasius, Gottfried. "Christ's Person and Work." In *God and Incarnation in Mid-nineteenth Century German Theology*, edited by Claude Welch, 31–114. New York: Oxford University Press, 1965.

Tienou, Tite. "Christian Theology in an Era of World Christianity." In *Globalizing Theology: Belief and Practice in an Era of World Christianity*, edited by Craig Ott and Harold A. Netland, 37–51. Grand Rapids: Baker Academic, 2006.

———. "Indigenous African Christian theologies: The Uphill Road." *International Bulletin of Missionary Research* 14 (1990) 73–77.

Tillich, Paul. *Systematic Theology.* Vol. 1.1, *Reason and Revelation.* Chicago: University of Chicago Press, 1951.

Torres, Sergio, and Virginia Fabella, eds. *The Emergent Gospel: Theology from the Underside of History.* Maryknoll, NY: Orbis, 1978.

Trembath, Kern Robert. *Evangelical Theories of Biblical Inspiration: A Review and Proposal.* New York: Oxford University Press, 1978.

Trujillo, Alfonso Lopez. *Liberation or Revolution? An Examination of the Priest's Role in the Socioeconomic Class Struggle in Latin America.* Huntington, IN: Our Sunday Visitor, 1977.

Tutu, Desmond. "Christianity and Apartheid." In *Apartheid Is a Heresy*, edited by John W. DeGruchy and Charles Villa-Vicencio, 39–47. Grand Rapids: Eerdmans, 1983.

Twomey, Gerald S. *The "Preferential Option for the Poor" in Catholic Social Thought from John XXIII to John Paul II.* Lewiston, NY: Edwin Mellen, 2005.

Udoh, Enyi Ben. "Guest Christology: An Interpretative View of the Christological Problem in Africa." PhD diss., Princeton Theological Seminary, 1983.

Umar, Muhammad Sani. "Weak States and Democratization: Ethnic and Religious Conflicts in Nigeria." In *Identity Conflicts: Can Violence Be Regulated?*, edited by J. Craig Jenkins and Esther E. Gottlieb, 259–279. New Brunswick, NJ: Transaction, 2007.

Vanhoozer, Kevin J. *The Drama of Doctrine: A Canonical Linguistic Approach to Christian Theology.* Louisville: Westminster John Knox, 2005.

———. *First Theology: God, Scripture, and Hermeneutics.* Downers Grove: InterVarsity Academic, 2002.

———. "'One Rule to Rule them All?' Theological Method in an Era of World Christianity." In *Globalizing Theology: Belief and Practice in an Era of World Christianity*, edited by Craig Ott and Harold A. Netland, 85–126. Grand Rapids: Baker Academic, 2006.

Vaughan, Olufemi. *Religion and the Making of Nigeria.* Durham: Duke University Press, 2016.

Vijayakumar, W. R. "Historical Survey of Buddhism in India: A Neo-Buddhist Interpretation." In *Ambedkar and the New-Buddhist Movement*, edited by T. S. Wilkinson and M. M. Thomas, 4–32. Madras: Christian Literature Society, 1972.

Vilela, Avelar Brandao. "Inaugural Address." In *The Church in the Present-Day Transformation of Latin America in the Light of the Council*, edited by Louis Michael Colonnese, 68–76. Bogotá: General Secretariat of CELAM, 1970.

Vinson, Laura Thaut. *Religion, Violence, and Local Power-Sharing in Nigeria.* New York: Cambridge University Press, 2017.

Volf, Miroslav. *A Public Faith: How Followers of Christ Should Serve the Common Good.* Grand Rapids: Brazos, 2011.

———. "The Social Meaning of Reconciliation." *Interpretation* 54 (2000) 158–72.

Volf, Miroslav, and Ryan McAnnally-Linz. *Public Faith in Action: How to Think Carefully, Engage Wisely, and Vote with Integrity.* Grand Rapids: Brazos, 2016.

Walls, Andrew F. *The Cross-Cultural Process in Christian History.* Maryknoll, NY: Orbis, 2002.

———. *Crossing Cultural Frontiers: Studies in the History of World Christianity.* Edited by Mark R. Gornik. Maryknoll, NY: Orbis, 2017.

———. "Kwame Bediako and Christian Scholarship in Africa." *International Bulletin of Missionary Research* 32 (2008) 188–93.

———. *The Missionary Movement in Christian History: Studies in the Transmission of Faith.* Maryknoll, NY: Orbis, 1996.

———. "The Rise of Global Theologies." In *Global Theology: Exploring the Contextual Nature of Theology and Mission*, edited by Jeffrey P. Greenman and Gene L. Green, 19–34. Downers Grove: InterVarsity Academic, 2012.

———. "Towards Understanding Africa's Place in Christianity." In *Religion in a Pluralistic Society: Essays Presented to Professor C. G. Baëta in Celebration of His Retirement from the Service of the University of Ghana, September 1971 by Friends and Colleagues*, edited by J. S. Pobee, 180–89. Leiden: Brill, 1976.

Warren, Max, ed. *To Apply the Gospel: Selections from the Writings of Henry Venn.* Grand Rapids: Eerdmans, 1971.

Webster, John C. B. "Building to Last: Harold Turner and the Study of Religion." In *Exploring New Religious Movements: Essays in Honour of Harold W. Turner*, edited by A. F. Walls and Wilbert R. Shenk, 1–18. Elkhart: Mission Focus, 1990.

———. *Historiography of Christianity in India*. New Delhi: Oxford University Press, 2012.

Westermann, Dietrich. *Africa and Christianity*. Oxford: Oxford University Press, 1937.

Wheeler, Mortimer. *Civilizations of the Indus Valley and Beyond*. London: Thames and Hudson, 1966.

Whitaker, C. Sylvester. *The Politics of Tradition: Continuity and Change in Northern Nigeria, 1946–1966*. Princeton: Princeton University Press, 1970.

Williams, Rowan. *Being Disciples: Essentials of the Christian Life*. Grand Rapids: Eerdmans, 2016.

———. *Faith in the Pubic Square*. London: Bloomsbury, 2012.

———. *On Christian Theology*. Oxford: Blackwell, 2000.

———. *Tokens of Trust: An Introduction to Christian Belief*. London: Canterbury Press Norwich, 2007.

———. *Why Study the Past? The Quest for the Historical Church*. Grand Rapids: Eerdmans, 2005.

Women's Organization for Liberation and Development (WOLD) Group. "Dalit Women." In *Towards a Dalit Theology*, edited by M. E. Prabhakar, 168. New Delhi: ISPCK, 1988.

Wright, Christopher J. H. *The Mission of God: Unlocking the Bible's Grand Narrative*. Nottingham: InterVarsity, 2006.

Yarbrough, Robert W. "The Gospel according to the Jesus Seminar." *Presbyterion* 20 (1994) 8–20.

Yardley, Jim, and Simon Romero. "Pope's Focus on Poor Revives Scorned Theology." *The New York Times*, May 23, 2015. https://www.nytimes.com/2015/05/24/world/europe/popes-focus-on-poor-revives-scorned-theology.html.

Yoder, John Howard. *Nevertheless: Varieties of Religious Pacifism*. Scottdale: Herald, 1992.

———. *Politics of Jesus*. 2nd ed. Grand Rapids: Eerdmans, 1994.

Zoe-Obianga, Rose. "The Role of Women in Present-Day Africa." In *African Theology en Route: Papers from the Pan-African Conference of Third World Theologians, December 17–23, 1977, Accra, Ghana*, edited by Kofi Appiah-Kubi and Sergio Torres, 145–49. Maryknoll, NY: Orbis, 1979.

Subject Index

Consejo Episcopal Latinoamericano
(CELAM), 131, 166
conscientization, 89–90
contextuality, xi, 1, 40, 67, 119, 209–10,
212
contextualization, 7, 14–15, 30, 103n5,
188
contextual theology
constitutive genre, xii, 7, 11–12, 14,
17, 26
explanatory genre, xii, 7, 10–11
rationales for contextual theology,
30–35
conversion, 10, 82, 90–91, 108, 121, 163,
164n163, 166, 190–91
council of Chalcedon (451 CE), 62n53,
67n64
council of Nicaea (325 CE), 62n53
Crowther, Samuel Ajayi, 102–3

Dalits, chap. 3
Dalit theology, xii, 5, 70, chap. 3, 209,
211–12
dalitness, 79, 84–85, 87n92, 90, 97–98
divine revelation, 2
Dubois, Abbe, 81–82
Dumont, Louis, 75

eschatology, 123, 157

Francis (Pope), 135
Freire, Paulo, 151

global Christianity, 5n9, *see* world
Christianity
Gutierrez, Gustavo, 2, 11, 67–68, 70, 95,
chap. 5

Harris, William Wade, 102
hermeneutics, 9, 21–22, 45, 115, 130,
140
biblical hermeneutics, 13
Marxian hermeneutic, 140, 145–48
theological hermeneutics, 13, 21,
105, 143
Hindu, 72–73, 75, 77, 82–83, 88, 91
Hinduism, 73, 83–84, 87n92, 90–91,
100, 174n10

Idowu, E. Bolaj, 8n19, 108, 110, 112n48,
117
Incarnation, 62n53, 67–68, 93–94, 119,
121, 155, 200n74
Indian constitution (1950), 77
Indus civilization, 74
inspiration
biblical inspiration, 19, 21;
divine inspiration, 18
inter-contextuality, 40
irruption of the poor, 140–43
Isasi-Diaz, Ada Maria, 29n85
Islamization, 176, 182–83

jāti, 72, 74–75
Jesus Christ
grammar of Christian theology, 61,
66, 68
mode of discipleship, 171, 174, 188,
191, 193–97, 206–7
model for contextual theologians,
40, 62, 68
John XXIII (Pope), 158
Jonathan, Goodluck, 182
Judaism, 59, 88, 124, 202

Kato, Byang, 8–9, 105, 112n48
kenosis, 98, 155
kenotic Christology, 62n54, 69
Kimpa, Vita, 102
kingdom of God, 37n1, 43, 57, 154, 157,
169, 196, 199
Kshatriyas, 72–75, 77, 86

Leo XIII (Pope), 158
Levine, Lee, 47, 146
liberation theology
Black liberation theology, 85, 95
Latin American liberation theology,
5, 13, 85, 94–95, chap. 5, 209,
212
Limbo, 24–25
loci theologici, 10, 14–15, 35, 54, 70

Macaulay, Herbert Olayinka, 180
Macdonald, John, 53
Manusmriti, 73, 90
Maritain, Jacques, 159–61

Printed in the USA
CPSIA information can be obtained
at www.ICGtesting.com
LVHW041625161123
764167LV00023B/158